Interpreting the Personal

INTERPRETING THE PERSONAL

EXPRESSION AND THE FORMATION OF FEELINGS

Sue Campbell

Cornell University Press   *Ithaca and London*

Copyright © 1997 by Cornell University

First published 1997 by Cornell University Press.
First printing, Cornell Paperbacks, 1997.

Library of Congress Cataloging-in-Publication Data

Campbell, Sue (Susan Leslie), b. 1956
    Interpreting the personal : expression and the formation of
feelings / Sue Campbell.
        p.   cm.
    Includes bibliographical references and index.
    ISBN 0-8014-3374-6 (cloth : alk. paper). — ISBN 0-8014-8408-1
(pbk. : alk. paper)
    1. Emotions. 2. Affect (Psychology). I. Title.
BF561.C35   1997
128'.37—dc21   97-26197

Printed in the United States of America

Cornell University Press strives to utilize environmentally responsible
suppliers and materials to the fullest extent possible in the publishing
of its books. Such materials include vegetable-based, low-VOC inks and
acid-free papers that are also either recycled, totally chlorine-free, or
partly composed of nonwood fibers.

Cloth printing   10 9 8 7 6 5 4 3 2 1
Paperback printing   10 9 8 7 6 5 4 3 2 1

For my sisters, Katy and Lori, in memory of our parents,
Pat and Bill Campbell

CONTENTS

Acknowledgments   ix

Introduction
"The Rich Smell of Hiddenness"   1

I
Feelings
Falling Off the Map of the Mind   13

II
Expression and the Individuation of Feeling   47

III
Forming an Emotion
Rereading Cyrano de Bergerac   75

IV
A Model for Affective Meaning   103

V
Freedom of Expression
Feminism, Externalism, and Social Constructivism   135

VI
Being Dismissed
The Politics of Emotional Expression   165

Appendix   189

References   193

Index   199

ACKNOWLEDGMENTS

It is a pleasure for me to think of the progress of this book in terms of the people who have supported it. I am particularly grateful to Ronnie de Sousa for the challenges of his work on the emotions and his generous criticism and encouragement of my views, and to Kate Morgan for her cheerful insistence that I could always be a better feminist philosopher. Naomi Scheman provided a thoughtful reading of an early version of the manuscript and encouraged me to pursue the work.

Sue Sherwin and Rich Campbell welcomed me to Dalhousie University by reading the manuscript from start to finish. They have supported my work and my life with great kindness and valued advice. My colleagues at Dalhousie are vigorous philosophers who provide a philosophical community that is sustaining and challenging. I am truly fortunate to be here and to have the Canadian Society for Women in Philosophy as a second philosophical home.

The manuscript was revised while I was on a Webster Fellowship in the Humanities at Queen's University, Kingston, Ontario. Susan Babbitt's determination gave a new life to the project, and the friendship and encouragement of Susan, Christine Koggel, and Maxine Wilson made Queen's a home for Jan, Stanley, Lili, and me. I thank Queen's and wish more scholars could benefit from these generous and necessary kinds of fellowships.

Alison Shonkwiler carefully guided the manuscript through the editorial process at Cornell. I thank Michael Stocker and Elizabeth Spelman for lively reviews. Karen Jones read the penultimate draft and provided astute, friendly, and detailed commentary. I hope she will see some very substantial improvements her reading has made. I am grateful to Roger Lamb for helpful comments on the material in Chapter 3 and to two anonymous reviewers for *Studies in History and Philosophy of Science* for helpful comments on the material in Chapter 1.

Parts of this book have been published elsewhere. An earlier version of the first half of Chapter 3 appears as "Love and Intentionality: Roxane's

Choice," in *Love Analyzed*, edited by Roger Lamb. Copyright © 1996 by WestviewPress. Reprinted by permission of WestviewPress. The sections on Darwin and James in Chapter 1 are reprinted from *Studies in History and Philosophy of Science*, vol. 28, no. 2, Sue Campbell, "Emotion as an Explanatory Principle in Early Evolutionary Theory" (1997), with permission from Elsevier Science Ltd, The Boulevard, Langford Lane, Kidlington oX5 1GB, UK. Much of Chapter 6 appeared originally as "Being Dismissed: The Politics of Emotional Expression," in *Hypatia: A Journal of Feminist Philosophy*, vol. 9, no. 3 (Summer 1994): 46–65.

Passages by Rick Bass are from *Oil Notes*. Copyright © 1989 by Rick Bass. Reprinted by permission of Houghton Mifflin Company/Seymour Lawrence. All rights reserved. Permission to reprint "Yellow Kitchen Gloves" by Michael Lynch is from Contact/II Publications. I am grateful for all these permissions.

I would like also to thank a number of people whose lives have kept mine good company over the entire course of this project. Richard Bosley taught me philosophy as a communal practice and remains a valued mentor. I have been talking philosophy with Rockney Jacobsen and David Checkland since I was an undergraduate. To have Rocky's philosophical company is to have a piece of gold in your pocket. David's friendship has helped shape many of my convictions about the value and responsibility of academic work. I miss Debbi Brown's irreverence but am pleased we are living parallel lives. Walking with Denise Blais in five cities has made some unsettled years steadier.

My sisters Katy and Lori, my niece Courtney, and my brother-in-law Barry fill my life with love, support, and humor. This book is, however inadequately, a testament to my parents, Lorna Patricia Campbell (née Gutteridge) and William John Campbell and to the very sociable household I grew up in.

Jan Sutherland, who edited the final draft, read this manuscript so often she knows what comes next, and I know, that whatever comes next, I'll have her good company and the cats will be on the kitchen table.

SUE CAMPBELL

Halifax, Nova Scotia

Interpreting the Personal

INTRODUCTION
"The Rich Smell of Hiddenness"

Why, if there are 19 of anything, is it not philosophy?
                    —J. L. Austin, "Intelligent Behavior"

FROM EMOTIONS TO FEELINGS

Feelings and emotions have neither been effaced from philosophical psychology nor yet been given an account that makes clear their connection to the other psychological categories that we organize into explanations of action and behavior. Theorists who reflect seriously on the nature of emotions do not find their reflections incorporated into the systematic treatments of mind and language that characterize current programmatic trends in this area of philosophy.[1] In standard anthologies that purport to give a comprehensive overview of philosophy of mind, treatments of the emotions are still barely represented.[2]

There is some historical explanation for the current resistance of emotion to philosophical analysis. Historically, the emotions often have been included in a description of the conative faculty because of their obvious role as powerful motives. Hobbes, for example, placed desire and emo-

---

1. They are notably absent, for example, from Dretske's *Explaining Behavior*, and Dennett's *The Intentional Stance*. Of philosophers who have recently offered the most influential positive, systematic accounts of psychological explanation, Davidson in *Essays on Actions and Events*, alone, is conscientious about including motivational attitudes other than desire. He says very little, however, about what differentiates the various pro-attitudes.

2. For example, Rosenthal has one selection on the emotions out of sixty-two offerings. Block contains no selection on the emotions out of forty-three articles. But see Hampshire, *Philosophy of Mind*. Theory of emotions has, however, become a fairly lively cottage industry. For recent comprehensive theories, see Solomon, *The Passions*, de Sousa, and Gordon. For recent special treatments, see Nissenbaum and Greenspan. For recent anthologies, see Rorty, *Explaining Emotions*, Calhoun and Solomon, and Harré. For recent feminist treatments, see Scheman, "Anger and the Politics of Naming," Spelman, "Anger and Insubordination," Jaggar, and Bartky, "Shame and Gender."

tion in the same psychological category, a genus of simple passions (appetite, desire, love, aversion, hate, joy, and grief), further distinguished by their different objects, relations to each other, and so on (Hobbes, chap. VI). As philosophy has come to adopt the ideal of a scientific psychology, the concept of desire, in a quasi-technical sense of a preference or pro-attitude, has continued to find a home within theory of action. Emotions and other affective experiences, however, have fallen out of this project of explanation as an assortment of leftovers. Emotions are no longer held to be a unified psychological category and thus do not constitute a reliable domain of investigation:

Emotions do not form a natural kind. (Rorty, *Explaining Emotions*, 1)

It may well be impossible to construct a manageable account of emotion to cover such apparently diverse phenomena. (Jaggar, 153)

The time has come to recognize that side-stepping cannot alter the fact that "emotion" has too many and diverse meanings to be useful as a pivotal concept in a scientific enterprise. (Sarbin, 86)

We might try to fix our domain of investigation by working with a list of the classic passions: love, fear, anger, envy, pity, jealousy, and the like. We could analyze some set of these passions and suggest something like typical conditions for emotional experience. But should we, like Gilbert Ryle, include vanity, a moral vice, or more appealingly, go back to Hobbes and reinstate pusillanimity, that temperamental characteristic of making a big deal out of small difficulties? It is difficult and suspect to provide an analysis of emotion or to use emotions in an explanatory structure for action or behavior without being very sure what we are talking about.[3]

Nevertheless, and despite the wide philosophical agreement and mutual cautions that the emotions do not form a psychological class, most theories of emotion do depend on analyzing some subset of a list of familiar emotions as a base from which to generalize about the nature of emotion more broadly. This methodology is sometimes explicitly noted:

3. It was, at one point, a practice actually to list the emotions, and these always carry the fascinating stamp of a particular theoretical agenda. Darwin's list in *The Expression of Emotion in Man and Animals* is of the passions that he thought would be universally shared and have a traceable evolutionary heritage in serviceable behavior. Hobbes's list in *Leviathan* centers on the theme of the risks of social intercourse. Aaron Hill, a Renaissance theatrical coach, offers a list of those passions that every actor ought to be able to master in "Dramatic Passions."

There are about four hundred words for emotion in English, and there are many words in other languages that seem to pick out something like emotions for which there are no English equivalents. . . . In this work, we will be dealing in detail with about a dozen emotions only. But our aim is exemplification, not salience to life's little problems or completeness in the scientific sense. *Much* remains to be done and what we offer here is a lead and an example. (Harré, 6)

As Harré's quote makes transparent, theorists who deal with feelings and emotions make a choice about what types of example will orient their understanding. Although Harré's anthology includes cross-cultural studies of emotion, like most others studies of emotion, it remains an example of attention to the well-established emotion categories.

I believe that there is a serious methodological problem with beginning an account of emotions with exemplars drawn from a list of the classic passions even when we expand that list to include non-Western emotions. Many passions and feelings do not fit easily into the relatively tidy categories provided by the standard emotions, and it is the complexities and subtleties of people's emotional lives that should orient our approach toward emotion theory. Consider the following passage from Janice Keefer's *Rest Harrow*:

It had taken Anna five minutes to scribble this far: half an hour later she still hadn't settled on a signature phrase. The essence of their relationship was, as far as she construed it, indeterminacy, incompletion. *Love, Anna.* How prescriptive, how closed that sounded, or worse, dictatorial: *Love, Anna!* How would she ever finish this letter. . . . How could she write "love" when she'd never said it? Besides, she still felt cross at him about the razor. In the end she settled for *As always, Anna.* (Keefer, 28–29)

It is only sometimes that we express our emotions, express "how we are feeling" by referring to a classic emotion, such as anger, jealousy, or love. Often our feelings are too nuanced, complex, or inchoate to be easily categorized. The complexity of an emotional life is both a value and a danger. It is through the attempted expression of our feelings that we come to understand and convey what is of significance to us. But when we try to express our feelings to others, we are frequently misunderstood, and our experience often is distorted.

My study begins from the conviction that any adequate theory of emotions should account for the value of the variety of feelings that give meaning to people's lives. To be politically adequate,. such a theory must further address how what is of most significance to us, as expressed through our feelings, can be either successfully communicated to others or can be subject to suppression, distortion, and manipulation. I will argue that traditional philosophical theories of the emotions fail on both counts. Typically, theorists concentrate on analyzing the features of a handful of classic emotions, such as love and anger, overtheorizing these emotions and neglecting a much wider range of feelings and the nature and importance of expression.

RICK BASS AND MURIEL

The philosophical neglect of feelings seems very odd since, at the same time and in different discourses, they are so thoroughly implicated in the structuring of people's lives. I cannot reliably construct my domain of investigation from the leftovers of philosophical lists because I want especially to attend to what might never have made it on to the list in the first place. Perhaps, then, it is time to step empty-handed into the particular testimonies of the passions through which people continue to relate their lives. I begin this study with two very different examples of the type of feeling that I believe provides an importantly new kind of start into an understanding of emotion. Here is the first:

> In the fall of 1985, my twenty-seventh year, I read indirectly from the poet-novelist Jim Harrison a quote from Kafka, about "freeing the frozen sea within us."
>
> I know how to find oil, but I'm a horrible speaker: I couldn't sell men's magazines on a troop ship. And I don't know if I can even write well enough to explain how oil is in some places, and not in others. I get frustrated. It seems sometimes that the best way to communicate the presence of oil—or perhaps of anything—is to revert to guttural *ughs* and growls, and just go out and by damn sink a hole in the ground, shove the pipe down there deep enough, until oil begins to flow up out of it, bubbling, with its rich smell of hiddenness, and the energy of discovery. And then to point to it: to say, There it is. Always, I want to do that. I want biceps to sheen; I want tractor-trailers to groan, bringing material in and taking oil out, and drilling breaks to squeal. (You're drilling through a hard formation: bearing down—then the drill bit pierces a softer formation . . . going faster, and it makes a barking, torquing, squealing sound—it sounds exactly like beagles. . . .)
>
> I want by stamping on the ground hard enough to make that oil come out. I want to skip legalities, permits, red tape, and other obstacles.
>
> Sometimes I feel almost out of control, and that what is down there is

between the oil and me. I want to go immediately and straight to what matters: getting that oil.

My father calls me "animal." I was a fencepost in the third-grade play. I bump into things often, and run over others, frequently.

But I know where oil is, and I want to try to explain to you what it feels like, how it is, to know this.

I just do not know how to do it—show you—because it is three-dimensional, or even beyond: it is future, undrilled, and I am present, knowing. I don't know yet, without drilling, how to bridge that gap.

It is the frozen sea within me. (Bass, 16–17; emphasis mine)

Bass is moved, to work and to write, by a powerful passion for finding oil, and this passion through which he structures his life ("If life, and living, is not like oil, then I do not know what is" [21]) will not appear on any classic list of the passions. It is given some philosophical legitimacy only when the absence of such passions from such lists is noted or commented on directly, and this happens rarely.

What difference does it make to a philosophical analysis of that phenomenon, of which emotions are the most congealed manifestations, if we consider all the feelings for which we do not have labels? What happens, that is, when we pay attention to the rich, detailed inlay of our affective lives which finds expression in art, gesture, metaphor, activity, and friendship with those we find like-minded? In this study, I try to understand the philosophical interest and importance of Rick Bass's passion for finding oil. To state my project generally: there is a common social practice where we ask people how they feel about various things and they tell us. When people tell us how they feel, they may do so as poetically and idiosyncratically as Bass does, or they may make mention of a classic emotion. Sometimes we understand how or what people feel, and sometimes we do not. And often people do not tell us how they feel, but rather show us through various modes of expression and we respond to them.

I wish to give an account of the above practices—of what I shall now call "affect"—as a category of interest in what people have to say about their lives, of understanding or explanation of people's behavior, and of interaction between or among people. I wish, in this way, as William James wished, to account for the aesthetic sphere of the mind "with its longings, its pleasures and pains, and its emotions" (James, "What Is an Emotion?," 17), and to do so in the awareness of the frequent absence of this sphere from continental maps of the mind.[4] Bass illustrates the point of departure for the ideas and arguments to follow: the conviction that there is

4. I borrow the notion of a continental geography as a metaphor for philosophy from Ryle (8), but there are many variations of it in the philosophical literature.

more to the analysis of affect than can be understood from an analysis of standard emotions. Like Bass, "I have fallen in love with . . . [an] underground geography" (Bass, 19).

The standard, classically listed emotions—anger, fear, and the like—are a subset of feelings, but, unlike feelings generally, they are conceptually well behaved. I mean by this that we have a shared vocabulary for referring to the classic emotions, which includes both emotion labels (such as "angry") and emotive property terms (such as "offensive"), and that the application of this vocabulary is subject to at least some objective standards. We can argue about whether some remark was offensive or whether someone has reason to be jealous. We also seem to have relatively well-defined ways of expressing the classic emotions, although I intend to call this assumption into question. Theories of affect have naturally centered on the potential for analysis of this important subset of feelings, even when these theories have had a broader mandate. I begin by examining theories that have a broad mandate, but that focus in on the classic emotions as paradigm analysands. These theories display systematic internal problems, particularly with respect to the individuation of affective states, that lead to the necessity of reexamining our approach to affect. These convictions are argued for and illustrated in Chapter 1 of my account.

Bass also illustrates the second concern that is the focus of my positive treatment of feelings in the remainder of the study: a concern with the relation between feelings and their expression. One of Bass's longings is to make us understand his passion for finding oil: one of the greatest pains of the aesthetic sphere is our inability to articulate our pleasures, pains, and longings. To understand affect, I shall argue, is centrally to understand both the activity of expression and the risks of expressive failure.

What Bass feels is a form of longing accentuated by his coupling of the longing for oil and the longing to find the means to express that original longing. But what he expresses in this passage also is the frustration of his longing to express himself, and that is one relatively well-defined feeling which he would not experience if he were not grappling with his own expressive resources and their limitations. Bass's attempt to express his passions and his perceived risk of expressive failure give character and intensity to the complex longing expressed. I will argue that this phenomenon—the involvement of our expressive opportunities and our modes of expression in the structuring of the feelings that are there to be expressed—is far more pervasive than has been thought. Chapters 2 and 3 are devoted to making a plausible case for the necessity of acts of expression to individuated feelings. The concern of the first part of the book is to link the concepts of feeling and expression in such a way as to make it possible to talk about the range of people's affective experiences.

6

I argue throughout this study, and particularly in Chapters 4 through 6 that the complex undertaking of understanding expressive success and failure requires a political analysis. Bass's prose is powerful, and this is certainly due partly to the duplicity of his literary personae: the sustained elegant linking of two longings—the passion for expression and the passion for hidden oil by a horrible speaker, a man whose own father calls him "animal," someone who doesn't read Kafka. Expression is a communicative activity, and there is no way to escape the legalities, permits, red tape, and other obstacles that successful communication involves. But what these obstacles amount to are different for the expression of feeling than for other communicative activities, and they differ a great deal for different people and for different groups of people. As the duplicity of Bass's oilman helps illustrate, one of the chief challenges to successful expression is the limitations imposed by the personae of gender. Bass is an oilman, a masculine figure characterized by emotional inarticulateness, a figure that can barely prevent itself from expressing deep passion by sinking back to guttural ughs and growls or just by damn sinking a hole in the ground.

Bass's masculine character is duplicitous, however. The posture of inarticulateness is an opportunity for Bass to dazzle us with his resourceful expression. Moreover, for all his posturing, Bass seems happily assured of his reader's will to understand him. Bass does not face the problems of confronting interpreters who attempt to distort or manipulate the importance to him of his own experience. Bass's expression is a free and privileged expression and contrasts starkly to the next example. Muriel's experience, to which I now turn, sharpens the need to attend to the ethical and political dimension of expression and interpretation.

Between Two Worlds, by Miriam Tlali, is a semi-autobiographical novel that describes the situation of urban blacks in apartheid South Africa. The black protagonist, Muriel, works at Metropolitan Radio, a shop that exploits blacks both as workers and customers. Muriel is highly competent and, over the course of the novel, her work responsibilities dictate increasing interaction with the white staff and more direct contact with the black customers who pay exorbitant interest for the goods sold at the shop. Muriel is "between two fires" (Tlali, 81), and, in the middle passages of the novel, she twice experiences a feeling that she describes as the "white-master's-well-fed-dog" feeling.

In the first instance, Muriel eagerly returns to work after six days at home with a daughter who has chicken pox. The boss, Mr. Bloch, fears small pox—"blacks suffer from all sorts of diseases" (Tlali, 89)—and bars Muriel from the shop until he calls his doctor. Later that day, a black customer says to Muriel: "You work nicely here, my sister. Like a white person. You must be very happy to work in such a place" (Tlali, 91):

> Such remarks were often made by my black customers. I hated them. They gave me that "white-master's-well-fed-dog" feeling that Mangaliso Sobukwe used to tell us about. I strove to conceal my true emotions. What could I say?
>
> "The little jobs they did not want to give us at first are being done by us these days," continued the customer, obviously proud.
>
> I felt like screaming. (Tlali, 91)

In the second passage that mentions the feeling, Muriel, tired of the humiliations of her position, has given in a letter of resignation. Mr. Bloch cannot understand why she is unhappy:

> "But why, why should want to leave? You are healthy and fat. We all treat you well. What's wrong?"
>
> Perhaps this was meant as a compliment but it made me get that "white-master's-well-fed-dog" feeling again. I corrected him. "I am fat because I eat the wrong type of food; not because I am happy." [. . .]
>
> How could I tell him that I was leaving because I did not want to make tea and be sent around to the cafés to buy refreshments for the white staff? None of them could understand it. (Tlali, 120)

In using the words "white-master's-well-fed-dog" feeling, Muriel, like Bass, attempts to communicate a distinctive kind of experience to the readers, one that would be difficult to understand through the emotion categories with which most of us are familiar. It is not simply an instance of anger, of humiliation, of frustration, or even of unhappiness. It is more ambivalent and complex than any negative emotion. Muriel's trope captures the ambivalence of her experience at Metropolitan Radio. It is, for example, in many ways far better to be a well-fed dog than a starved and abandoned one.

Muriel's feeling bears obvious relation to a number of feelings, and perhaps we might think of it as a complex emotion. We could then understand it by coming to see how the various aspects of her work leave her frustrated and humiliated on the one hand, content and eager to continue on the other. However there are general reasons, I think, to resist any reductive analysis of the feeling to experiences that might be more familiar to the reader. Some of these considerations are ethical and have to do with our responsibilities as interpreters.

The first reason to resist an analysis of the feeling into what we might consider to be more basic emotion categories is the role of the feeling in the novel. Muriel expresses the "white-master's-well-fed-dog" feeling to the reader at a key point: her first attempt to resign from her position. She does not follow through on this resignation. Once we try to understand Muriel's feeling, a great deal of the information imparted to us in *Between Two Worlds* takes on a clearer pattern. Events are easier to understand in relation to each other because we understand their effect on Muriel. Moreover, actions that would require separate explanations—why Muriel returns joyfully to work and in a short time is despairing enough to resign—are seen to be related. Muriel's feeling is an explanation for both. The narrative role of Muriel's expression of her feelings is to unify the action of the novel and guide the reader's interpretation of events. To try to analyze her feeling into more basic emotion categories seems wrong-headed.

A second set of reasons is more directly ethical and political. The particular form that Muriel's experience takes partly is the result of her very restricted expressive opportunities. Muriel strives to conceal her emotions from customers for she is constantly told she must be loyal to the firm. Her present feeling is in response to not being able to express how things are for her. Moreover, Muriel expresses "white-master's-well-fed-dog" feeling on two occasions where people precisely misunderstand how she views her working life and how it affects her. Both the black customer and Bloch misdescribe to Muriel her attitude toward her own life. The customer calls her happy. Muriel's response is to the reader. Her response communicates that she is being misdescribed and misunderstood and helps us see what allows the misunderstanding. Her response also corrects the misunderstanding the reader might have. The passages are a warning against our using our own understandings or experiences to assess Muriel's experiences at Metropolitan Radio. For both black and white readers, the novel is meant to educate our understanding.

Bass's experience appears to be the experience of a very particular, perhaps idiosyncratic, feeling. Muriel takes her experience to be that of a type of feeling, one which would be an importantly shared experience for urban blacks in apartheid South Africa. The sharing of the feeling is marked in the first passage. It is the feeling "that Mangaliso Sobukwe used to tell us about." Although we may have no emotion category that captures the feeling, it is not idiosyncratic; it is distinctive and local, and this aspect of our understanding will be less well developed if we look on the feeling as some amalgam of categories with which we are familiar. To correctly understand and interpret the experience Muriel expresses to the reader, we need to understand the compromised position of urban blacks such as Muriel in apartheid South Africa; we need to understand the context in which the experience of being a "white-master's well-fed dog" is formed and shared. *Between Two Worlds* is meant to give us this understanding. If we don't have some sense of "white-master's-well-fed-dog" feeling by the end of the novel, we have not been good readers.

In Chapter 4, I argue that to understand affective experience as meaningful requires an understanding of the communicative and interpretive circumstances, individual and political, in which such meaning is created. I propose a general model for the individuation of feelings or the establishment of affective meanings that can accommodate the uniqueness of feelings while suggesting how emotion categories arise. The model is meant, then, to be adequate to feelings that are indiosyncratic and feelings that are local, as well as to emotions that may be very widely shared across times and cultures. The conditions of expressive success and the risks of expressive failure are examined within an approach to philosophy of mind that makes interpretation central to the formation of meaning. The role of political limitations in the expression of feeling, particularly, the power of our interpreters to affect how we feel, is the explicit theme of Chapters 5 and 6.

Terminology and Central Claims

In the first of the two passages, Muriel refers to the "white-master's-well-fed-dog" feeling as an emotion. In this study, I similarly use the word *feeling* to refer to all experiences people might categorize as emotions. Feeling is, in common popular usage, a synonym for emotion, and this is the way I use here. When we think of emotions, we most naturally think of what I call the standard emotions or classic passions. I will take the category of feeling to include standard or classic emotions, such as anger, jealousy, and love, and also to include such feelings as the "white-master's-well-fed-dog" feeling and Bass's passion for finding oil. The category is thus inclusive of the standard emotions but much broader. To keep salient to the reader that my interest is in this broad category of experience, I also use the words *affect* or *affective* to mark out my area of interest. No choice of terminology is without its risks. Feelings, for example, have been analyzed by many philosophers as sensations, and thus, as quite distinct from more complex emotional states. In Chapter 1, I will critique the tradition of theory responsible for this separation.

It is more difficult to define, in a preliminary way, the other central concept of this study: expression. The core meaning of expression seems to be to make manifest or evident, and to talk of expressing feeling is a very central use of the word *expression*. However, in a way that is parallel to the fate of "feeling," the meaning of "expression" often has been narrowed in a way that distorts our understanding of the activity of expressing feeling. Making a feeling evident has sometimes been interpreted as involuntarily revealing the feeling, perhaps by the expression on your face or by a gesture or exclamation. In Darwin's theory, which I look at in Chapter 1, expression is contrasted to intentional or deliberate activity. But Muriel and Bass express their feelings and do so in a deliberate and sophisticated way. In Chapter 2, I begin to give an account of expression that can make sense of what Bass and Muriel do.

I now briefly outline the central claims of this study. For those who approach this work from a discipline other than philosophy, these claims will be clearer as they are argued for in detail in the chapters that follow.

Because of the neglect of the broad category of affect in philosophy of mind, and the consequent necessity of making this category visible to give an account of it, my study has a certain heuristic structure. It might, for convenience, be regarded as a courtroom presentation. I first isolate gaps and inconsistencies in the testimonies of previous theories (Chapter 1), adduce a variety of considerations for an alternative description of the category of affect (Chapters 2 and 3), and only then make my formal summations as to the nature of this category (Chapters 3 and 4), as well as a plea for its reform (Chapters 4, 5, and 6). Because of this structure, it will be useful to list the central claims as they would appear in conceptual relation to each other.

Affect and Explanation.

Our interest in how people feel is our interest in the importance to them of the situations and occasion of their lives. A way of phrasing this thesis, which I shall defend later, is that we have an interest in people as autobiographers. This is the role of affect as an explanatory category. This role does not compete with the role of intentional explanation, nor does it just underlie it.[5] It is different in important ways (one person is not replaceable by another) and supplementary (affective explanation systematizes a great deal of behavior as organized behavior).

Affect and Individuation.

Personal significance is a type of meaning, and its determination is subject to the same public conditions of interpretability as other types of meaning. How we feel is to be understood in terms of how we behave

---

5. For an important argument that the emotions first make salient for agents the beliefs and desires referred to in intentional explanation and thus ground the possibility of intentional explanation, see de Sousa.

insofar as this behavior is interpretable. Expression individuates or forms feelings, and expressive behavior is itself publicly individuated.

Expressive Success and Failure.

The successful determination of affective significance requires that expressers and interpreters respond to events as having a similar significance, or, alternatively, that they understand each other's expressive vocabularies. These conditions make the determination of affective significance difficult and unreliable.

Affect and Emotion.

Emotions are a species of the genus feeling, where the significance of occasions is widely shared. Their shared significance is reflected in a shared vocabulary of labels and properties and communal norms governing appropriate expression. That some occasions are of communal significance does not, of course, prevent them from being of great personal significance. On emotive occasions, personal significance either coincides or clashes with social significance.

Expression and Control.

If what we feel is to be understood in terms of how we express ourselves, people can control our feelings by controlling our modes of expression. Some of the control over affective possibilities resides in the power of interpreters to affect the ways in which we can view occasions. Other types of controls are exercised by the sorts of expressive resources we are allowed and by the ideologies that govern expression of feeling.

Because of a methodological attachment to the classic emotions as paradigm analysands for the category of affect, much of what is involved in the determination of affective meanings has lain below the level of philosophical attention. In this study, I attend particularly to people's expressive resources and opportunities and to the complex role of public interpretation in the formation of personal experience. In doing so, I hope to reveal a political dimension to the experience and constitution of the personal that has not yet been adequately theorized.

I
FEELINGS
Falling Off the Map of the Mind

It is not easy to deal scientifically with feelings.
Freud, Civilization and Its Discontents

THE DISAPPEARANCE OF FEELINGS

In 1890, William James spoke with assurance of the value of feelings to a scientific psychology. In chapter 1 of *The Principles of Psychology*, James defines psychology as "the Science of Mental Life, both of its phenomena and their conditions" and lists as phenomena "such things as we call feelings, desires, cognitions, reasonings, decisions, and the like" (James, 1:1). To map this last remark to contemporary philosophical psychology, desires, beliefs, decision procedures, and intentions have continued to find a home in philosophical explanation of action. Emotions, however, have barely maintained a foothold, and all other feelings have disappeared. The disappearance of feeling has left us unable to account for the ways in which we understand others and ourselves.

In this chapter, I relate a part of the philosophical story of the disappearance of feeling. The story has three interconnected themes. I first link the neglect of a broad range feelings and the corresponding neglect of expression in theories of emotion to the persistent and mistaken methodology of focusing on a handful of classic emotions as paradigms of feeling. William James, for example, whose theory I consider, wished to offer a comprehensive theory of the "aesthetic sphere" of the mind, but uses as analysands only those feelings so strongly categorized "both from within and without that they may be called the standard emotions" (James, "What Is an Emotion?," 17). James, like many other philosophers, assumes our feelings are easily categorized by both ourselves and others into set, stable types of experience and behavior. He thus pays no attention to how feelings are formed through expression. The inability of theories such as James's to address how feelings are formed manifests itself, I argue, in a corresponding inability to say how feelings are distinguished one from another. The problem of how affective states are individuated has contributed to the disappearance of feelings as an interesting and viable explanatory category in contemporary philosophy.

Second, I contend that the type of philosophical attention feelings have received has led to a diminished and confused assessment of this psychological category. Understanding behavior through the category of affect often is elegantly parsimonious. In reading Bass, we come to understand a complex variety of his activities over time through his passion for discovering oil and his longing to express this passion. When he relates that he drove his company car into the swamp, and that this is only one of the many company cars that he has ruined, we do not attempt to understand his behavior as primarily an exercise in practical reasoning—he wanted to get to the other side and believed that the road was safe—and then wonder how his passion for oil fits under this higher level of explanation. It is the affective level of explanation under which subsidiary explanations of particular pieces of behavior must be placed (Bass, 23). Similarly, we come to understand many of Muriel's actions at Metropolitan, both her eagerness to return to work and her resignations, through coming to understand that she feels like a "white-master's well-fed-dog." Like Leibniz's god, in understanding behavior through the category of affect, "the simplicity of the means counterbalances the richness of the effects" (Leibniz, 413). But philosophers have not been successful at giving an account of this kind of explanation that preserves the features of simplicity and comprehensiveness. They have instead often fragmented the category of affect to give a philosophical account of it.

The fragmentation of affect is clearly illustrated in the conclusion to Ryle's chapter on emotions in *The Concept of Mind*:

> There are two quite different senses of "emotion," in which we explain people's behavior by reference to emotions. In the first sense we are referring to the motives or inclinations from which more or less intelligent actions are done. In the second sense we are referring to moods, including the agitations and perturbations of which some aimless movements are signs. In neither of these senses are we asserting or implying that the overt behavior is the effect of a felt turbulence in the agent's stream of consciousness. In a third sense of "emotion," pangs and twinges are feelings or emotions, but they are not, save *per accidens*, things by reference to which we explain behavior. (114)

In Ryle, whose theory I also consider in this chapter, we see the coincidence of two aspects to the contemporary treatment of feelings. The idea

of using affect as a comprehensive, simple explanation of a variety of behaviors, some practical, some highly perturbed, has been lost. We also see
that feelings have dropped out of the category of motives entirely. Feelings are categorized with sensations; they no longer play any role in the
explanation of behavior. They are, instead, and this is the third theme, a
part of the problem of consciousness, that is, a part of the challenge of
providing an account of those states that give to psychological life a seemingly private and indisputably phenomenological character. The contemporary treatment of feelings as sensations, or as the same type of thing as
sensations, is plentifully exampled in the literature:

> feelings are by definition a matter of conscious awareness . . . emotions
> differ from feelings, sensations, or physiological responses in that they are
> dispositional rather than episodic. (Jaggar, 155)

> Cognitivist theories are often contrasted to the view that emotions are like
> feelings of dizziness or spasms of pain since they do not involve any kind of
> cognitive state . . . (I shall refer to this view without prejudice as the "Dumb
> View.") (Spelman, "Anger and Insubordination," 265)

In this chapter, I confine myself to trying to understand the philosophical
momentum toward this view of feelings.

The overall theme that unifies the next four sections of this chapter, in
which I consider the accounts of affect in Darwin, James, Ryle, and Alston, is
how feelings have gradually lost any role as simple and comprehensive
explanations of behavior. I chose these four theorists because, given the
initial high hopes of a scientific psychology for the category of affect, I am
interested in the real story of the disappearance of feeling. I locate the roots
of the reduction of feelings to sensations and their consequent entangle-
ment with the problem of consciousness in the requirements on an account
of behavior imposed by evolutionary theory, the first philosophical moment
when our affective life begins to cling only tenuously to a map of the mind.
James, Alston, and Ryle are among the few modern theorists who share a
perplexity about the nature of feelings that drove them to attempt to deal
with the concept of affect directly. All four theorists are unable to preserve a
general explanatory relation between feelings and behavior.

Darwin, James, Ryle, and Alston all have different philosophical agendas
in which feelings and emotions play a role. I try to give enough background in each section to display the most important commitments of the
theories without become too immersed in the complications of each project. At the same time, I tell a story about the treatment of feelings as a
plot of its own woven through these accounts.

Darwin's Use of Expression

Darwin's *Expression of the Emotions in Man and Animals* legitimated the scientific study of communicative behavior in animal species. Ironically, however, and despite his title, Darwin had no interest in the variety of behaviors that could count as expressive of a single emotion or in the variety of behaviors that could count as emotional. He limited his study to a few emotions that he thought were reliably expressed in patterns of behavior common across races and sometimes across species. As a consequence, emotions become redundant in explaining behavior. Both Darwin's methodology and it problematic consequence were bequeathed to James. I trace the structure of the problem in Darwin, partly to illuminate the context in which James proposed his own more influential account of emotions, partly because Darwin's theory is a clear and striking example of some of the difficulties in making theoretical room for the emotions in explaining behavior.

In the concluding reflections to *Expression*, Darwin admits that he has "often felt much difficulty about the proper application of the terms, will, consciousness, and intention" (356), but he never suggests that the term *emotion* is similarly problematic. He took himself to be dealing with an obvious kind of psychological phenomenon and did not theoretically justify his use of the term. In other words, he adapted a folk-psychological category to a scientific theory. Darwin's use of *expression* also is unreflective. He simply assumes our ability to recognize certain behaviors as reliably expressive of emotion.[1] He writes, for example, that "man himself cannot express love and humility by external signs, so plainly as does a dog, when with drooping ears, hanging lips, flexuous body and wagging tail, he meets his beloved master" (10). This recognition assumption leads Darwin to focus on behaviors that might reveal an emotion independently of any intention to express that emotion—for humans, primarily facial expressions and bodily postures. Deliberate and sophisticated expressive acts such as those of Muriel or Bass do not fall within the scope of Darwin's account of expression. In sum, Darwin did not provide a rich or reflective account of either emotion or expression.

More curious, viewed in the context of evolutionary theory, the project of *Expression* seems renegade. Evolutionary theory restructured the criteria for adequate psychological explanation. With the emergence of this theory, the accounts given of the relation of psychological states to behavior were required to meet stringent conditions. Since natural selection can

---

1. Darwin, in fact, speculates that our capacities to recognize certain emotional expressions are innate (357).

operate only on overt behavior, the particular demand of evolutionary theory is that psychological states play a clearly defined functional role with respect to biologically serviceable movement. Unlike previous philosophical accounts of the nature of consciousness, evolutionary accounts must start from the evidence of behavior within an environment. Animal behavior, supported by appropriate physiological studies, forms the evidential base for the postulation of various psychological categories as evolutionary mechanisms and for the individuation of various states within those categories. The new scientific psychology "takes mind in the midst of all its concrete relations" (James, *Principles*, 1: 6). However, Darwin believed that in emotionally expressive behavior, he had found patterns of behavior not tied to local environments, but that were common to different races, and indeed different species.

Darwin's commitments to these patterns of behavior is evidenced in an inquiry circulated in 1867, designed to ascertain whether "the same movements of the features or body express the same emotions" in different races: "Is contempt expressed by a slight protrusion of the lips and by turning up the nose, and with a slight expiration?" (16). Shame, indignation, grief, astonishment, depression, fear and so on are inquired about in the same manner. Darwin's search for patterns of behavior not tied to local environments seems to be in tension with what his theory would recommend as methodology, and our understanding of this approach depends on seeing the importance of emotional expression to evolutionary theory.

Emotional expression played a complex and intriguing role in the defense of species transformation.[2] If Darwin could argue for the likelihood of a common progenitor, he had a forceful way to refute special creationism with its commitment that species came into existence in their present condition. Variation in animal behavior, however, competitively supports both evolutionary theory and special creationism as either the result of adaptation and selection or as evidence of the rich detail of the creator's plan. What was needed was evidence that would adjudicate.

Darwin argued that the common behavior patterns expressive of human and animal emotions were, in fact, evidence for the descent of different species from a common progenitor. The near universality of types of expression across races indicated inheritable structures and the common ancestry of races (Darwin, 15, 359). Moreover, the common form of some human and animal expressions, for example, the exposing of the canine,

---

2. See Richards, Fridlund, and Montgomery for discussion. Fridlund and Montgomery differ on the primary explanation for the focus on nonadaptive evolution. Fridlund (117) attributes it wholly to Darwin's response to Sir Charles Bell, whereas Montgomery (47) leaves a significant role for Darwin's desire to defend an associational account of mind.

indicated a common progenitor for diverse species as well as diverse races: "The community of certain expressions in distinct though allied species . . . is rendered somewhat more intelligible, if we believe in their descent from a common progenitor" (Darwin, 12). It remained to give a precise explanation of a type of inheritable structure that could occur so pervasively.

Emotional expression was a potentially powerful ally to the theory of evolution, not only because of purportedly unique and pervasive behavioral patterns, but also because these patterns seemed to allow for the postulation of a principle of explanation within evolutionary theory that would support the idea of a common progenitor. This principle—use inheritance—had been favored by Darwin, at an earlier stage of his thought, as the primary mechanism of species transformation.[3] He accepted, in part, a Lamarckian model of evolution according to which active modifications can be inherited. With respect to expression specifically, Darwin proposed that complex repeated actions evolve, over the course of generations, into inheritable habits. Darwin's major principle of explanation for emotional expression was the principle of "serviceable associated habits":

> Certain complex actions are of direct or indirect service under certain states of the mind, in order to relieve or gratify certain sensations, desires, &c.; and whenever the same state of mind is induced, however feebly, there is a tendency through the force of habit and association for the same movements to be performed, though they may not then be of the least use. (28)[4]

Habit is an appealing evolutionary notion. First of all, habits have an obvious relation to serviceable behavior in that complex actions can be performed with a minimum of reflection. Habits are efficient. Second, as habits are developed, they could, if one accepts the idea of inheritable habit, support the claim that inheritable structures gradually evolve. Darwin's challenge was to justify the existence of *inherited* habit by excluding the possibilities that behavior that seemed evidence for this inheritance could be explained by reference to some other mechanism. It is in the explanation and defense of emotionally expressive habit as heritable that

3. It was only in the 1880s, when faced with the problem of accounting for the complex instinctual behavior of some insects, that Darwin began to prefer natural selection over use inheritance as the primary mechanism of species transformation. See Richards and Montgomery for an account.

4. Darwin used two other principles to explain incidents of expressive behavior that appeared to have no connection with serviceable habit. These secondary principles are "antithesis" and "direct nervous discharge." I do not discuss them in this treatment as they have even less connection to serviceable behavior than Darwin's primary explanatory principle.

nonpurposive behavior begins to dominate the theory and we begin to lose our understanding of the evolutionary role of emotion.

To argue for inherited habit, Darwin must exclude the alternatives that the relevant behavior is the result of intention, imitation, recent habit, or adaptive instinct bestowed by the creator. Intention or imitation would support the thesis that the behavior was learned, hence not inherited. These psychological mechanisms could explain the development of habit, but not its perdurability, and such behavior remains consistent with creationism. Adaptive instinct would potentially support creationism. It is only when the explanation of common behavior can be narrowed by excluding the above possibilities that such behavior serves as strong evidence for inheritability. But any serviceable behavior can conceivably be explained by these mechanisms, however much the commonality of behavior across races and species begins to beg for an account.

Conversely, the less purposive the behavior, the more likely it is to have been inherited. There would be no other explanation for the behavior. Darwin stressed that expressive habits were not only frequently of no service, they were "often of much disservice" (67). Darwin is, thus, throughout *Expression*, particularly impressed by such phenomena as zoo animals scratching concrete in a gesture of burying their feces who nevertheless will not cover them up when there is material available: "if we rightly understand the meaning of the above cat-like habit, of which there can be little doubt, we have a purposeless remnant of an habitual movement, which was originally followed by some remote progenitor of the dog-genus for a definite purpose, and which has been retained for a prodigious length of time" (Darwin, 44).[5]

Although Darwin stressed purposeless behavior in his general theoretical remarks, he did give many examples of serviceable animal expression.

---

5. Alan Fridlund has recently argued that Darwin's tactical anticreationist stance in *Expression* entrenched a commitment to vestigial habit that led Darwin to ignore the value of communicative behavior as the most plausible evolutionary account of expression. Darwin, in fact, gave many examples of animal display behavior in *Expression* and allowed in the conclusion to *Expression* that humans put expressive movements to use in communication and that such behavior "is certainly of importance for the welfare of mankind" (Darwin, 366). Nevertheless, he did not want to characterize communicative behavior as serviceable movement that would explain the existence of the expressive patterns. I thus agree with much of Fridlund's analysis, but my concerns here diverge from his. Fridlund does not attend to the fact that it was perceived patterns of behavior associated with classic emotions such as fear and anger that inspired Darwin to put emotional expression to use in an anticreationist attack via the mechanism of use inheritance. My argument in what follows is that, given Darwin's commitment to these purported patterns of behavior, it would have been difficult for him to relate emotions to serviceable behavior because he had nothing to justify the postulation of emotions as a distinct psychological mechanism needed to explain behavior, whether this behavior is serviceable or not.

Furthermore, when the habit is itself no longer serviceable, there may still be serviceable expressive behavior consisting in our attempt to repress the habit. Darwin attempts to leave room, within the account of inherited habit, for expressive behavior that is serviceable, but has difficulty showing that this behavior is emotional, that is, that we need emotion to explain it.

When Darwin describes expressive behavior as serviceable habit, there is reason to question whether the reference to emotion, as a distinctive state of mind, is necessary to explain the behavior. In his initial descriptions of once-serviceable animal habits that have gradually become of no service to the animal, there is almost no mention of emotion.[6] Dogs, for instance, preparing to sleep on a hard surface, scratch and turn as if to create a hollow as an ancestor might have done on the plains, and cats, in a gesture associated with suckling, often push their forefeet against a warm soft surface. The initially useful habits do not seem particularly emotional and there is no mention of emotion in Darwin's descriptions.[7] When Darwin does make reference to emotion in the description of the habitual behavior, we can once again ask whether this reference is necessary to explain the behavior. For example, Darwin notes that many animals draw back their ears when "they feel slightly savage," but the reference to feeling does not here add to our understanding of a behavior that is serviceable for animals who use their teeth in fighting (whether this fighting is serious or in play).

Finally, there is, at least, no preparation in Darwin's account for postulating emotions as the explanation of movements used to repress disserviceable habit. In *Expression*, emotions are associated for the most part with spontaneous patterned behavior. Movements used to repress habit would suggest a conscious recognition that the behavior is not serviceable. Darwin himself says, "Here it is obvious that the consciousness and will must at first have come into play" (353) and often remarks that it is those muscles least under the control of the will that continue to reveal the vestiges of the disserviceable pattern (173). In other words, with any serviceable behavior, Darwin has an adequate explanatory framework that appeals only to instinct, volitional action, and the habit consequent on repeated actions and in response to similar stimuli. Some of this behavior

6. There are many reasons why a habit might lose its value: a change in environment through domestication, a change in natural environment over generations, or simply the changes in circumstances an individual animal confronts through maturing.

7. John Dewey was a particularly astute critic of the nonexplanatory role of emotion in this section of Darwin's theory: "I wish to point out that in the case of 'serviceable associated habit,' the principle of explanation *actually* used . . . is that of survival, in the form of attitudes, of acts originally useful . . . *qua* act—as serving life. . . . *The reference to emotion in explaining the attitude is wholly irrelevant.*" ("A Theory of Emotions," 154–55; emphasis in original).

may be expressive in the sense of revealing a state of consciousness. That the state is emotional rather than perceptual or intentional would need more of an account than Darwin offers. The attempt to connect emotion to serviceable behavior fails on grounds of explanatory redundancy.

This criticism leaves Darwin with the thesis that emotions are the explanatory principle of purposeless habit, a thesis that appears to meet the theoretical constraints of locating a unique place for emotions. Rather than playing a clearly functional role with respect to biologically serviceable movement, emotions become the marker for behavior patterns that are no longer serviceable. I say "marker," for even here emotions do not seem helpful in actually explaining the behavior. It is more plausible to suppose that similar stimuli trigger the habitual behavior on perception of these stimuli, and James will argue for this option. Vestigial fear responses, for example, would trace those responses an ancestor used to escape from perceived danger. It is the perception of apparent danger that would trigger the vestigial response in a descendant. Reference to an intervening state of mind, fear, serves to mark a range of behaviors that may no longer be of service, but does not add to their explanation.

An obvious puzzle raised by Darwin's account is why it is that emotional explanation risks being the redundant level of explanation. Why is it that for expressive behavior, whether serviceable or disserviceable, we can usually give an adequate explanation that does not mention emotion. I suggest that Darwin had done nothing within the theory to establish the grounds for postulating emotion as a distinctive principle of psychological explanation. In looking for an option to intention or instinct that would render plausible the notion of ancestral behaviors, Darwin postulates inherited habit. But according to Darwin, habit requires a repeated state of mind for its expression and this may be perceptual/sensational or intentional. Darwin does nothing to theoretically ground the emotions as a kind of distinctive psychological category where states of mind within that category could explain behavior. The problem with finding a distinctive role for emotion is shielded by Darwin's assumption that expressive behavior is a special type of behavior, an assumption that appears to be supported by the unique and common behavioral patterns to which Darwin makes reference.

Emotions, however, are not adequately grounded as a psychological category by reference to distinctive behavioral patterns, and this becomes evident in problems with identifying and individuating emotions. First of all, the purported universality of emotional expression across species is not manifest in very much of sameness of movement. Darwin claimed at the start of expression that "the same state of mind is expressed throughout the world with remarkable uniformity" (17), but, clearly, Darwin's loving dog does not express his affection in the same way as a loving person. It did not seem to trouble Darwin, though it ought to have, that the expressive behavior he noted as common to diverse species really had very little in common across species. Darwin offers touching, for example, as one of the few natural expressions of love, but a cat's rubbing against my legs and a partner's embrace are very diverse sorts of movement (Darwin, 213). Outside of some of the facial gestures Darwin discusses, the cross-species behavioral commonalities noted by Darwin appear only as commonalities when described generally as expressions of fear, love, or anger. However, calling something "love" or "fear" first requires that we recognize quite diverse bodily movements as expressions of love or fear. Darwin has, in a sense, begged the question of what those bodily movements express and of how we come to recognize what they express.

It is the postulation of the sameness of mental state, love, for example, which is displayed by Darwin to account for the commonality of the behavior. What the various behaviors have in common is that they are postulated as expressions of the same mental state. However, because the only grounds for ascribing mental states is behavior, there is no way to exclude that different behaviors are, in fact, indicative of different mental states. The separation that results is this: the feelings common to races and species must be picked out—individuated—independently of the different ways in which they are behaviorally manifested: feelings begin to become autonomous from their expressions. However, Darwin has no adequate theoretical means for providing alternative grounds for the individuation of feelings, leaving, again, as the sole support for their individuation the informal fact that we do recognize emotional behavior.[8]

I suggest that Darwin's dependence on the recognizability of expressive behavior and his failure to recognize or deal with problems of individuation are consequences of his commitment to a handful of classic emotional expressions where our familiarity with the representation of emotion through these classics expressions belies the diversity of our expressive lives. Had Darwin taken the rich variation of emotional expression in humans as his starting point, the anticreationist agenda of *Expression* might have been sacrificed to a more viable account of the emotions. Darwin's theory, instead, combined a simplistic picture of expression as universal spontaneous, patterned, gesture with a difficulty in locating a unique place or role for the emotions in the explanation of behavior. My

---

8. Once again, Dewey was quick to point out the problem in Darwin, suggesting that it is only through expression that the individuation of feeling can proceed: "the very phrase 'expression of emotion,' as well as Darwin's method of stating the matter, begs the question of the relation of emotion to organic peripheral action, in that it assumes the former as primary and the latter as secondary" (Dewey, "A Theory of Emotion," 152).

analysis of Darwin suggests that an adequate theory of feelings must combine an account of the explanatory role of feelings with a more complex and realistic understanding of expression. Instead, in the work of William James, the problems of Darwin's methodology became an entrenched part of philosophical tradition.

JAMES AND THE PROBLEM OF EPIPHENOMENA

William James wrote in "What Is an Emotion?, that "we have already a brain scheme in our hands whose applications are much wider than its authors dreamed" (18). It was his ambitious wish to use this scheme for an account of an area of mind that he considered to be either ignored or bungled by nineteenth-century psychologists: the aesthetic sphere, with "its longings, its pleasures, its pains, and its emotions" (17). James considered that the sphere had been so ignored by empirical psychologists that they might reply that they either had "as yet bestowed no thought upon the subject, or that they had found it so difficult to make distinct hypotheses that the matter lay for them among the problems of the future" (17). James, however, not only failed to locate a distinctive sphere of psychological activity, but, according to a subsequent generation of critics, also offered an account that could not differentiate an emotion from any kind of bodily sensation. History has cast James as the figure responsible for the decomposition of emotions into feelings and feelings into sensations. As James evidently wished to give an account of affect that secured it some significant place in psychology, his influence seems to have eclipsed and mocked his own motivations. The difficulties in James's account can be traced to his attachment to the classic passions.

James initially attempted to give an account of affect that was not restricted to the classic passions, that would, instead, explain a broad and significant area of human experience. He includes, in the aesthetic sphere, intellectual pleasures and pains such as the delight in a proof or the torment of an unfinished problem, the feeling of "all-overishness" when a friend goes near the edge of a precipice, and feelings of anticipation of other feelings (James, "What Is an Emotion?," 18, 26). *The Principles of Psychology* has many chapters that indicate the importance that James attributed to the emotions. Notably, we must be willing to act on emotional experience to form good moral habit, certain emotions are criterial for setting the boundaries of the self, and emotion is crucial to James's theory of belief. (See *The Principles* chap. 4, "Habit," chap. 10, "The Consciousness of Self," and chap. 21, "Perception of Reality.") Finally, James took expressive behavior to be serviceable and attributed our new understanding of this to evolutionary theory, to the adaptation of animals to their particular environments (James, "What Is an Emotion?," 20). Emotions are to be treated as a type of instinctual behavior.

Despite James's admirably broad mandate for an account of affect and his recognition of the importance of an account of feeling to both psychology and ethics, James chooses as his primary analysands for the aesthetic sphere only those feelings that have a distinctive bodily expression, emotions already so strongly categorized "both from within and without that they may be called the standard emotions" (James, "What Is an Emotion?," 17). James, like Darwin, restricts his account to the classic passions to make theoretical use of set patterns of behavior that he believed to be reliably activated by species-specific environmental stimuli. Like Darwin, James ends up unable to account for this behavior as affective behavior. In James, we also see the beginnings of modern terminological preferences. James uses "emotion" to refer to the classic passions, such as fear, anger, and grief, and "feeling" to refer to all affective states, *including* the classic passions. This usage, by no means hardened in James, creates a terminological distinction between emotion and feeling that subsequent theorists exploit by using "emotion" to refer to motivational affective states and "feeling" as the label for the sensory component of those states.

James did not initially entertain the idea that expressive behavior was of no service, although he will be pushed toward this view by time he writes *The Principles of Psychology*. He did see the problem of explanatory redundancy, and his own account can be read as a determined attempt to avoid it. If we critically situate James in relation to Darwin, we can describe his project as follows: James had inherited the problem of finding for emotions a unique role within evolutionary theory. Darwin's account makes obvious the potential difficulties with this project. To recapitulate briefly: (1) Within an account of serviceable behavior, Darwin could not differentiate emotion from any other state of mind that might occur frequently enough to lead to complex, repeated, and inheritable behaviors. (2) Darwin could not maintain a secure explanatory connection between an affective state and the behavior expressive of that state. (3) Darwin did not give an account of affective behavior as serviceable behavior and likely could not have.

James attempted to speak to the first two of these difficulties by: (1) offering a unique account of emotions at the physiological level; and (2) securing the relation between emotion and behavior through an analysis that reduced the affective state to the physiological accompaniments of the affective behavior. James's reduction took part in two stages, and it is the second stage that has become notorious. I examine each one separately.

In stage one, James attempted to reinstate the special status of emotions, using a strategy of physiological decentralization so that the failure of emotions to be a well-defined competitor to either cognition or perception in explaining behavior would not deprive us of a possible account of them. He denied two levels of physiological specialization to the emotions. Within the framework of a psychological model of cognitive and volitional functions mapped, respectively, to a physiological model of sensorial and motor centers of the brain, James denied that there is any third brain center that is the seat of emotional experience. He also denied that there is any process that can be singled out as emotional in either of the other centers. James did, however, make a choice of centers and chose the sensorial one—emotional brain processes "are nothing but" sensorial brain processes "variously combined" (James, "What Is an Emotion?," 18).

Three things are worth noting about this physiological formulation. First, James chose to place emotional processes in the informational center of the brain. The processes in this center are those that are ordinarily taken to cause behavior. Second, the ambiguous formulation, "such processes variously combined," suggests that there might be a principle of organization that makes emotional processes unique. Third, the lack of specialization at a physiological level need not translate to a lack of specialization at a functional level although the aesthetic sphere of the mind is never explicitly given a functional definition. In other words, James's physiological reduction of the emotions is compatible with arguing all of the following: that emotions play a unique role in the explanation of behavior, that emotions can be uniquely characterized physiologically, and that emotional behavior can be uniquely characterized. It is important to see that James's ontological reduction of the emotions need not be an attempt to eliminate their role in explaining behavior.[9]

9. As another example of the reduction of an explanatory term, we can keep in mind the popular example of the reduction of the chemical notion of valence to a particular microphysical property. I find Daniel Dennett's description of this reduction useful for its emphasis on two different types of theoretical answers: "Sometimes terms are embedded in more powerful theories, and sometimes they are embedded by explicit definition. What do all chemical elements with the same valence have in common? First answer: they are disposed to combine with other elements in the same integral ratios. Second answer: they all have such and such a microphysical property (a property which explains their capacity so to combine)" (Dennett, "Three Kinds of Intentional Psychology," 43–44). The first and second answers are both equally good responses to the question about valence. Dennett characterizes the first as a conceptual answer that defines the notion of valence within a theory— biochemistry. He characterizes the second as a causal/reductive answer that explains the capacity mentioned in the conceptual answer by giving an account of it within the ontology of a more powerful theory—physics. When such a reduction succeeds—and this requires, minimally, that some substantive number of explanatory notions within a theory can be reduced in a similar fashion—chemists may continue to use, and may, for practical reasons,

James obviously meant to effect an ontological reduction of the affective sphere to the physiological. This is clear from both his methodology and his prefacing remarks about the defects of current psychological accounts in the *Principles*: "They give one nowhere a central point of view, or a deductive or generative principle. They distinguish and refine and specify *in infinitum* without ever getting to another logical level. Whereas the beauty of all truly scientific work is to get to ever deeper levels" (James, *Principles*, 2:448–49). It is evident from the importance James attributed to the emotions that he did not mean to eliminate their explanatory role as well. However, an ontological reduction works to preserve the value of the emotions in explaining behavior only if the reduction gives us some deeper understanding of the motivational capacities attributed to the emotions. James, however, precisely fails to give an account of the relation of emotions to behavior—the very relation that his reduction might explain. Instead, he urges a further level of reduction.

In stage two, James's innovation is to reverse the normal understanding of the causal role of emotion in accounts of action. Darwin had offered a familiar picture of emotions as psychological states that cause behavior. James's striking suggestion is that an emotional state is simply a state of kinaesthetic awareness of our behavior. Emotions are not causally interposed between perception and movement:

> Common sense says, we lose our fortune, are sorry, and weep; we meet a bear, are frightened and run. . . . The hypothesis here to be defended says that this order of sequence is incorrect, that the one mental state is not immediately induced by the other, that the bodily manifestations must first be interposed between, and that the more rational statement is that we feel sorry because we cry. (James, "What Is an Emotion?," 19)

Nor, however, is movement the cause of an emotion: "The more closely I scrutinize my states, the more persuaded I become that what moods, affections and passions I have are in very truth both constituted by and made up of those bodily changes we ordinarily call their expression or consequence" (James, "What Is an Emotion?," 24). James removes emotions from a causal account of action entirely, and, instead, offers a conceptual connection between emotion and expression, reducing the

---

be obliged to use the concept of valence. For, although the laws of chemistry may be special cases of the laws of physics, they may be related in no simple fashion. For example, the laws that relate complex organizations of particles may require the techniques of biochemistry for their discovery (Sellars, 21). The power of physics to explain valence validates both the explanatory power of physics and the continued explanatory use of valence within chemistry.

former to the sensations that either make up or accompany the latter. But this, obviously, is not to give emotions a special functional role in explaining behavior.

The standard criticism of James's failure to give emotions a significant psychological role follows in a straightforward fashion from the second stage of reduction. If emotions are not part of a causal sequence resulting in action, but are, in fact, our feeling of the bodily changes that are the sensory processes accompanying action, then emotions are mere epiphenomenal accompaniments to action and have no useful biological role. A recent commentator characterizes a Jamesian emotion as "a mere *epiphenomenon,* an inconsequential by-product of physiological excitation. . . . With this ablation, emotion concepts would seem to be of little value in the explanation and prediction of behavior" (Gordon, 88–89). Surely James could not think he had functionally defined emotion with this account.

It is not clear whether James meant the decomposition of emotion into sensation to stay at rest. He refers to the expression of each emotion as "integral" and claims that "no shade of emotion, however slight, should be without a bodily reverberation as unique, when taken in its totality, as is the mental mood itself" (James, "What Is an Emotion?," 21). I argue that James holds that the various sensory processes that make up any particular emotion at the physiological level are synthesized into a distinctive feeling or kinesthetic perception. As with Darwin, however, the inability to define emotions functionally becomes symptomatically reflected in problems with their individuation. One of the most influential critics of James, William B. Cannon, argued persuasively that it is not possible to distinguish one emotion from another or to differentiate an emotional experience from any other category of experience involving sensation, by attention to the feelings themselves. In other words, James is called to account for having failed to provide grounds for individuating emotions.

I believe that the way to understand James is to reconsider the fundamental question of whether he was trying to make a special place for emotional explanation within an evolutionary account of mind and behavior. James criticizes standard views of emotion understood under a certain description: that a mental perception excites a mental affection and this latter state of mind gives rise to a bodily expression—we meet a bear, are frightened, and run. What James took to be the standard accounts of emotion, with a mental affection interposed between perception and action, conflicted with his theory of ideo-motor action and also gave the emotion a conceptual independence from its potential behavioral effects. In *The Principles,* James eloquently asserts that "our sensations and thoughts are but cross-sections, as it were, of currents whose essential consequence is motion" (James, *Principles*, 2:526). James's parallel claim in "What Is an Emotion?" is that by abstracting from the experience of fear all the sensations that accompany the movements that reputedly are the effect of fear, we are left with nothing we could call a feeling. Movement is essential to it. Without the bodily changes expressive of and consequent upon the perception of the bear, for example, the emotion of fear simply collapses into cognition: "We might then see the bear and judge it best to run" (James, "What Is an Emotion?," 19). To view James's theory appropriately as an answer to Darwin, we must see that what distinguishes action characterized as an emotional process from action that is not so characterized is the absence of a pure psychological state as a sufficient explanation of the action. In so far as emotions fit into the explanation of action, they must have some special place that accommodates their bodily basis. But however valuable this aspect of James's approach, the hint is never pursued. James makes no attempt to illuminate the distinctive motivational role of the emotions.

The most glaring gap in James is his failure to account for the sphere in which he has an interest: the aesthetic sphere with its longings, its pleasures, its pains, and its emotions. This is a perplexing omission. I suggest, though, that we can account for James's choice and his failure to ground emotion as a category of explanation partly as a consequence of a prior methodological decision to analyze set patterns of emotional behavior. This decision would have been natural for a theorist following Darwin, and has the following independent motivation within James's theory. The methodological decision clearly supports the argumentative strategy of a certain sort of thought experiment: calling for his readers to abstract the elements of a type of experience with which they are already thoroughly familiar. "Can one fancy the state of rage and picture no ebullition of it in the chest . . . no clenching of the teeth, no impulse to vigorous action" (James, "What Is an Emotion?," 23). What would grief be "without its tears, its sobs, its suffocation of the heart, its pangs of the breast bone?" (James, "What Is an Emotion?," 22). In "What Is an Emotion?," James urges these experiments as the "vital point" of his theory (23).

James never felt obliged to offer an account of our ability to synthesize our sensory reverberations into an emotional experience. As a rhetorical choice in support of the thought experiments that were his primary argumentative appeal, he had deliberately restricted himself to sets of behaviors where the problem of synthesis would be, coincidentally, least likely to arise. Nevertheless, the problem of individuation still arises, even granting the characteristic bodily symptoms that James depends on. That is to say, if having an emotion is, as James says, having "variously combined" sensorial brain processes and, so, variously combined sensations, then we need from such an account two things. First, we need an account of which combinations of sensations, or which secondary feelings, are emotions and which are not. Second, we need an account that, in the end, would allow us to distinguish that combination of sensations or that feeling which is anger from, say, that combination of sensations or that feeling which is fear. James's critics take him to task for failing to provide either.

James's failure to provide an individuating principle for the emotions appears to be a near repetition of the problem I identified earlier in Darwin's account. Emotions are individuated within the theory as behavioral patterns partly by appealing to an inner state. In James's theory the state is the feeling—what would grief be without it tears?—essential to his thought experiments. However, the inner state depends, reciprocally, for its individuation on our accepting the initial behavioral description. The actual relation of an emotion to the various behaviors that might be expressive of it is inadequately theorized.

The question remains of whether there was a potential to the approach of using patterns of behavior that James simply failed to exploit, and I will try and say briefly why I think not. I have identified two problems related to the reliance on patterned behaviors. First, the problem of individuation. Assumptions of individuation are built into the theory by initially specifying certain behaviors as criterial for grief, fear, love, and so on. These assumptions have no independent grounding. Second, the problem of explanatory redundancy. These theories give the misleading impression that emotional behavior is more set and specific as to pattern than it is. Pointing to some highly unique pattern of behavior will make it seem as though emotions are necessary to explain the behavior and so seem to justify emotions within the theory. That they have not been adequately justified will become apparent in a competing sufficient explanation for the behavior that does not mention emotions.

There is a deep problem with the methodology. Generally, what we want for a scientifically sound account of a psychological category is a functional description of the category that will help provide a way to individuate the members of that category so they can be used to explain action or behavior. When we explain a person's behavior with the psychological category of belief, we note their behavior within an environment, attend to what information they are receiving from their environment, and individuate the belief by hypothesizing the information that in conjunction with other factors would lead to that behavior. Despite the acknowledged defects of this type of explanation, it offers grounds for individuating belief by offering a functional account of a psychological category and using this category to explain particular behaviors within their environments. Darwin and James precisely did not start from the evidence of behavior in an environment, seeing what would then be necessary to account for this behavior. That is, they did not take mind in the midst of its concrete relations. In their accounts, behavior is schematized and abstracted from its circumstances. Asking which emotion explains a schematized pattern of behavior and how the emotion explains it is like saying, with no further information: someone twirls around four times. Which belief explains this piece of behavior, and how does it explain it? There is no sense to the question of what psychological state (i.e., both what type of state and what specific state) in fact explains a piece of abstract schematized behavior. Insofar as these behavioral patterns are the core of an account, that account is bound to fail. Some of James's early critics, notably D. Irons and W. L. Worcester were, as James himself notes "struck by [the] variability in the symptoms of any given emotion" (James, "The Physical Basis of Emotion," 519).[10]

I would speculate that James recognizes the problem with his methodology by the time of his presentation of the theory in *The Principles of Psychology*. At this point, James seems defeated about locating a theoretical explanatory role for the emotions. Despite the considerable use he has put them to in many parts of his psychology, the demarcation offered between instinct and emotion is that instinctive reactions, and not emotional ones, "enter into practical relations with exciting objects" (*Principles*, 2:442). James now explicitly avoids the problem of explanatory redundancy by opting for the second horn of the dilemma inherited from Darwin, namely, that expressive behavior is not serviceable. This seems to me to abandon the project of "What Is an Emotion?" and, in fact, many emotions so evidently motivate serviceable behavior that James reclassifies fear, jealousy, shame, and romantic and parental love as instincts.

Interestingly, by the time he wrote the *Principles*, James also had given up on the idea that set behavioral patterns are criterial for the presence of certain emotions. This is evident in subtle changes of wording: James is now not interested in emotions "thoroughly characterized from within and without," but with "coarser emotions . . . in which everyone recognizes a strong organic reverberation" (*Principles*, 2:451). The change also is evident in James's explicit remarks "that our descriptions have no absolute truth; that they only applied to the average man; that every one of us almost has some personal idiosyncrasy of expression" (*Principles*, 2:447–

10. The critiques to which James refers are D. Irons, "Professor James's Theory of Emotion," and Dr. Worcester, "Observations on Some Points in James's Psychology. II. Emotion." Interestingly, James suggested that various fears, angers, and so on "preserve enough *functional* resemblance . . . in the midst of their diversity to lead us to call them by identical names" ("The Physical Basis of Emotion," 520; emphasis in original).

48). Rather than explore these idiosyncracies, however, James continues to use the representation of set behavioral patterns to motivate the thought experiments that he takes to constitute the distinctive contribution of his account.

RYLE: THE FRAGMENTATION OF AFFECT

Gilbert Ryle shared James's dislike of purely mental causes, but he also vigorously opposed any analysis of the psychological as a realm of inner, private experience. Ryle's *Concept of Mind* was highly influential in the history of the treatment of feelings, and his analysis of mind is dominated by one particular explanatory concept: that of a disposition or propensity to behave in a predictable and law-like fashion: "[W]hen we speak of a person's mind, we are not speaking of a second theatre of special-status incidents, but of certain ways in which some of the incidents of his one life are ordered. His life . . . is one concatenation of events, the differences between some and other classes of which largely consist in the applicability or inapplicability to them of logically different types of law-propositions and law-like propositions" (167). Ryle's promotion of dispositions was so successful that the concept still dominates our modern treatment of psychological predication.[11] I believe it has contributed to our difficulty in understanding feeling and emotion.

Ryle's interest in affect was as expansive as that of James's. Ryle wished to analyze everything that could be included under the category of feelings and emotions (83). Like Darwin and James, he assumed that the more familiar emotions could be understood in terms of predictable patterns of behavior and could, therefore, be subsumed under a dispositional analysis. Ryle also was explicitly influenced by James's reduction of feeling as an alternative methodology for dealing with affective states that could not be analyzed in a law-like way (Ryle, 84). Finally, like his predecessors, Darwin and James, Ryle was, in the end, unable to give an account of the relation of even the classic emotions to the behavior expressive of them. However, as Ryle's treatment was not a reduction of all feelings but, rather, the use of James's reduction to eliminate feelings that could not be handled as dispositions, Ryle also fragmented the category of affect. His theory displays in progress the strategy that becomes the dogma of subsequent theories of the emotions—the subordination of feelings-as-sensations to emotions-as-motives.

11. For its widespread use in psychological explanation, see Davidson, "Actions, Reasons and Causes"; Dennett, "Three Kinds of Intentional Psychology"; and Dretske. Its use in theory of emotion is extremely pervasive.

I first trace the fragmentation of affect in Ryle. I then raise the general question of what counts as organized behavior, a question suggested by the inability of Darwin, James, and Ryle to understand expressive behavior in a way that makes sense of affective explanation. Ryle's preference for dispositions as a general explanatory framework for behavior is explicitly linked to his understanding of whose point of view we credit in taking behavior to be organized. That we do not take into account the person whose behavior is under scrutiny is evident in Ryle's dismissal of auto-biography as an alternative organizing framework. I argue later in this study that it is a person's own point of view on his or her behavior that is critical to making a place for feelings in our understanding of mind.

To cover some familiar ground, although the reason Ryle appears to evince little direct interest in why we have a psychological vocabulary is his conviction that such terms as "belief," as in "he believes the ice is unsafe," and "vanity," as in "he boasted from vanity," are narrowly miscategorized as referring to mental occurrences and especially to mental causes, and more broadly miscategorized as referring to either mental or physical oc-currences. He proposes, instead, that the locutions in which such terms appear should be analyzed as propensities and dispositions to behave in certain ways in certain circumstances. With most psychological attribu-tions, the relevant complex of dispositions cannot be specified but only indicated by example. Someone who has the belief that the ice is unsafe, for instance, might keep to the edge of the pond, call her children away from the middle, and keep an eye on the life belts (Ryle, 45). She might, however, perform an entirely different set of actions. Ryle is both a con-ceptual and an epistemological behaviorist. Psychological states are dispo-sitions to behave, and we come to know others and ourselves by witness-ing the manifestations of these dispositions in actual behavior.

How will this model of mind work to explain feelings and emotions? Ryle, of course, must deny that feelings are *psychological* occurrences be-cause his ontology leaves him no room for this category. As James under-stood, however, many feelings and emotions have a strong bodily dimen-sion. They thus seem to be partly experiences or occurrences and are resistant to recategorization as dispositions. Muriel, for example, de-scribes her feelings both in language of the body and as occurrences or events: "it made me get that 'white-master's-well-fed-dog' feeling again." Ryle is aware that feelings, and our use of feeling vocabulary, is a problem for his theory and devotes an entire chapter to feelings and emotions:

This scrutiny is necessary because adherents of the dogma of the ghost in the machine can adduce in support of it the consent of most philosophers and psychologists to the view that emotions are internal or private experiences. Emotions are described as turbulences in the stream of consciousness. (83)

Ryle draws heavily on the idea that emotions are not a homogeneous kind in order to segment the category of affect so that some of its terms can be categorized as propensities. He includes as emotions all terms that might be put into the biography of a specific person as explaining her behavior, such as vanity, punctuality, and an interest in symbolic logic. Such terms, which Ryle classifies as inclinations or motives, can be given a fairly straightforward analysis as dispositions to behave:

> [O]n hearing that a man is vain we expect him, in the first instance, to behave in certain ways, namely to talk a lot about himself, to cleave to the society of the eminent, to reject criticisms, to seek the footlights and to disengage himself from conversations about the merits of others. (86)

The classic emotions are categorized, by Ryle, as agitations or moods, that, like inclinations, are analyzed as propensities to behave. As a final category of emotions, Ryle allows feelings, and admits them as occurrences, but only if they are describable in the vocabulary of bodily sensations: "In a third sense of 'emotion,' pangs and twinges are feelings or emotions, but they are not, save *per accidens*, things by reference to which we explain behavior" (114).

We have, then, a fracturing of the category of affect through the use of the distinction between occurrences and dispositions. Feelings are reduced to sensations and cannot justify feeling locutions as explanatory locutions. Feelings play no role in explaining intelligent behavior. Ryle's nods an appreciation to James for this reductionist approach. However, Ryle simply eliminates feelings in favor of sensations and precisely denies them the explanatory role that James had hoped to locate.

Ryle attempts to bring some order to our understanding of feeling by picking out the use of feelings to talk of sensations as primary and trying to understand all feelings through this model. All emotions can be spoken of as feelings by the person experiencing them, however, and I argue that Ryle's strategy does not offer a coherent explanation of this fact.

Ryle grants that, when we attribute an emotional disposition to someone, we expect the person will have a propensity both to undergo and to do certain things. What the person will undergo are feelings—the only occurrences in the genus of affect. A person will have feelings associated with compassion, for example, and these feelings will be analyzed as bodily sensations. However, the person also will have a propensity to avow that they feel some way ("I feel compassion"), and the feeling, here, purportedly refers to the emotional disposition. Feeling avowals form, for Ryle, our very best evidence for the attribution of affective dispositions (105), but these locutions threaten the distinction between dispositions and occurrences that is crucial to Ryle's behaviorism. Ryle is obliged to deal with the problem of crossed vocabulary: if emotions and feelings are logically different sorts of things—dispositions and occurrences—why do our locutions use the same terms to refer to both? How is feeling vain related to being vain (an inclination), feeling angry to being angry (an agitation), feeling depressed to being depressed (a mood)? Ryle must give an answer that leaves plausible his analysis of emotions as dispositions. If feelings are occurrences (which Ryle grants), if a feeling of vanity is a particular kind of feeling, and if we can predicate vanity of ourselves or others by indifferently speaking of vanity or the feeling of vanity, then Ryle risks losing a dispositional analysis for an immensely broad category of psychological terms.

Ryle regards the category of motivated behavior as the rough equivalent of the category of intelligent behavior (114). It seems much wider than what we would allow as behavior expressive of the classic emotions. The expansion of the class of affective dispositions to include character traits such as vanity, however, appears to offer a possible strategy for preserving the distinction between dispositions and occurrences, where psychological terms nonetheless refer to dispositions alone:

> Certainly, we . . . expect the vain man to feel certain pangs and flutters in certain situations; we expect him to have an acute sinking feeling, when an eminent person forgets his name, and to feel buoyant of heart and light of toe on hearing of the misfortunes of his rivals. . . . [However,] to put it quite dogmatically, the vain man never feels vain. (Ryle, 86–87)

The feelings a vain man has are not feelings of vanity, even though they are associated with vanity and may, through this association, come to be spoken of as feelings of vanity. A strong motive for Ryle's reinstatement of a broad category of motives is the opportunity to argue that the feelings associated with affective propensities decompose into feelings that need not use the same labels, thus protecting these propensities from an analysis that would mention occurrences of the same name.

The strategy used with vanity, however, is inadequate to handle all the terms that Ryle will allow as emotional propensities, and this motivates the final reduction of feelings to sensations. Buoyancy and pique are moods, and so also propensities, and thus it is necessary to protect these propensities, as well, from an analysis that would mention occurrences of the same name. Having admitted that feelings are occurrences, Ryle's only possible strategy for preserving a dispositional account of affect is to push the reduction of feelings to a level where their description need involve no terms that cross-refer to inclinations, agitations, or moods (104). To accomplish this result, Ryle's final account of feelings is that they are sensations that serve as "signs" of moods and agitations. As sensations, they can then simply be described as tingles, pangs, and tickles. This strategy leaves several problems unresolved. I mention three.

First, the role of our feeling language becomes unclear. Ryle's reduction does not explain why I say "I felt angry" rather than "I felt a tense tingle before I hit her." Ryle's suggestion, that, because certain motive terms "rank as species of emotion; they come thence to be spoken of as feelings" is wholly unsatisfactory—it merely amounts to saying that emotions *do* come to be spoken of as feelings without telling us why (85).[12] Nor does Ryle explain the kind of behavior I am engaged when I use the language of feeling. Feeling avowals form, for Ryle, our very best kind of evidence for the attribution of affective dispositions (105), but they report neither the presence of a dispositional state, nor the occurrence of the sensations into which that feeling decomposes. They avow, express, or evince feelings, but express none of the things that, according to Ryle, feelings really are, namely sensations. Ryle is certainly right about the importance of avowals, but he has done nothing to legitimize them within his own theory.

Second, feelings such as those experienced by Muriel and Bass are not good candidates for Ryle's analysis. They seem to have fallen through a gap. The plausibility of a dispositional account relies on our having expectations about how others will behave. When we understand others as angry or in love, we may well have expectations that often are satisfied. Anger is a shared and familiar category of experience where expectations as to how angry people should behave become embedded in social norms. The norms of anger—who can be angry with whom and in what ways—help regularize angry behavior, increasing our power to predict be-

---

12. Ryle's claim that sensations are the signs of moods and agitations seems to be offered as a point about a reliable connection, but we associate sensations with a dispositional state through a hypothesis that secures only a very contingent connection. What makes certain sensations a throb of compassion rather than a headache, is their association with compassion, but compassion is, of course, a determinable disposition, which is not realized in a set pattern of behavior. These sensations, therefore, could not indicate compassion with sufficient reliability (as they could, in fact, in James) ever to be a sign of compassion. Even more seriously, and quite independently of whether feelings could be coherently reduced to sensations, sensation, itself, is a problematic category for Ryle. Because they are neither dispositions nor public occurrences, sensations fall outside of Ryle's structure of psychological explanation. The reduction of feelings to sensations leaves Ryle with a type of occurrence, sensations, that threatens his conceptual behaviorism.

havior in this category. I have questioned our reliance on familiar behavior patterns in attempting to understand emotions. At this point, I would add that whatever case Ryle can make here will apply only to a small group of classic emotions. There is no indication that Bass's and Muriel's feelings are shared or understood widely enough to give rise to conventions that would render behavior sufficiently predictable for a dispositional analysis. The option on Ryle's account is to regard these feelings as sensations that do not explain behavior. But I have argued that Muriel's and Bass's feelings provide a very important level of explanation of a diverse range of their behaviors.

Finally, what remains of the analysis of motivated behavior, which for Ryle meets up with the category of intelligent behavior, simply seems to be that we act from reasons: to say that he boasted from vanity is to say that "wherever he finds a chance of securing the admiration and envy of others, he does what he thinks will produce this admiration and envy" (Ryle, 89). But what makes this reason an emotional one?

Donald Davidson in "Actions, Reasons, and Causes" argues famously that teleological or motive explanations of actions do not exclude that the primary reason for an action also is the cause of that action. Davidson points out that motive accounts such as Ryle's, which are meant to replace causal accounts, intersect with causal accounts in a shared description of what counts as the primary reason for an action: a certain pro-attitude toward actions of that kind in conjunction with some kind of cognitive recognition (believing, knowing, remembering, and so on) that the action is of that kind. This intersection is possible because the category of pro-attitudes in Davidson is very broad:

> Fortunately, it is not necessary to classify and analyze the many varieties of emotions, sentiments, moods, motives, passions, and hungers whose mention may answer the question, "Why did you do it?" in order to see how, when such mention rationalizes the action, a primary reason is involved. . . . If Ryle's boaster did what he did from vanity, then something entailed by Ryle's account is true: the boaster wanted to secure the admiration and envy of others, and he believed that his action would produce this envy and admiration; true or false, Ryle's account does not dispense with primary reasons but depends on them. (Davidson, "Actions," 7)

I am not interested here in the role of mental causation in a theory of affect, but only with Davidson's note that Ryle's account of vanity depends on primary reasons. But the specified pro-attitude in this case is not the vanity, but a desire it gives rise to: the desire to secure the admiration and envy of others. The primary reason could equally well be compatible with character traits such as insecurity or that brand of feistiness that thrives on adversaries, or the higher-level objective of wanting to be the winner in a game of ritual boasting. What makes this a case of *affective* reason or motive? And what makes this a case of one specific category of affective reasons among others? The compatibility of a specific desire pro-attitude with a range of higher-level motives or objectives broadens our explanatory commitments.

My concern about Ryle is not that his account of inclinations depends on primary reasons, but that he has no fuller analysis of the category of affect that would help us see why a certain primary reason is a candidate for an affective predication such as compassion, jealousy, or, by his account, vanity. It is alright for Davidson, in the context of his objectives, to default on a fuller analysis of the varied categories of pro-attitudes by saying, for instance, "these are the sorts of things a jealous man wants to do" (Davidson, "Actions," 7). Although Ryle would, no doubt, say exactly this as well, the failure to locate affect uniquely in the explanation of behavior, when this is what you are trying to give an account of, cannot be redressed by appealing extraphilosophically to the claim that we know what jealousy is. Obvious reasons should not be deemed so obvious as to be ignored. The obvious answers to, "How does a jealous man act?," are two more questions: (1) "What is he jealous of?"; and (2) "I don't know. Who is it?" Philosophers have paid little attention to what seems the rather obvious fact that there are few set patterns of behavior even for the classic emotions.[13]

In summary, Ryle appears to hold an account of feelings much like the one offered by James, but it is both considerably less unified and less explanatory. James's reduction is the reduction of an entire psychological category. Ryle's fragmentation of the category of affect eliminates emotions and feelings from his map of the mind. In *The Concept of Mind*, emotions as inclinations are clearly reintegrated into the explanation of behavior, but at considerable cost. Ryle, no more than Darwin or James, locates a unique role for affect within an account of motivation, and it is time to pause and look at this issue.

Ryle operates exclusively with a contrasting set of distinctions for an analysis of a psychological vocabulary. Either psychological terms are analyzed as dispositions to behave, where the behaviors are the public occur-

---

13. Tormey, who is concerned with expression (see Chapter 2 of this book) is more astute on this point: "it would be misleading to analyze expression as a simple two-term relation, implying that X expresses Y if X is, say, some pattern of behavior and Y some mental state or process characteristically manifested in behavior of the type of which X is a member . . . this is equivalent to assuming, a priori, that all expressions of fear . . . must have something in common" (28–29).

rences that both evidence our psychological attributions and are predictable on the basis of these attributions, or psychological terms are mental causes of which the behaviors are effects. Ryle argues for the wholesale replacement of the latter strategy by the former. Davidson's remarks bring out the important point that we do have various and very different categories of explanation for action and behavior and that some of these categories may overlap in their appeal to primary reasons and in the behavior for which they account. Darwin, James, and Ryle all run afoul of the problem of explanatory redundancy in their accounts of affectivity. This brings up the general question of why we would use one category of explanation rather than another. What are the different explanatory purposes and commitments that need to be sorted to avoid this redundancy? Davidson claims that what we want from an explanation of action is an interpretation that makes sense of that action by giving it "a place in a pattern," "a familiar picture" (Davidson, "Actions," 10). I wish to raise the question of whose point of view counts in legitimizing a certain collection of behaviors as a pattern.

In the Introduction to *The Concept of Mind,* Ryle uses both geographical discourse and narrative discourse to describe his project. Ryle's positive description of his philosophical task shows an unsurprising allegiance to the former:

> To determine the logical geography of concepts is to reveal the logic of the propositions in which they are wielded, that is to say, to show with what other propositions they are consistent and inconsistent, what propositions follow from them and from what propositions they follow. The logical type or category to which a concept belongs is the set of ways in which it is logically legitimate to operate with it. (8)

However the idea of narrative is used to formulate the problem of mind and of mind–body interaction:

> [the mind's] career is private. . . . A person therefore lives through two collateral histories, one consisting of what happens in and to his body, the other consisting of what happens in and to his mind. (Ryle, 11)

> [A]ctual transactions between the episodes of the private history and those of the public history remain mysterious, since by definition they can belong to neither series. They could not be reported among the happenings described in a person's autobiography of his inner life, but nor could they be reported in someone else's biography of that person's overt career. (Ryle, 12)

A certain continued commitment to some types of narrative to the exclusion of others lies hidden below the weight of the geographical model.

Ryle has reason to be suspicious of narrative. The idea of a theater of the mind is rendered more plausible by the idea of a mind's career or history, because this suggests that the mind's career is narratable and that we thus have access to it. Ryle seems to think that we can dispense with the idea of narrative once we have exploded a particular kind of narrative: the myth of the mind. But although narrative is not the discourse of resolution in Ryle, it seems fair to me to regard the book as a description of the possibilities of narratives about other people's lives and our own lives: "a man's bodily life is as much a public affair as are the lives of animals and reptiles and even as the careers of trees, crystals, and planets" (Ryle, 11). A sort of ordinary question then arises: what are the possibilities for biography and autobiography in Ryle?

The possibility of biography is firmly endorsed. To have a career, life as a public affair, a history, is to be in a position where one's life could be described in a narrative, and everything necessary to an understanding of the life as related in that biography could be included. Reference to emotions, for instance, would provide the motives that explain action sufficiently to give the narrative a plot. Also, and crucially, narrative has a point of view, and this is implicit in Ryle's description of the ordinary and competent understanding that we have of people.

Those who construct narratives about us do not occupy some neutral observational standpoint. They have a stake in understanding us. They are, to use Ryle's list from his Introduction, our teachers, examiners, historians, novelists, confessors, noncommissioned officers, employers, partners, lovers, friends, and enemies. They "appraise [our] performances, assess [our] progress, understand [our] words and actions, discern [our] motives . . . see [our] jokes" and, important, influence our minds by their "criticism, example, teaching, punishment, bribery, mockery, and persuasion" (Ryle, 7). The one important person that is allowed no special narrative standpoint about my life is myself.

I make the observation, at this point, that we do not have to allow that people know special things about their own lives, or know them with some special authority, or come to find things about their own lives in some special way to allow that they can organize the things they know about themselves from a particular narrative standpoint. The explanatory purposes that ground our use of affective explanation may oblige us to take this standpoint into account, and, in taking this standpoint into account, we might solve the problem of explanatory redundancy. If this is the case, it would explain why set patterns of behavior that are the behaviors of no particular person are precisely the wrong place to begin an account of affect. I pursue the possibility of an autobiographical standpoint as the special organizational principle associated with affective explanation in Chapter 4.

ALSTON AND EPISTEMIC WARRANT

If we attempt to raise affect to a philosophically manageable level of generality by choosing the standard emotions as our paradigm analysands, we risk losing the domain of feeling entirely. In "Feelings" William Alston attempts, in reply to Ryle, to rehabilitate feelings as a central and positive notion within philosophy of mind by reinstating some of the complexity that had been lost from the time of James onward. Alston's article, written in 1969, remains one of the most sustained treatments of feelings in the philosophical literature and is a testament to their neglect. Alston, however, accepts far too much from the preceding tradition of treatment to accomplish his project.

Jamesian agents are lonely creatures. By the time Alston and Ryle discuss the concept of feeling, the landscape of philosophical psychology had undergone considerable evolution, resulting in the formal separation of empirical psychology from philosophy of mind, the latter focusing its attention on the analysis of ordinary concepts as those show themselves in our ability to employ a shared vocabulary of psychological terms. The need to establish the possibility of this shared vocabulary leads to a different kind of analysis of psychological states, one mediated by our shared ability to manipulate the general terms of our language.

Within this new philosophical order, feelings remain no easier to place. The explanation of our ability to identify and distinguish our felt states becomes exacerbated and located in the issue of mental privacy. If my acquaintance with my states of consciousness is through a type of inner perception where there need be no public manifestation of these states, whereas your acquaintance with these same states is solely through my behavior, how do we share a univocal vocabulary for referring to these states?[14] When I say I feel homesick and you say you feel homesick, how do we guarantee that our use of the word "homesick," fixed for each of us by such different modes of experience, has the same meaning? Without the guarantee of a stable vocabulary, where "homesick" has a meaning in our language that we all understand and share, what gives me the resources for identifying my own states? Feelings have played a particularly vexing

14. See, for example, Hampshire, "The Analogy of Feeling"; Aune; and Austin, "Other Minds." For the still-lively nature of this issue, as well as a proposed solution, see Davidson, "Three Varieties of Knowledge."

role in this dilemma as paradigms of conscious states that, because of their bodily basis, resist analysis into explanatorily useful abstractions—the fate met by beliefs and desires. It is important to note that the problem of identifying our conscious states, as it arises in discussions of the concept of feeling, arises only, however, if we accept the reduction of feelings to mere states of consciousness. Alston accepts this reduction and attempts to find a functional role for feeling within it.

Alston is well aware of writing at the end of a particular tradition where feelings have been reduced and wishes to remove himself from this tradition by arguing for the complexity of feelings. He recognizes that he is dealing with a significant gap in the philosophical literature. The role has been set by the reduction of feelings to sensations, thereby leading philosophers to deny that such states as emotions could be feelings, for sensations lack the necessary cognitive structure to ground action. They lack, for instance, the propositional content that would explain why we act. We act in anger because we believe that we have been insulted. Philosophers who are anxious to show that emotions or motives are not simply feelings assume that feelings themselves are simple analysands in a map of the mind, and it is this particular reduction that Alston wants to resist. The issue is where to reinstate their complexity.

Alston's account of the complexity of feelings is an attempt to meet the requirements of shared and univocal vocabulary for psychological states where the stability of meaning is not compromised by the complete reduction of feeling to private experience. He also accepts Ryle's tough prescriptive requirements on contemporary philosophical analysis as concerned with the logical geography of concepts and propositions. Alston's account of feelings is an account (1) of locutions; and (2) of how some propositions, in this case datable first-person feel statements such as "I feel angry," support other propositions. That is, it is an account of how to wield the concept of feeling legitimately within publicly understood propositions.

The evolutionary treatment of the emotions provides the background for the curiously static role of feeling in Alston's theory. In James, the reduction of emotion to the sensory accompaniment of action has the following consequences: (1) it fails to involve emotion in the explanation of behavior. (2) It reduces emotions, functionally, to a source of information about ourselves, or, at most, ourselves in relation to our environment, and then, only if we have the resources for synthesizing our experience into something we can uniquely identify as affective experience. Finally, (3) feelings that have no standardized expression lack a principle of recognition and thus become completely mysterious. Attempts to treat feelings directly begin to focus on the second consequence, and their epistemic status in self-knowledge rather than on their explanatory role in behavior. The second consequence is the only consequence of the Jamesian reduction that provides an indication for a positive account of affect. It is thus the epistemic possibilities of feeling that are exploited by Alston.[15]

Alston derives his positive epistemic account from a feature of a particular group of feelings, feelings reported by phrases of the form "I feel f" where "f" is some adjective or adjectival phrase "the nominal form of which designates a kind of state of a person" (Alston, 5). "Anger," for instance, is the nominalization of "angry." In other words, Alston limits his account to feelings already so well characterized that they have nominalized forms or can be designated by general terms. Alston then rejects an analysis of such feelings as either complexes of bodily sensations or special unanalyzable qualities of consciousness. His negative argument is that such an analysis reduces the concept of each feeling to the concept of those elements of which the feeling is constituted. For instance, the concept of feeling angry becomes the concept of a certain set of bodily sensations, making no reference to the state of being angry, which includes cognitive elements and publicly recognizable patterns of behavior, and to which the concept of feeling angry is obviously related in some way.

Alston's proposal is that, although feelings are nothing but noncognitive modifications of consciousness, first-person feel locutions give epistemic warrant to first-person state locutions; that is, if I feel angry, I will be inclined to believe that I am angry, and this belief will have prima facie warrant. Alston's account thus focuses on the role of feeling as a source of information about ourselves. But Alston nowhere gives an account of the sorts of things feelings are by virtue of which we could understand their epistemic authority in self-knowledge. Feelings are, in Alston's theory, just whatever enables persons to make reliable judgments about whatever emotional state they are in: "It is just a fact about human beings that they are sometimes able to make reliable judgements about certain kinds of things without having any evidence on which to base those judgements. When the kind of thing in question is a state of the individual that is not itself a conscious state, we call this condition which enables him to do this

---

15. For a modern attempt to use this strategy, see Clarke: "Evidence that emotional feelings should be understood as informational units similar to sensations is available from evolutionary biology. . . . As Darwin argued, such communication provides an evolutionary advantage to social animals. If emotional expression communicates information to other members of one's species, it is reasonable to expect that subjective experience of an emotion functions to inform the subject of the same information" (669). Like Alston, Clarke is left minimally with the task of offering some account of how feelings, which he describes as nonpropositional information units, perform this function.

a feeling" (21). The functional role of feelings is found within the explanation of self-knowledge, not of behavior. Furthermore, according to Alston, to be angry is not to have a feeling at all. The classic emotions are not themselves felt, although feelings provide us with the warrant for thinking we are in an emotional state.

As Alston's analysis is an account of the ways in which general terms may be used in a proposition, it is the analysis of a *concept* of a feeling. Feelings become complex because feeling concepts include the concepts of the states for which they provide epistemic warrant. To provide an intersubjective feeling vocabulary, the concept of the state (of, say, anger) is made conceptually prior to the concept of the feeling (of anger), in much the same way as the concept of being red might be thought more basic than or prior to the concept of something's appearing red. Alston attempts to reinstate complexity in the account of feelings by making every particular feeling concept complex in a similar way.

Alston's account both reflects and attempts to exploit, a treatment of affect that has been unable to give an account of how this psychological category relates to organized behavior. This history has reduced affect to a part of the problem of consciousness. However, I contend that Alston is unable to make a persuasive general case for feelings as warrant conferring modifications of consciousness. There is no epistemic role for a great many feelings and no possibility of utilizing Alston's account because there is no corresponding state of the sort that Alston requires. The kind of analysis on which Alston embarked requires, at minimum, that he deal with states at all levels of the analysis that are sufficiently well characterized to yield concepts. But I have already started to suggest that many feelings are not like this. Consider, now, this example from Sylvia Plath's "Cut":

> What a thrill—
> My thumb instead of an onion.
> The top quite gone
> Except for a sort of hinge
> Of skin,
> A flap like a hat,
> Dead white.
> Then that red plush. . . . (23)

What is the feeling Plath expresses in "Cut"? The difficulty in answering this question is not merely taxonomic, as nowhere on a standard list of the classic emotions will we find its name. The opening suggests exhilaration ("What a thrill—"), but this is immediately undercut by the lines that follow, describing what should be a frightening wound in a dry and matter-of-fact voice, and a simile that reduces the horrifying to triteness ("like a hat"). We do not have a name, or a well-defined category of affect to attach to this type of feeling. Alicia Ostriker, in *Writing Like a Woman*, suggests that in "reading 'Cut,' one feels the weird sinking hilarity which is an immediate response to any accident" (84). When Ostriker characterizes the feeling as one of "weird sinking hilarity," her description seems perfectly appropriate, and we recognize the feeling expressed.

We could, following Alston, say that Plath's feeling of weird sinking hilarity warrants her in believing that she is in a state of weird sinking hilarity, but that would be to suppose that Plath is as good a critic as Ostriker. Further, even if Ostriker's description strikes us as right, it would be a mistake to think that what she has done in providing the description is to locate the feeling for us in an already prepared taxonomy of affective states. It would be closer to the truth to say that Ostriker has, in coining an apt phrase, prepared a new category of affect, and we may now recognize as belonging to that category fleeting feelings we have had. Ostriker has, perhaps, in labeling the feeling, provided us with a new expressive resource that we could not otherwise sort out from an affective soup of hurt, surprise, shock, confusion, and speechlessness.

Like the accounts of Darwin, James, and Ryle, Alston's account of feeling suffers from overattention to the familiar classic emotions, for which the problem of recognition is least likely to arise. His epistemological thesis—that to have a feeling is thereby to be warranted in having a belief about the character of one's own psychological states—could never have suggested itself if his entire range of examples had been restricted to feelings such as Bass has for oil or Plath has on the occasion of a cut. As a result, Alston and his predecessors overlook the serious problem of how we recognize or identify a feeling and its expression. That oversight is related to the further neglect of the close nature of the relation between a feeling and its expression.

By arriving at an apt characterization of Plath's feeling, Ostriker had to function as a critic, not a taxonomist. Likewise, in giving expression to her feeling, Plath functioned as a poet, not a taxonomist. In the chapters that follow, I develop the thought that the relationships between the feelings we express, their expression, and the interpretive skills and projects of others are much tighter than the history of the treatment of feelings would lead us to expect.

From evolutionary theory, we might expect an account of affect that seeks a functional role for feelings in the evolution of serviceable behavior. Darwin, because of his anticreationist agenda provided an evolutionary narrative in which feelings account only for the disserviceable remnants of once-serviceable behavior. The behavior expressive of emotion is disruptive of, rather than integrated into, the overall pattern of behavior.

In James, feelings can not even disrupt otherwise organized behavior—they are the mere epiphenomena of behavior the organization of which is explained by other psychological means. Our *talk* of feelings can no longer be part of explanations of behavior, and there is nothing left for such talk to be but descriptions or reports of the presence of feelings, so the only useful scrutiny of such talk is epistemological scrutiny.

Alston illustrates the result of this transformation: feeling locutions are warrant conferring locutions and nothing more. The emotions themselves, which were once supposed to be feelings, become unfelt states for which feelings are evidence. Ryle draws out the metaphysical implications of the transformation I have traced from Darwin through James: feeling talk is talk about a disorganized array of unrelated matters, none of which are themselves feelings. There is no place left for feelings on the map of the mind.

But no one along the way wants to give up the idea that emotions are motivationally linked to behavior, so emotions and feelings (as these latter shrink to mere sensations) start to drift apart—emotions drift in the direction of beliefs and desires, and feelings drift in the direction of qualia, the nonfunctional epiphenomena of consciousness.

At the same time, the absence of feelings is felt. Darwin, James, Alston, and Ryle, however differently motivated in their accounts of affect, are united in their inability to account for the individuation of the states that fall under the concept of affect, even when these states are tokens of classic emotions. Their dependence on what they take to be our quite ordinary abilities to recognize these states, behaviorally or phenomenologically, obscures the fact that they have not provided an account of their individuation. In Chapter 2, I offer such an account.

Finally, Darwin, James, Ryle, and Alston all have superficially different motives for founding an account of affect on familiar feelings that are so well characterized that they have associated concepts and/or are designated by general terms ("as the sun, for Piaget's children, bears its name in its center" [Merleau-Ponty, 4]). But the persistence of this phenomenon in the treatment of affect points to a difficulty in finding a methodology adequate for analyzing a grouping of psychophysical phenomena that may be composed in part, by very particular as well as locally shared responses. I have suggested that we need a more adequate understanding of affect as a category of interest and explanation, and I pursue this suggestion in later chapters.

II

EXPRESSION AND THE INDIVIDUATION OF FEELING

I think of myself as using poetry as a chief means of self-explora-
tion . . . the poem, like the dream, does this through images and
it is in the images of my poems that I feel I am finding out more
about my own experience, my sense of things. But I don't think
of myself as having a position or a self-description which I'm
then going to present in the poem.

Adrienne Rich

Whenever there is a gap in our understanding of the conceptual
scheme, a gap that we cannot close by the discovery of a middle
term, there is an unsolved philosophical problem. We close the
gap when we bring to light an unnoticed overlapping between
the conditions of application of one concept and the conditions
of application of another, an overlapping that we had hitherto
overlooked. . . . But it is only a truly philosophical curiosity, if the
irritating gap in the conceptual scheme occurs at a crucial point
in systematizing a whole set of concepts according to some uni-
form principle.

Stuart Hampshire, "Feeling and Expression"

The term *expression*, even if one discounts its aesthetic uses, has a
broad range of application. We express not only feelings, moods,
sentiments, emotions—in fact, the whole of our affective lives—
but also beliefs, opinions, intentions, and needs. To note that we
express such states as needs is to point out how naturally we use the term
expression with a wide range of psychological states, and there seems no
reason to count one type of state as more expressible than another. I thus
start from the assumption that there is nothing special about the nature
of expression that has to do with its unique connection to a particular
type of psychological state. However, the variety of psychological states
that can be expressed does provide an interesting clue about expression
by drawing our attention to the corresponding variety of resources that we
use to express ourselves.

Our expressive resources, the means by which we express our psychological states, include language, nonlinguistic action, and involuntary behavior over which we can, nevertheless, exercise some control, such as smirking, grimacing, whimpering. I express my opinions through language, my desires through action, and I can express my affection for you in a variety of ways—by talking romantically, buying you flowers, or smiling at you when you enter a room.

I make these initial points about the range of application of the notion of expression primarily to indicate that expressing, on our natural use of the term, is an activity and a ubiquitous one. I introduce the idea of *expressive resources* to open the possibility that the formation of various types of psychological states and the grounds on which they are predicable by others and interpretable to ourselves may depend on our access to and use of different types of expressive resources. Neither you nor I have any reason to believe that I desire to quit smoking, if I never, at any time, engage in any *action* that could so be interpreted. My kitten Lili, having no access to linguistic resources, may have something like beliefs, but cannot be credited with any opinions (Tormey, 72).

Perhaps because expression is so ubiquitous, our understanding of the notion is not well delineated. There are few philosophical accounts of expression outside aesthetic theory; both within and outside aesthetics, most accounts deal only with the expression of feelings or emotions. If we concentrate on the expression of emotion and the resources peculiar to this activity, we may develop a view of expression that is inadequate to explain the expression of other psychological states. Theories of expression have, in fact, suffered from a limited focus on expression of feelings.

As we saw in Chapter 1, theorists have depended with little success, on our abilities to recognize set patterns of behavior associated with classic emotions to try to give an account of these emotions. Darwin, James, and Ryle thought that certain kinds of behaviors were recognizable as reliably expressive of particular emotions. These theorists could not give an adequate account of the relation of emotions to behavior partly because they allowed the role of emotional explanation to piggy-back on the idea of unique behavioral patterns.

Attempts to fix the individuation of expression to give an account of feeling have a parallel in accounts of expression. It is, as I shall show, a deep supposition of many philosophical accounts of the nature of expression that our everyday emotions of love, fear, and the like, are individuated independently of how they are expressed by us in action or behavior. However, I contend that *expression is the activity through which our psychological states, including our feelings, become individuated for both others and our-*

selves. By *individuated,* I mean formed or created as the particulars they are in such a way that they can then be recognized or identified. An account of feeling or expression that attempts to hold one of these as individuated, in order to give an account of the other, precisely misses the point where these concepts intersect.

In this chapter, I concentrate on accounts of expression from within philosophy of mind. I first critically assess the accounts of Richard Wollheim, William Alston, and Alan Tormey. These three theorists offer general accounts of the concept of expression that nevertheless focus centrally on the expression of feelings. All three assume that our feelings are individuated prior to their expression.

I approach these accounts with two concerns. First, I advance a political concern about what types of criticism of our emotional lives these theories can explain or even accommodate. When we express our feelings, criticism of the way we express ourselves often is criticism of the moral adequacy of our feelings or of the moral quality of our emotional lives. I have in mind such criticisms as Wilde's famous attack on Lord Alfred Douglas: "You were, and are I suppose still, a typical sentimentalist. For a sentimentalist is simply one who desires to have the luxury of an emotion without paying for it" (quoted in Tanner, 125). I argue here and in Chapter 6, that there is a significant political dimension to expressive criticism. This type of criticism gives an urgency to understanding the relation between feeling and expression, for theories that assume that psychological states are individuated independently of expression cannot explain how expressive criticism is criticism of the quality of our responses.

Second, these three theories fail in a fundamental way to realize their objectives. Interestingly, although Wollheim ("Expression"), Alston ("Expressing"), and Tormey all agree that expression is an activity, they do not approach the nature of the activity directly and cannot, in the end, give a coherent account of this activity. The assumption that our psychological states are individuated before they are expressed makes it impossible, I argue, to give an account of the activity of expressing.

Although I am primarily interested in affective states, I also am concerned with the appropriate place of an account of expression within philosophy of mind. My account of expressing feelings reflects this broader concern. My criticisms should lead us to consider that expression is the activity through which our psychological states, including our feelings, become individuated for both others and ourselves. I present Charles Taylor's work on action as the expression of desire as outlining a more satisfactory general approach to expression than is found in accounts of expression of feeling. Finally, I remind the reader of a different tradition of theorizing about expression, the expressionist theory of art, which provides additional support for my approach and allows me to draw out some of its political importance.

The concern of this chapter and the next is to link the concepts of feeling and expression in such a way as to make it possible to talk from within philosophy of mind about the range of people's affective experiences. This linkage cannot be directly defended on the basis of an agreement on the logic of the concepts, for there is no such agreement. The claim that expression is an activity of individuating feelings is a central positive proposal of the study and one with an obvious and appealing consequence. The richer and more discriminating our ways of expression, the richer and more nuanced our affective lives.

Expression and Individuation

In *The Prose of the World*, Merleau-Ponty illustrates a perplexity in theory of expression by describing the filming, in slow motion, of Matisse making a single brush stroke on the canvas. Matisse, himself, was apparently moved in watching the film. The brush "could be seen meditating, in a suspended and solemn time . . . beginning ten possible movements, performing in front of the canvas a sort of propitiatory dance, coming so close several times as almost to touch it, and finally coming down like lightning in the only stroke necessary" (Merleau-Ponty, 44).[1] The "only stroke necessary" implies, as Merleau-Ponty well knows, that Matisse made the *right* expressive choice, and this notion of correctness may, in turn, tempt us to posit a referent in comparison to which we, or at least Matisse, can know that this was the right choice. This referent we may call "the object of expression," whatever it is, and how and wherever it exists—a sentiment, a scene outside the artist's window, or a vision in the artist's mind. Whatever this object, Matisse's brush strokes accurately represent it to us.

We are less tempted than we once were to disfigure the artist into a ghostwriter of the real world or a mere scribe of inner artistic vision. The complexities, mysteries, and integrity of artistic choice and creativity make a view of a preexistent referent copied into art naive, and this is precisely why Merleau-Ponty uses this example to make a point about the nature and problem of expression:

[For] if at the end of the film Matisse believes that he really chose, on that particular day, between those possible strokes and, like Leibniz's God,

1. Although Merleau-Ponty put aside this work in the early 1950s, there is no evidence that this was a gesture of repudiation.

solved an immense problem of minimum and maximum, he is mistaken. . . . It is true that the hand hesitated, that it meditated. It is therefore true that there was a choice, that the stroke was chosen so as to satisfy ten conditions scattered on the painting, unformulated and unformulable for anyone other than Matisse, since they were defined and imposed only by the intention to make *this particular painting which did not yet exist.* (44–45; emphasis in original)

In other words, the particular with reference to which we judge expressive success and failure is formed through the very act of expression, and Merleau-Ponty means this to be a fully general comment about the nature of expression.

In this section, I trace a more critical route to the same point that Merleau-Ponty eloquently presents by this example. However sophisticated our view of artistic expression, that our everyday feelings of fear, anger, love, and the like are fully individuated as particulars before they are expressed by us in talk or in action remains a deep supposition and systematic distortion of many nonaesthetic accounts of the nature of expression.[2] The presupposition of individuation gives us the illusion that we can explain expressive failure at the cost of leaving us unable to account for a pervasive and politically significant kind of criticism of people's affective lives.

We judge people to be sentimental, overemotional, or inarticulate, that is, we judge them to have various "diseases of the affections" through the way they express their feelings. These criticisms have moral weight and often divide roughly along gender or group lines. Western women of a comfortable socioeconomic class, may, for example, be thought more prone than men of this class to sentimentality or emotionality. I am curious about how this type of criticism works. We know all we know of a person's affective life from their expression of it, but a term such as *emotionality*, rather than having a restricted application to a person's expressive behavior or to some range of affective states of a person inferred from their expressive behavior, is often used to condemn a person's emotional nature. That is, when we refer to someone as sentimental or overemotional, or, one might add, as oversensitive, morbid, or bitter, we often imply that they have a bad emotional character. What licenses this type of condemnation? My thesis is not that such criticisms cannot fairly be made of people. It is rather that their being made so often of women is an

2. I borrow the notion of systematic distortion from R. G. Collingwood, *The Principles of Art:* "A theory which has commended itself to a great many intelligent people invariably expresses a high degree of insight into the subject dealt with, and the distortion to which this has been subjected is invariably thoroughgoing and systematic" (107).

invitation to ask whether there is a political dimension to their use. Standard accounts of the relation between feeling and expression are in no position to answer this question because they cannot, in the first place, easily accommodate explanations of this kind of criticism.

The distorting agent in accounts of expression is the assumption that psychological states are individuated before they are expressed, that the expression of a psychological state is an instance of revealing or disclosing that state and is in no way formative of it. So Richard Wollheim begins his article "Expression" by stating that we can do one of three things with the fluctuating and imperious feelings of our inner life: "We can put them into words: we can manifest them in our actions: or we can keep them to ourselves. We can conceal them, or we can reveal them" (227–28). Similarly, Alan Tormey, in *The Concept of Expression*, describes the activity of expressing ourselves in this manner:

> There is something "inside" which is ex-pressed, forced out, and which in turn reveals what remains inside. But human expression is revealing in a dual sense. If we hear an outburst of nervous laughter *as* an expression of embarrassment we are aware both that something is occurring "inside" the person, and that there is some event or situation, real or imagined, by which he is embarrassed. (28)

Finally, William Alston, in "Expressing" wishes to test the hypothesis that there is no significant difference in linguistically expressing a feeling and reporting its presence, that is, asserting that one has it.

A word choice of "reveal" or "manifest" to describe expressing does not prove that these philosophers hold a feeling to be separate and independent of any act that expresses it; however, this is the most natural reading of their wording, and Alston's view seems prima facie committed to the prior individuation of the state reported. Moreover, all these views contain symptomatic commitments and problems best explained by the presence of this distorting presupposition. Alston, for example, claims that expressions "are a reliable indication of some feeling or attitude," where "to say that x is an indication of y is to say that from x one can (fairly safely) infer the existence of y" (Alston, 20). For Tormey "to say that behavior expresses a belief, in the way I am using this concept, is to say that the belief and the behavior can be linked inferentially" (76, note 13). To say that we can infer the presence of x from the presence of y typically implies that y is not constitutive of x. I provide further support for my reading of these theories later in this section; however, I will first say how the assumption that a feeling is individuated prior to its expression makes difficult a diagnosis of diseases of the affections.

I have said that the broad stroke criticisms of emotionality and sentimentality often seem to be condemnations of a person's emotional nature. However, since it's not at all clear from the start what criticisms of a person's emotional nature are meant to be, we should first consider that a criticism of sentimentality might be a comment on the limited range of feelings that a person has, or it may be a comment on the limited range of occasions that a person finds moving. Both these diagnoses seem compatible with reliable single-case inferences from expression to feeling and their accretive effect on our assessment of a person's emotional nature.

In his thoughtful article, "Sentimentality," Michael Tanner, beginning with our vague notion of sentimentality as involving self-indulgent emotions somehow had on the cheap, considers both the above possibilities and rejects them as no more than partially explanatory. With respect to the range of feelings expressed, Tanner postulates that unsentimental emotions such as anger sometimes can provide a secure basis for accusing someone of sentimentality.[3] With respect to what we are affected by, Tanner points out that the seeming triviality of the response cannot always be traced back to the triviality of its occasion. For example: "It is surely clear that the death of a child, at least one of Little Nell's mettle, is something towards which strong feelings are appropriate" (Tanner, 130). Nevertheless, Dickens's portrayal of her death is sentimental, as is our response to this portrayal.

Tanner limits the adequacy of accounts of sentimentality that are focused on type of response or occasion of response to make room for the additional reflection that the self-indulgence of sentimentality often is located in a triadic relation among feeling, object, and action. Specifically, he suggests that a feeling is sometimes sentimental when it becomes freed from appropriate governance by the nature of its object or occasion and is, consequently, inappropriately expressed in action. To illustrate Tanner's suggestion, I expand on one of his own examples: Othello's final speech and suicide.

The feeling that motivates the final action of the play is remorse over the murder of Desdemona, but, because of Othello's expression of remorse, the remorse is in a distorted relation to its occasion. Othello's jealousy was unwarranted, and the murder is such an outrage that a quick quiet suicide might be an appropriate expression of this remorse. But instead, Othello pauses . . . to taste his remorse reflectively in speech.

---

3. I do not find this claim particularly convincing. Whatever sentimentality is, it seems most naturally to infect an emotional life characterized by the possibility that passive response does not change the character of that emotion. Passivity in anger very often changes anger to a different emotion: resentment, frustration, or depression.

Dislocated from the tragedy of the murder, it becomes, instead, the opportunity for reflection on the tragic figure that he, to himself, presents as "one that lov'd not wisely, but too well" "whose hand . . . threw a pearl away/ Richer than all his tribe" (Act V, Scene 2). The remorse is no longer controlled by its occasion, but festers in an inappropriate act of self-indulgent expression that taints even the suicide that follow with sentimentality. Tanner concludes that "an inner life which is self-generating and insufficiently related to the world of action is corrupting and dangerous" (Tanner, 144).

Although expression is not Tanner's explicit concern, I find his reflections apt to the theme of this chapter. Both Othello's speech and suicide are expressions of remorse. Othello's remorse is inappropriately expressed, and, consequently, Othello is a sentimentalist, a condemnation of his emotional nature. But it's difficult to see how a view that both presupposes individuation of Othello's remorse before his attempt to express it and allows for expressive failure can support this criticism of Othello. Under the assumption of individuation, we can reliably infer that Othello feels remorse, and we can criticize his expression of it, but, perhaps Othello just isn't very good at expressing himself. The remorse is clearly appropriate. How are we then justified in criticizing more than its expression? In other words, why isn't sentimentality just a stylistic criticism? A tempting response is that we can infer something further about Othello's remorse from its expression, and condemn the remorse by this further inference. But there is nothing other than the expression that *makes* the remorse sentimental. To call Othello's remorse "sentimental" is a direct, rather than an inferential, criticism.

If these suspicions about the noninferential nature of certain criticisms arise for sentimentality, they are more piercing for emotionality, a condemnation of someone's emotional nature more straightforwardly made and held at the expressive level. Perhaps an emotional person expresses some dominant range of emotions, but another person who expresses this same range might be considered passionate, vital, or, to use a term of Tanner, "emotionally generous." And, as with sentimentality, we can be as emotional about major incidents as about relatively trivial ones. Unlike sentimentality, however, emotionality does not have connotations of emotions somehow had on the cheap. Rather, the condemnation seems to focus on some excess to one's expressive life that is not merely related to how often or forcefully one expresses oneself. A life of anger tiresomely unmistakable by continual expression in physical withdrawal or verbal hostility is not overemotional as we now use the term. But what about a person who cries all the time? Emotionality suggests that some persons do not have adequate control over their emotional life, as evidenced not by the frequency or even intensity but by the *mode* of expression, and these persons nearly always are women.

Once again, I deny that this criticism is plausibly inferential. We can imagine two women, A and B, each with a single expressive resource— one chops wood, the other cries—and we can further imagine, with appropriate modulations in these activities and some minimal verbal help, that we can infer only identical information about each feeling that they coincidently express. "Anger at *X*," says A chopping wood, B crying. "Slight depression," says A chopping more methodically, B crying quietly. There is no difference here in what we can *infer* as to the type, intensity, or objects of their respective feelings. One type of expression *reveals* no more than the other about the particulars of the feelings. The sole difference is in the *mode* of expression, and to call the crier overemotional is to condemn her affective life solely and directly by condemning the mode of expression. But this means that the relation between feeling and expression is more intimate than disclosure or revelation.

The argument of this section, that expressive criticisms such as sentimentality are at the same time criticisms of the feelings expressed, creates problems for the claim that feelings are individuated prior to and independent of expression. Views that include the independence assumption also are unable to give an account of expression as a distinctive activity. A brief look at this second difficulty leads me to propose an account that focuses directly on analyzing expression as an activity.

Expression is a term taken to have received its meaning by contrast either to communication or to some particular form of communicative activity, such as asserting.[4] We might suppose, then, that an elaboration of this contrast will illuminate expressing as a type of activity. Classic accounts of expression, however, have focused, not on a direct analysis of the activity, but on what states are expressed and, most prominently, on our expressive resources as a way of delimiting the concept of expression. The obliqueness of these approaches requires comment. I use Wollheim's and Alston's work to display the problems of attention to resources. Tormey's book-length treatment presents special problems, although he holds the presupposition of individuation as strongly.[5]

4. Ernst Gombrich, for example, proposes the following as a "crude representation of the expressionist theory of art" in contrast with the communication of information (57):

EXPRESSION	COMMUNICATION
EMOTION	INFORMATION
SYMPTOM	CODE
NATURAL	CONVENTIONAL

5. Briefly, Tormey's view would require a more complex presentation, because there is so much that is right about it. Tormey denies that there are peculiarly expressive resources and affirms that we can express a wide variety of psychological states. He thus sees quite clearly

Wollheim and Alston each concentrate on the relation of language, facial expression, and gesture to expression. If some resources, for instance facial expressions, are peculiarly expressive, and others, perhaps linguistic assertions, cannot be used expressively, this might provide some understanding of what it is to perform an act of expression. Both Wollheim and Alston grant that interjections are usually expressive, but differ over the general role of linguistic assertion in expression.

In brief summary, Wollheim believes that paradigmatically expressive activity involves involuntary, but controllable, behavior, such as smiling. Expression and communication are, for Wollheim, contrasting modes of revealing our psychological states ("Expression," 227–30), and this contrast can be seen precisely in the different resources we use for each. Alston ("Expressing") on the other hand, denies that facial expressions are genuinely expressive (they merely display feelings) and argues that linguistic assertions such as "I am annoyed" are every bit as expressive as such interjections as "Damn!" or "Bully!" He believes that expression is communication, but denies that there is any significant difference between linguistically expressing a feeling and asserting that you have it, in other words, reporting its presence (17, 37).

Alston affirms that expression is a communicative activity: Wollheim denies this. But what the views share is more interesting. Neither philosopher gives an account of expression as a distinctive activity. Neither view locates a unique place for expressing within the realm of linguistic activity. Wollheim uses a contrast between nonlinguistic and linguistic activity, but categorizes both as different modes of the same general activity—self-revelation ("Expression," 230). As these philosophers hold that expression is an activity, but give no distinctive account of it, they fail in a fundamental way to realize the objectives of their approach. Neither view can give an account of expression as distinctive in function from other modes of giving our lives public presence or voice, and neither view can be right as a general account of expression.

Alston's account focuses on expression of feeling in language, and he thus misses some points that can be seen more clearly in focusing on the expression of belief in language. He fails to take account of the indirection that is possible in linguistic expression, but would render a proposition ill-suited to report. "Looks like there won't be a ballgame tonight" can stand as an expression, but not as a report of my belief that it will rain

---

that, if expression is to be uniquely located, we must locate a unique activity. He also argues that expressing and reporting are different activities. However, because he holds the presupposition of individuation, he, no more than Wollheim or Alston, can locate this activity. Tormey ends, very oddly for a philosopher who allows the expression of belief and opinion, by denying that expression is communication.

(Tormey, 68–70). Also, linguistic utterances are not typically regarded as expressing and reporting the same thing. When I sincerely say, "The cat is hungry," I am performing two different speech acts. What is reported is what makes my utterance true. I am thus reporting that the cat is hungry and expressing my belief that the cat is hungry (Dennett, *Consciousness Explained*, 305). Finally, Alston's view, as it is stated, assumes that, given adequate linguistic resources, when we are in a position to express our psychological states linguistically, we are in a position to assert that we have them. Although this is consistent with Alston's later work on feeling locutions as providing a warranting function for psychological reports, it seems to me an implausibly strong view.

Wollheim's view cannot begin to account for the range of psychological states expressed. In fact, he allows in passing that straightforward assertions such as "I'm angry" are sometimes expressions of thought and that a thought may give to a feeling much of its "distinctness and inner elaboration" ("Expression," 232). This admission makes obvious that a contrast between expressing and some other kind of activity cannot be made by denying linguistic resources to expression, for we express our beliefs, opinions, and thoughts. If expression is to be contrasted to other activities, this contrast must be able to operate within the linguistic realm.

My diagnosis of the failure of treatments of expression to give an account of expressing as a unique activity, and hence their default focus on resources as an attempt to locate expression, is their assumed individuation of the state expressed. For under this assumption it is nearly impossible to locate a distinctive function for an expressive use of language: to linguistically communicate the nature of our psychological states will seem to roam indifferently, as it does to Alston, over expressing or reporting them. But it also is impossible to defend a view that contrasts expression with communicative activity while doing justice to the range of states expressed and the necessary admission of language to expressive resources. Finally, if we can express our opinions and beliefs through assertion, this fact simply indicates that assertion is too encompassing a description of our linguistic acts to contrast to expression. The distinction that Alston misses—our capacity to linguistically express without reporting suggests that, in the linguistic realm, this is where the contrast should be located. Reporting also clearly assumes individuation of the state reported, for a second party may report, with greater or lesser accuracy, my beliefs, opinions, intentions, and feelings.

If the presupposition of prior individuation not only blocks our understanding of such criticisms as emotionality, but also depletes room for any positive account of the activity of expressing, we surely have sufficient reason to abandon this presupposition. If our psychological states are not prior to and independent of acts of expression, then they are somehow formed or individuated through these acts. Expression is partly formative of our beliefs, opinions, intentions, and feelings.

Reversing the relation of dependence between expressive activity and psychological content makes room for a positive account of expression as a distinctive activity, and makes it possible to see how expressive criticism can straightforwardly be affective criticism. If Othello's remorse is individuated or characterized by Othello's speech, then we can say that the speech makes the remorse sentimental.

I propose, then, as an account of the relation between the activity of expression and the state expressed that expression is the activity of articulating that state through language and/or behavior. A successful act of articulation is discrimination sufficient for the individuation of a psychological state. I have not stated the conditions for a *successful* act of articulation. However, as a rough marker, it is only after grasping what constitutes the expression of a belief, need, or feeling that I am in a position to report that state, and a second party may be in that position at exactly the same time. It is possible for me to express jealousy and for you accurately to report how I feel, or what I must believe, without my even recognizing the states I have succeeded in individuating. This account of expression as articulation assumes, of course, a view of the mind in which our psychological life is simply not transparent to us or neatly taxonomized into various categories of entities. Our activities give character and content to the flow and flux of our psychological lives, forming those states that we later taxonomize into beliefs, desires, intentions, emotions, and whatever other categories suit our explanatory purposes.

I conclude this section by acknowledging a potential objection. Wollheim and Tormey deny that expression is communication.[6] The objection arises from my claim that, because we use language to express ourselves, we cannot sustain a contrast between expression and communication, but must say what kind of communicative activity expression is. Expression seems clearly communicative some of the time. I express my needs to you, my opinions of you to others, and my intentions publicly so as to commit myself to undertaking action. Nevertheless, expression also seems sometimes to take place independently of an intention to express ourselves, and we may then doubt that it is communicative. To answer this objection, I now turn to Charles Taylor's account of expression.

6. "Expression is not communication; nor does it require communication to occur successfully" (Tormey, 92).

TAYLOR'S ACCOUNT OF EXPRESSING

The suggestion that expression is the activity of individuating certain kinds of psychological states is not original.[7] I think, in fact, that it is quite widespread. The idea is accepted, in weaker or stronger forms, for many psychological states through a discussion of the relation of what I have termed *expressive resources* to the existence of these states—the relation of language to belief, for example. In *Thought and Action*, Stuart Hampshire argues that "the expression of a belief is not the inessential act of clothing it with words; it is the only way of making the belief definite, as a belief in this statement rather than that" (quoted in Tormey, 75). In general, and here Hampshire is somewhat of an exception, discussions about the constitutive relation of behavior to psychological states rarely take place under the heading of "a theory of expression." It thus is difficult to see the pervasiveness of the view I am offering. I have emphasized that we express the full range of our psychological states, and to make the nature of my proposal about expression more perspicuous, I turn now to one of the few accounts that moves an interest in expression away from emotions and feelings: Charles Taylor's account of action as the expression of desire in "Action as Expression."

Taylor begins his account by pointing to uses of the term *expression* that we will accept as standard or unproblematic: "my face expresses joy, my words express my thoughts or feelings, this piece of music expresses sadness, longing, resoluteness" (Taylor, 73). He points out that our use of the term recommends the following basic formula: expression makes something manifest through an embodiment (Taylor, 73). Taylor argues for three refinements to this formula for cases of genuine expression, all of which I accept.

First, to use the concept of expression is to indicate that something has been made manifest to us noninferentially. I may infer that you've had a bad day because you don't eat your dinner, but I see your frustration in your clenched face. When I reason inferentially, "there is something else which I know or which is plain to me in a more direct way, and which I recognize as grounding my inference" (Taylor, 74). It is obvious that you're not eating, and I use this behavior as evidence that you are upset. Its status as evidence for an inference is clear in some way. Perhaps I consider other

---

7. For feelings and emotions, the suggestion is hardly original, having been put forward about the emotions as early as 1938 by R. G. Collingwood in *The Principles of Art*; however, Collingwood puts the point too strongly and epistemologically: that prior to expression of a feeling, all we are conscious of is a perturbation of whose nature we are entirely ignorant (Collingwood, 109). See the discussion on Collingwood in the next section.

hypotheses the behavior might support, for instance, that you don't like what I've cooked. When something is manifest to us through expression, we are not engaged in an inferential process. Othello's sentimentality is not identical with his expression of remorse, but neither is there some further feature of this expression that permits us to infer that Othello is a sentimentalist. We see the sentimentality directly in the expression.

The second refinement, and here I use Taylor's own example, is that what is manifest can only be manifest through expression. This is a stronger condition than the first. We can "look at a construction and see that it is highly unstable and will shortly fall" (Taylor, 74). The array expresses the impending fall. We can, also, however, observe the actual fall. By contrast, in what Taylor calls cases of genuine expression, what is expressed is manifest only through the expression. I can express my disapproval of your eating habits in a variety of ways, through my words or my actions, but my disapproval can be manifest only through expression. There are not two possible phases of my disapproval, one in which you hear it in my words, and one, twenty minutes later, in which you encounter it free of any expressive medium.

Taylor approaches a third and final condition on what he calls genuine expression through a discussion of expressive resources. Expression is a part of "the way of life of beings who have to be in a sense open with each other" (Taylor, 79). Certain sorts of activities, such as speech, facial expressions, and gesture, are, as Taylor puts it, apt for communication and become shaped partly or wholly by their role in communication. We come to respond to these activities as communications: we respond as interpreters. This is an extremely important point. Taylor uses the example of smiling. Smiles, he argues, are ontogenetically apt for communicating openness, and the activity of smiling has been shaped by our need to communicate plus the aptness of smiling for communicating something in particular: openness. In seeing a smile as expressive, I see it as manifesting not just friendliness, but also the disposition to communicate. It is this second level of manifestation, a consequence of our form of life as communicators, that invites the interpretive activity associated with expression and has, as a consequence, that many types of behavior are expressive independently of particular intentions to communicate on particular occasions. I may smile unconsciously when I intend to keep a straight face and my smile communicates friendliness. Taylor's third refinement, then, is that expression makes manifest what is expressed in a way not reducible to an agent's intention to communicate.

Taylor's account is oriented toward understanding the relation between action and desire, specifically, why we consider action an expression of desire. First, because action is a natural response to desire, action offers an accessible physiognomic reading. If you reach for the hammer, this action manifests to me that you desire the hammer, though I may not know why you desire it. Second, desires are not manifest outside of a context of expression: "The desires that we predicate of agents are not discriminable spatio-temporally from the person who acts, in whose behavior we read the desire" (Taylor, 82). Finally, and with respect to Taylor's third refinement, in the normal or basic case, we identify desires through the actions they typically cause or produce. "And this is the only way that a desire can be characterized. If I didn't have this normal situation as one of my possibilities, and at least sometimes as an actuality, I couldn't have the language of desire that I have" (Taylor, 84). Because the action bears the identifying marks of desire and we have no alternative way of characterizing desire, the action itself communicates the desire independently of the agent's intention. Taylor's felicitous way of putting the point is that "action doesn't just enable us to see the desire; it *is* the desire, embodied in public space" (Taylor, 87). My alternative way of characterizing this conclusion is that action as expression individuates desire.

There are features of Taylor's account that I like very much. First, Taylor suggests that to understand the importance of expression, we need first to understand our form of life as communicators and the extent to which this form of life requires interpretive activity that is grounded in the development of shared and recognizable expressive behaviors. Our understanding of expression as communication has as much to do with the fact that expression invites interpretive activity as it has to do with our intentions to communicate. This feature of Taylor's account addresses the concern about communication with which I concluded the last section. My smile may communicate my friendliness even if it is not my intention, in smiling, to communicate my friendliness.

Second, I read Taylor as also suggesting the view that expressive behavior is in some sense constitutive of what is expressed, in that what is expressed cannot be manifest independently of expression, and, moreover, expressive activity allows us to fully individuate or characterize what is expressed.[8] Taylor's analysis of expression seems to me a fruitful way to elaborate contemporary philosophical intuitions about the role of behavior in the constitution of the psychological. Most contemporary philosophers hold some version of the thesis that behavior is constitutive of the mental. Ryle's analysis of psychological terms as dispositions to behave is one example of how this commitment can be elaborated. Those who re-

---

8. This goes beyond what Taylor explicitly endorses. Taylor offers a view of action as individuating desire to give weight to his claim that action meets the third condition of his account. However, I take Taylor's work on desire to be a strong support for my general point that expression individuates.

ject Ryle's behaviorism with its accompanying denial of an inner life will still want to hold that the truth of psychological ascriptions is answerable, in some way and in to some degree, to behavioral manifestations knowable to persons other than the subject of the ascription. To argue for a certain necessary link, as Taylor does with action and desire, between a psychological state's manifestation in an embodiment and the individuation of the state manifested is one promising way of working out this intuition.

Accounts of expression have not developed, however, in the direction of Taylor's work on desire. Indeed, something odd happens in accounts of expression. Taylor, Wollheim, Tormey, and Alston all begin from the intuition that to talk of the expression of feelings is to make a very standard use of the notion of expression. In other words, a discussion of expressing feeling seems like a good place to start an account of expression. Moreover, a theory of expression seems like the right place to discuss how behavior is constitutive of the mental. But theorists who continue to stick very closely to the expression of feelings in formulating their accounts of expression do not usually advance the view that our expressive activities help constitute our feelings. Instead, I have argued, such theorists take our expressions to be revealing of our feelings.

Why, then, might theorists believe that our feelings are independent of our acts of expression, that I may never do anything that could be interpreted as expressing a feeling while still having that feeling, and feelings that receive no expression might be a persistent rather than occasional feature of my psychological life?

Few theorists would now endorse a parallel account of the privacy of belief or desire. At bottom, I believe we all wish to guard the idea that our affective lives can be fully formed and remain intact without the interference of others, and even without others' knowledge that we have such lives. In later chapters, I argue that the security derived from our commitment to private emotional lives is largely illusory. However, I do not think that this commitment to privacy is the whole story of why theorists have not seen a constitutive role for expression when they talk about expressing feelings.

Interestingly there are two features to Taylor's account that provide clues as to why accounts of expressing feeling have not developed in the direction of Taylor's work on desire. I have accepted Taylor's conditions on expression, but think the way he arrives at his view of the relation between desire and action will create difficulties for understanding the relation of feeling to expression. In particular, Taylor's focus on the naturalness of certain expressive resources and on the idea of an unproblematic "happy" case will not illuminate the complexities of emotional expression.

Taylor seems to think of some behaviors as more naturally expressive of others. He begins his account of expression by discussing smiling, which he takes to be ontogenetically apt for communicating openness. He also argues that, as we naturally act on desires, actions can be seen as genuinely expressive of desire. References to naturalness support Taylor's general point that genuine expression is communicative in a sense not reducible to agent intention and support the more specific proposal that actions express desires.

I agree with Taylor that the aptness of certain behaviors for communication both grounds and explains the possibility of our form of life as communicators and that discussions of unlearned responses such as smiling are a good place to begin a discussion of expression. Nevertheless, we have developed sophisticated modes of expression that are equally a part of our form of life as communicators. Taylor, in fact, acknowledges the sophistications of our expression of desire in his discussion of mime:

[There] is a kind of manifestation which is foundational for genuine expression, in that it is presupposed by it. This is the "natural" level of expression, on which genuine expression builds, always with some degree of the arbitrary and the conventional. Mime and style take this up and make a language in which we can say to each, as it were, what we believe ourselves to be. (Taylor, 89)

Moreover, part of our form of life as communicators involves our development as interpreters who see and read a great deal in all kinds of human behaviors. What is manifest to us about others is often finely keyed to the particularities of expressive and interpretive context and cannot be understood simply by considering the nature and development of certain expressive behaviors. Taylor does not discuss the very important role for an understanding of expression played by our interpretive activities. I may take a certain way in which you sign off your electronic mail as expressive of your impatience with me or as expressive of your desire to see me soon because I am familiar with and skilled at interpreting your style in the particular context of our communications through E-mail.

The ways in which we sometimes naturally express our feelings is an understandable place to begin a general account of expression, but with feelings, in particular, it is dangerous to limit our discussion to those behaviors that are foundational for the project of expression. The idea that certain gestures and facial expressions are uniquely expressive of feelings leads too easily to a view of formed and hidden emotions inadvertently exposed through a smile or gesture. Charles Darwin's assumption that people's expressive behaviors could be universally and readily recognized as expressive of particular psychological states led him to highlight a very restricted group of behaviors: facial expressions and some bodily gestures. Darwin tended to use expression to mean the sign of an emotion in contrast to behavior motivated and rationalized by emotion. His view seems to have little to do with the expressive sophistication of Bass, Muriel, or Plath. Darwin's account is adequate neither for the ways in which we express ourselves nor for the range of states expressed. I prefer the term "expressive resources" to "expressive behaviors" to highlight the sophistication of our modes of expression.

I further argue that claiming that some behaviors are especially expressive as a way of understanding the concept of expression is unnecessary if one can specify the objective of expressive activity. My account of expression as the activity of individuating psychological states relocates the importance of resources precisely because the account is applicable to a broad range of psychological states. The importance of a discussion of expressive resources follows on the function of expressive activity as making manifest what is expressed. Some resources may be more crucial than others to the individuation of different types of states. An expression of opinion may require language; the expression of desire may typically require action. There is an ambiguity in the notion of resources that are uniquely expressive. A brief discussion of this ambiguity should set to rest the possibility that the concept of expression can be understood adequately through the idea that there are uniquely expressive resources. Supposing for a moment that there are such things as resources unique to an activity, they might be understood as: (1) resources that could only be used for that activity; or (2) all the resources that might be needed for a particular activity, and that therefore, might be said, in some way, to characterize that activity. Suppose, for instance, that depending on (1) as a strategy, you hand me an edger, and say "We use this only for painting." Even if this were true, I know little more about the activity of painting than before the display of this tool. Whether there is a notion of the resources of an activity that would be rich enough to give a complete description of that activity seems very unlikely. You might, for instance using (2) as a strategy, hand me the paint, the pan, the edger, the roller, the brush, the plastic, and the masking tape and say, "That's all you'll need." But without a specification of the objective of the activity, I most likely still could not figure out what to do with all this equipment. Perhaps the conflation of (1) and (2) makes the strategy of trying to understand an activity through resources unique to that activity look plausible, but I can think of no case where additional specification of the objective, goal, or function of an activity is not an essential part of our understanding it.

Once the objective of expressive activity is specified, we can investigate the appropriate resources for each psychological category. That they differ importantly from category to category is certainly central to understanding the conditions for successful expression, and I will have much more to say about the expressive resources that we use in individuating our affective states. However, there are no uniquely expressive resources in the sense of strategy 1. For feelings, we might think there are uniquely expressive resources for two reasons. First, some linguistic resources are used primarily to express feeling—expletives are a favored example. But, as linguistic artifacts, expletives can be put to many uses. We might use "Damn!," for instance, as a signal to start the insurrection, as a disguised order, or even descriptively in a certain code. We could make it stand for "She said to meet her in the parking garage." To the objection that these latter uses of "Damn" are no longer the use of an expletive, we need only respond by conceding the point. If "expletive" is understood so that the term is only a use of an expletive when it expresses feeling, then the category of expletives is defined in terms of the activity of expressing feelings and so cannot be used to define that activity. Second, facial expressions and bodily gestures seem natural, in the sense of unlearned, and reliably enough correlated with feelings to be signs of these feelings:

> The emotive meaning of words can best be understood by comparing and contrasting it with the expressiveness of laughs, sighs, groans, and all other similar manifestations of the emotions, whether by voice or gesture. It is obvious that these 'natural' expressions are direct behavioristic symptoms of the emotions or feelings to which they testify. (Stevenson, 37)

However, all expressive resources may be used for at least one other activity—pretending to be in a state that one is not, in fact, in. I have spent some time on the issue of resources because of the way the idea of direct or natural expression confutes attempts to understand expression as an activity.

Taylor's account of the relation between action and desire depends on what he calls a normal or basic case. We often act freely on our desires, and this fact allows us to identify desires by the actions they tend to produce. I am not interested in assessing this claim about desire and action. I would point out that there may be a difference in the freedom with which we express desire and feeling. Taylor's reliance on a "happy" case where we do express freely is the second feature of his approach that provides clues as to why theorists have not taken expressions of feelings to be constitutive of feelings. An important source of the assumption that feelings are individuated prior to and independently of our expression likely has to do with the kind and degree of expressive failure to which many of us are routinely subject when we try to express our feelings.

There are at least two kinds of breakdown in the relation between expression and feeling that we need to understand. The first is that we often take ourselves to be unsuccessful when we express our feelings. Someone can be trying to explain how he or she feels may say, "No, I'm not expressing this right," or say of his or her tears, "That was a complete overreaction. I wasn't really that upset. I must just have been tired." Bass says, "I just do not know how to do it" (Bass, 17). The conditions of expressive success and failure will be a major theme of the second half of this study. I have clearly sided with Merleau-Ponty: the particular feelings that we succeed at expressing or fail to express are formed only through our acts of expression. Without a prior referent against which to measure expressive success or failure, the account of expressive failure becomes more interesting, complex, and political.

Second, there are many circumstances in which we believe that we cannot express our feelings but must conceal them instead. Muriel says, "I strove to conceal my true emotions" (Tlali, 91). The phenomenon of concealment may seem like a special problem for the type of account I am offering. "What we feel is, by and large, what we express" is a claim of ontological dependence—feelings are formed through their expression. There are, however, weaker and stronger versions of this claim: (1) that feelings, to be individuated, must be expressible; and (2) that feelings, to be individuated, must be expressed. The second claim obviously is an implausibly strong claim, at least for the classic emotions. To conceal an emotion is precisely not to express it, and concealment is such a common phenomenon with certain emotions, such as anger, that we have alternative labels such as "resentment" that actually imply the element of concealment. Given that "conceal" actually is a contrastive notion to "express" that operates within the same domain, it is not possible to widen the notion of "express" to include it by, for example, supposing that fantasies of revenge are expressions of anger.

I offer the following claim as plausible, based on the contrastive nature of concealment: there is some behavior on which the existence of a feeling depends. This behavior need not count as expressing the feeling; it may be behavior that counts as concealing the feeling. But if one neither conceals nor expresses the feeling, neither suppresses nor displays the expression of the feeling, then one does not have the feeling.

I shall return to the phenomenon of concealment as well as to other questions of expressive failure. Taylor's work provides the direction for an account of expressive success and failure—we need an understanding of our form of life as communicators as this relates particularly to communication of our feelings. We need to understand the circumstances—individual, social, and political—in which affective meaning is formed and interpreted.

THE EXPRESSIONIST THEORY OF ART

The accounts of expression I discussed earlier in the chapter are silent about the expression or individuation of the kinds of less familiar feelings I have presented, such as Bass's passion for discovering oil, Muriel's "white-master's-well-fed-dog feeling," or Plath's weird sinking hilarity. I now refer to feelings not grouped under emotion concepts as "free-style" feelings, to contrast the mode of their expression with the idea of a set pattern of behavior. As I have indicated in discussing examples, free-style feelings need not be unshared. My concern is that an impoverished account of the ways in which we express ourselves contributes to our inability to speak of the range of feelings that people express. Conversely, if we acknowledge the sophistication of our expressive resources, we are more likely to see the nuance and variety of people's affective lives. At the same time, we are less likely to think that people could have such lives without expressive and interpretive activity. There is one area of theory I have not yet discussed, where acknowledging both the sophistication of expression as an activity and the complex nature of affective experience leads to a view close to my own.

My defense of expression as formative of feeling is influenced by the tradition of expressionist theories of art with its insistence that artistic expression is the activity of communicating experiences without mediating categorizations. In my presentation of the expressionist theory of art in this final section of this chapter, I employ a somewhat unusual strategy. I quote extensively from three theorists, Curt Ducasse, John Dewey, and R. G. Collingwood, to display the common points among these theories, politically and philosophically, that have influenced my own account.

The expressionist theory, originally proposed by Eugene Veron (1879), was widely defended in the first half of this century by Ducasse, Dewey, and Collingwood. Taken as a group, their theories offer a re-entrance into a theory of expression in two ways: (1) the theories are important to understanding expression as a concept with a political history and a complex meaning. I examine how the complexities of the meaning of "expression" have facilitated its political use in theories of art. (2) Furthermore, to say, with rough synonymity, that art is *expressive* and that art is *the language of feeling* is to suppose a conceptual connection between expression and feeling, and I wish to comment on what has allowed for a conceptual connection in this particular body of theory. I believe there is something alluring about the idea that a great deal of art is expressive, with the rider that the key notion of "expression" is not determinate enough in meaning for an analysis of this notion within aesthetics to have settled, one way or another, the viability of an account of aesthetic activity based on expression. In this section, I show that "expression" does not have so much a core meaning as a core appeal. I am guided by Collingwood who wrote that the meaning of a word "is never something upon which the word sits perched like a gull on a stone; it is something over which the word hovers like a gull over a ship's stern. Trying to fix the proper meaning in our minds is like coaxing the gull to settle in the rigging, with the rule that the gull must be alive when it settles: one must not shoot it and tie it there" (7).

The core appeal of the notion of aesthetic expression is the possibility of a shared experience, or a shared response to experience, where the sharing is initiated or made possible by an artist who communicates the nature of this experience in a highly unique and particular way through her or his art. The possibility of this kind of shared experience is an important political possibility, but is not regarded in this way by theorists who have criticized expressionist theories of art. Alan Tormey, for example, comments as follows: "The history of the philosophy of art could, without excessive distortion be written as a study of the significance of a handful of concepts. The successive displacement of 'imitation' by 'representation,' and of 'representation' by 'expression,' for example" (97). This quote itself contains something close to a distortion by not highlighting the more important historical point that the use of "expression" was not motivated by the conceptual inadequacy of the notion of representation as a description of artistic activity but rather by the perceived moral and political inadequacies of previous aesthetic theories and practices.[9]

The appearance of the expressionist theory, in Eugene Veron's *Aesthetics* (1879), was a response to the theory that artistic activity should aim at the creation of beauty. Instead, claimed Veron, "What properly constitutes artistic genius is the imperious need to manifest externally by directly expressive forms and signs the emotions felt" (Veron, 35; quoted in Ducasse, 22). Veron's theory is unapologetically an aesthetic manifesto that promotes sincerity, spontaneity, and originality in art as an antidote to excessive classicism. The theory also is a moral manifesto: "[The response to art] . . . rests largely on sympathy. It depicts emotions, sentiments, charac-

---

9. Collingwood writes: "For I do not think of aesthetic theory as an attempt to investigate and expound eternal verities concerning the nature of eternal objects called Art, but as an attempt to reach, by thinking, the solution of certain problems arising out of the situation in which artists find themselves here and now" (vi).

ters. It manifests in artistic form the peculiar interest that man has for man. The beautiful then becomes a secondary matter" (Veron, 109; quoted in Ducasse, 22).

The substance of Veron's manifesto for a renewed art is quoted extensively and with vigorous approval by Curt Ducasse who introduces his *Philosophy of Art* with a Preface that makes clear the role of his aesthetic theory in his overall commitment to philosophical liberalism:

> The name Liberalism is perhaps the least unsatisfactory of the various labels with which might be tagged a philosophical standpoint which, endeavoring to push relativistic analysis as far as it will go . . . quickly finds itself confronted everywhere by the fact that individuals as such are the only absolutes to be found, and alone transform the endless "ifs" of the relativistic scheme into "sinces." . . . The present volume attempts to exhibit the meaning of it [Liberalism] in the field of aesthetics. (ix)

Finally, John Dewey in *Art as Experience* and R. G. Collingwood in the *Principles of Art* share a common concern that the theories and institutions of art that separate aesthetic activity from daily activity lead to impoverished lives. Both believe that aesthetic activity, as practiced by the artist, is a heightened and self-conscious participation in an activity people engage in daily: "Art is thus prefigured in the very process of living" (Dewey, *Art as Experience*, 24). "Every utterance and every gesture that each one of us makes is a work of art" (Collingwood, 285).

Dewey and Collingwood further hold that expression is bringing to consciousness the significance of experience in a way that this significance can and should be shared, for the experiences themselves are communal experiences:

> [the artist] undertakes his artistic labour . . . as a public labour on behalf of the community to which he belongs. Whatever statement of emotion he utters is prefaced by the implicit rubric, not "I feel," but "we feel." (Collingwood, 315)

> [W]orks of art are the only media of complete and unhindered communication between man and man that can occur in a world full of gulfs and walls that limit community of experience. (Dewey, *Art as Experience*, 105)

Expressionist theories share, from political and moral commitments to liberalism or to a certain form of community, a vision of community where individuals can understand or share each other's very particular affective experiences without the mediation or guidance of critics and institutions, and, crucially, without these experiences being brought under generic emotion concepts.

The distortion of the theory in its summary presentations, involving both it depoliticization and de-democratization, is evident in Ernst Gombrich's "Expression and Communication" (1965), perhaps the best known postmortem to the expressionist theory. Gombrich introduces the theory ("the Romantic idea that art is the language of emotions") by quoting a lecture in which the critic Roger Fry uses the wireless as an analogy for the theory. Fry speaks of the artist as the transmitter, the work of art as the medium, and the spectator as the receiver who often possesses such an imperfect instrument that it can only respond to "crude and elementary emissions." Gombrich, after noting that "If anyone had a right . . . to think of his mind as of a sensitive instrument, it was this great critic" (Gombrich, 56), accepts Fry's analogy as explaining the basic appeal of the expressionist theory: "It suggests that the artist broadcasts his message in the hope of reaching a mind that will vibrate in unison with his own, and that his medium (the work of art) is only the means to achieve this end" (Gombrich, 56). Gombrich's presentation suggests that expressionist theories contain much of what, in fact, they took themselves to be objecting to: the importance or necessity of the great critic as guide, and the artist as distanced from community and looking for a single mind, perhaps as isolated as himself, with whom to share an experience in some way too sophisticated for most people to understand.

I stated that the concept of expression, as used in aesthetic theory, has more of a core appeal than a core meaning. What makes the notion of expression an ideal concept through which to defend the possibility of an unmediated relationship between artist and community is, in fact, the *complex* meaning of the word. The English word *expression* has its roots in the Latin *ex-primere*, and means both to squeeze or press out (as women express milk and we express the juice from grapes), and to delineate, depict, or symbolize. Furthermore, as an adjective, *express* means exact or precise (as in "an express likeness"). The English word expression is the intersection of these derivations, and this intersection is heavily exploited in expressionist theories (Wollheim, *Art and Its Objects*, 26–28). Thus briefly, the aesthetic expression of feeling is the material emergence of the feeling, coming out under pressure, in a form that is an exact likeness of the feeling or makes the individual nature of that feeling obvious.

Thus the core appeal of expression for these theories plays on two aspects: (1) the necessity or centrality of the aesthetic impulse in life—what might be called the ordinary importance of art; and (2) the possibility of sharing someone else's particular experience in a direct way because the activity of aesthetic expression makes that experience manifest and, what's more, makes possible, encourages, or demands this sharing. It is, of course the second aspect that has been attacked for its lack of coherence in several ways. For the present study, however, the important questions set by expressionist theories are: What is it for us to be able to interpret or understand a particular affective experience without bringing it under an emotion concept? Is there some coherent notion of response that illuminates this possibility? Like expressionist theorists I regard this possibility as politically important. My reasons for this are more fully discussed in Chapters 4 and 5. Briefly, (1) emotion categories are normative categories legitimized by those who have the power to determine what kinds of occasions are (or have been) of communal significance; (2) there are many occasions of personal and shared personal significance that are not of communal significance; and (3) there are many experiences of communal significance that do not find room within these basically conservative categories.

The second value of the expressionist theory of art is the conceptual linking of expression and feeling made possible through regarding expression as an activity and feelings as unique. The classic expressionist theories that I have discussed all give an account of expression as an activity that individuates, objectifies, or embodies an affective experience in a way that contributes to its uniqueness. All are, as well, intensely committed to vindicating the importance of the uniqueness and variety of affective experiences. All expressionist theories are committed to the existence of nuanced and nameless feelings that are neither reducible to sensations nor the sorts of states that are adequately captured by the categories of the classic emotions. Expressionist theories are the only body of theory in which the free-style feelings that I wish to defend make a sustained philosophical appearance. I quote, extensively, to display the centrality of this commitment. For Ducasse:

> *The feelings experienced by human beings are endlessly various, and only a very few, such as love, fear, anger, etc., have received names.* This is a fact which is most important to realize clearly and to bear constantly in mind throughout the present volume, for otherwise the philosophy of art set forth in its pages is bound to be completely misunderstood. . . . The feelings which are unlabelled, are so for various reasons. . . . The chief reason, however, is probably that they are *individuals without a kind.* The names, Anger, Love, Anxiety, etc., are not proper names but names of kinds, and cases of those kinds are not noticed by us as individuals but as cases-of-a-kind. The *individuality* of each is overlooked by us as generally as are the unlabelled feelings. (195–97; emphasis in orginal)

According to Dewey:

> Save nominally, there is no such thing as *the* emotion of fear, hate, love. The unique unduplicated character of experienced events and situations impregnates the emotion that is evoked. Were it the function of speech to reproduce that to which it refers, we could never speak of fear, but only of . . . fear-under-specified-circumstances-of-drawing-a-wrong-conclusion from just-such-and-such-data. A lifetime would be too short to reproduce in words a single emotion. (*Art as Experience*, 67)

Finally, Collingwood sets his commitment to the individual nature of the feelings in a discussion of why expressing an emotion is not at all like describing it because

> description generalizes. To describe a thing is to call it a thing of such and such a kind: to bring it under a conception, to classify it. Expression, on the contrary, individualizes. The anger which I feel here and now, with a certain person, for a certain cause, is no doubt an instance of anger, and in describing it as anger one is telling truth about it; but it is much more than mere anger: it is a peculiar anger, not quite like any anger that I have ever felt before, and probably not quite like any anger I shall ever feel again. To become fully conscious of it means becoming conscious of it . . . as this quite peculiar anger. (112–13)

To summarize, feelings are regarded as unique by these theorists in one or both of these senses: they are regarded as individuals without a kind (or as individual kinds) or as particulars that cannot be adequately individuated by placement under concepts. With respect to the first, Ducasse is right that there are many feelings—I would add many shared feelings—for which we do not have concepts or labels. However, I do not find it felicitous to regard these as individuals without a kind. This way of putting it has the potential to create too sharp a separation between these unlabeled feelings and emotions. The model I offer is a more complex continuum. The second sense in which these theorists regard feelings as unique seems true of any particulars outside of individual kinds. Nonetheless, there are two potentially interesting aspects to this claim: (1) that for some reason we think we can fully individuate feelings through their categorization and that this is false:

> Anna's unhappy; Anna's worried, but not like Mummy; Anna's worry is like a pocket handkerchief balled in a pocket, something she can squeeze and squeeze and throw away when she's done with it. (Keefer, 107)

and (2) that categorization is, in fact, unnecessary (or may be antitheti-cal) to the individuation of feelings. I pursue these themes in later chap-ters. I am satisfied to point out here that a focus on the uniqueness and variety of feelings and a view of expression as an activity that either indi-viduates these feelings or makes their individuality manifest are insepar-able commitments of expressionist theories.

In expressionist theories of art, whether feelings have been taken to be individuated in the sense of formed prior to the acts of expression that embody or particularize them has depended on other and more general commitments of these philosophers to the status of the mental. Thus, these theories vary in their support for the central thesis of this chapter: that expression is the activity of forming or creating our psychological states. Ducasse's view on this, for example, is that the states are already formed. This commitment is reflected in his parallel views of language, as a medium not through which we think, but in which we encode thoughts. Hence, he prefers expression as an activity of objectification rather than individuation. Collingwood's view is less definite but involves a strong commitment to unconscious feeling such that a feeling might be individu-ated, although we would not be able to recognize it as the feeling we have until its expression. Dewey alone is thoroughly opposed to the idea that individuation could take place in any independence of expression or ar-ticulation through a medium: "Erroneous views of the nature of the act of expression almost all have their source in the notion that an emotion is complete in itself within, only when uttered having impact on any exter-nal material" (*Art as Experience*, 66–67).

There is a final aspect to expressionist theories that I would like to note briefly. The emphasis on experience that is actually shared rather than, for instance, understood or responded to seems like an oddly excessive and implausible commitment. Nevertheless, all three theories hold as one that the artist, at least, must respond to the artwork in such a way that the artwork mirrors back the experience. Expressionist theories face the prob-lem of what counts as successful articulation or embodiment of a feeling within a medium. It seems to me likely that the notion of shared experi-ence, where the limiting case of the person who shares the experience is the actual artist, plays an important theoretical role in settling when artic-ulation or objectification is complete. I make this observation to highlight the importance of some notion of shared response for theories that es-chew categorization as marking the success of individuation. In Chapter 4, I shall be concerned more generally with this issue.

In this chapter, I have considered the role played in accounts of expres-sion by the assumption that feelings are fully formed prior to their expression. At the same time, I have tried to show, at several points, that what is problematic in those accounts of expression is made less problematic as we relax our attachment to that assumption. To show this much is not, however, to provide anything but the most indirect case on behalf of the contrary view that our expressions of feeling are deeply implicated in the character of the feelings themselves.

III

FORMING AN EMOTION
Rereading Cyrano de Bergerac

I never loved but one man in my life,
And I have lost him—twice. . . .
　　　　　　　—Roxane in *Cyrano de Bergerac,* Act V

In *The Rationality of Emotion,* Ronald de Sousa asks the intriguing
question: Could you be in love and not know with whom (110)? If
this were possible, the character of your feeling, as well as its
object, would be thrown into question. We do not normally allow
that a person can knowingly be in love without their knowing whom they
love, for we believe that their finding a certain person cherishable both
causes their love and supplies it with an object. There are two points here.
The first is that many emotions, and love certainly, are essentially object
directed. I am not in love prior to having found someone to love. The
second point is that I take it to be a common view that it is the way in which
we appraise a certain object or situation that gives an emotion its character.
According to Alison Jaggar, for example, in a summary of contemporary
theories of emotion, "[we] define or identify emotions not by the quality or
character of the physiological sensation that may be associated with them,
but rather by their intentional aspect, the associated judgement" (155).

To state, however, that our love depends on how we view a person—our
attitudes, perceptions and beliefs about that person—or that our fear depends on our appraising a situation as dangerous might make it seem that
the emotions are completely formed through our appraisals of objects,
people, and situations and independently of our acts of expression. Many
philosophers are, in fact, committed to this thesis. In Chapter 2, I argued
against accounts of expression that assume that a feeling is individuated
prior to and independent of its expression. In this chapter, I show that
one of the most important trends in contemporary emotion theory—cog-
nitive/perceptual accounts of emotion—also contains a version of this
problematic assumption.

To examine and defend the role of expression in the *formation* of emotion, I take up de Sousa's question for a case of love gone badly wrong—Roxane's love in Edward Rostand's *Cyrano de Bergerac*. The case should be viewed philosophically as it is theatrically: the drama of a failed effort to individuate the appropriate object of an emotion. My analysis is meant to go some distance toward further persuading the reader that acts of expression help form feelings. On my reading of the play, Roxane's love develops through her expressive actions. After performing a certain number of such actions, Roxane cannot easily withdraw her claim that she loves. However, Roxane's expressive actions do not fulfill the role of establishing an appropriate object for Roxane's love. Consequently, her love is ill formed. Diagnosing the failure of Roxane's love makes it possible to show the role that expression plays in forming emotion, particularly the role that expressive action plays in establishing an object. The conclusion I draw from the study of *Cyrano* is modest: that on some occasions, we must allow expression a role in determining the intentional object of an emotional state, and hence, in determining the character of that state.

The alternative to my account is, of course, that Roxane's actions do not play a role in determining whom she loves. That Roxane's actions play no role in determining whom she loves is the alternative to which I take many contemporary cognitive/perceptual accounts of emotion, those, for example of Amelie Rorty ("Explaining Emotions," 106–8) and Ronald de Sousa (115) to be committed. On a cognitive/perceptual view, beliefs, perceptions, or appraisals both cause and establish the information content of our emotions. That I appraise the bear as dangerous causes my fear, makes the bear the object of my fear, and gives my emotion its individuating description: I am afraid of the bear. Expression plays no role here. On this type of alternative, when Roxane expresses her love, she is expressing or revealing what is already true to say of her prior to her actions. It is true to say of her that she loves someone in particular, although she herself may be mistaken about whom this is. She may even express her love to the wrong person. My analysis of *Cyrano* is meant to be a challenge to cognitive/perceptual models. I argue that these models are inadequate to handle the complications of Roxane's love, and I argue against them more generally.

Nonetheless, there is much to be said for the idea that the causal antecedents of our feelings play an important role in giving them the character they have. In the last section of this chapter, I offer a proposal about what this important role is: a person's emotional history—their biography—plays a role in fixing emotional properties in the world and a role in determining that person's responses. Both the associational nature of emotional properties and our emotional development give important positions to causation, but do so without our needing to suppose that the causes of particular feelings form their objects independently from our expression. I do not deny the importance of the causal history of an emotion. Rather, I place the importance of this history within an account of expression.

A detailed analysis of a case such as Roxane's is important to an account such as my own, which attempts to find some unity to the category of affect. Many feelings are not object directed. Attending to the ways in which emotions acquire objects through appraisals, as cognitive/perceptual models do, does not create more space for free-style feelings in an account of the relation of affect to behavior. Furthermore, because the accounts given of emotion and object are various, complex, and divisive, examining the object-directedness of emotion further motivates the view held by many philosophers that emotions are not a unified psychological class:[1]

> If one takes in the full range of phenomena present in this class, it becomes evident why the conception of emotion's directedness has fared so badly in the literature on emotions. It is simply far too varied. . . . Because the content of the concept far exceeds the limits of a plausible analysis, I propose that we abandon the project. . . . This decision is not regrettable if one views the class of emotions as a heterogeneous class of mental attitudes and respects their diversity accordingly. (Nissenbaum, 80)

If we can see how expression of a classic emotion is articulation in behavior sufficient to individuate a psychological state, we have the possibility of a more unified account of the notion of affect, and I hold out very strongly for this possibility.

ROXANE'S LOVE

My analysis of *Cyrano* offers the following thesis: the complete individuation of an emotion includes a specification of its object and, in some cases, it is the actions of the subject of the emotion that establish who or what that object is. A spirited story of love that does not successfully establish an object, although it seems, at times, to have one, is *Cyrano de Ber-*

1. See also Rorty, "Explaining Emotions," and de Sousa who agrees with her: "The dramatic structure of the formal objects of emotions has another important consequence. . . . In view of the diversity in logical structure of different emotions . . . it would be better, though messier, to concede a sense in which emotions do not form a kind in the same way as do wants or beliefs" (de Sousa, 185). Gordon also has doubts about the usefulness of trying to locate a univocal notion of object directedness (45).

gerac. Cyrano, hidden, writes and speaks as Christian, and the two men win Roxane, the woman whom each loves, together. Christian is beautiful and brave, but, in love, he is ineloquent. Cyrano is brave and eloquent, but grotesque. When Roxane, in the throes of infatuation for Christian, cries out: "He is beautiful and brilliant—and I love him" (Act III), she is foretelling the increasing complexity of a situation where she comes to love for qualities that are not instantiated by a single individual, but by two different men. There is no doubt that each man loves Roxane uniquely. Whether Roxane loves one of them uniquely is the problem of the play, and the playwright seems to answer no. By the end of *Cyrano de Bergerac,* Cyrano and Christian are both dead, the closure to a misbegotten love. I take the ending of the play to confirm our intuitions that Roxane's love has not been successfully object directed and, therefore, cannot be completely formed. The play offers several options of whom Roxane might love. She might love Christian, Cyrano, both men, or neither. Roxane, herself, concludes

> I never loved but one man in my life,
> And I have lost him—twice. . . .
> (Act V)

I will try to make some sense of her diagnosis.[2]

The play offers three opportunities to analyze what goes wrong with Roxane's love. I consider the three crucial scenes: the balcony scene of "Roxane's Kiss" (Act III), a scene at the battlefield where Christian dies (Act IV), and a scene at the monastery where Cyrano dies (Act V). What goes wrong, however, is complex and involves both appraisal and expressive action. The conventions of romantic love that govern the treatment of love in *Cyrano* require that Roxane's love should have a single object. There are times when her appraisals seem to pick out a single object, at the beginning of the play Christian, at the end Cyrano, even though many of her appraisals of Christian are inaccurate. But Roxane's love develops through object-directed action that fixes both Christian and Cyrano as objects of her love.

Cyrano is a heroic comedy in the grand manner, but its treatment of love is relatively subtle. Though no one character articulates, in speech or

---

2. One possible explanation of the failure of Roxane's love is that, as a matter of fact, the qualities for which Roxane comes to love are necessary to the sustenance of her love, and these qualities are separately instantiated in two different people. In "Love and Intentionality: Roxane's Choice," I argue that the difference between the qualities of the two men is so drastically and deliberately undercut, that by Act IV, the qualities relevant to Roxane's love are instantiated by either man.

action, a view of love adequate to the complexities of the dramatic situation, Cyrano comes closest to doing so. He envisions a situation where he and Christian must win Roxane together, for neither has completely those qualities for which Roxane will come to love; nevertheless, he supposes that Roxane, in loving, will come to love a person, and that person will be Christian.[3]

> I know—
> Afraid that when you have her all alone,
> You lose all. Have no fear. It is yourself
> She loves—give her yourself put into words—
> My words, upon your lips!
>
> (Act II)

Cyrano assumes that the qualities for which Roxane loves will cause her love, that in loving, she will love a person, and must assume as well that what sustains her love will not necessarily be the same as what caused it. Cyrano concludes from this, however, that although both men may be required to win her, one can keep her. But this will depend on whether Roxane's expressive acts are successful in fully forming her emotion by establishing an object for it. Cyrano counts too much on his own agency in structuring the possibilities for Roxane's love and takes too little account of the importance of Roxane's agency.

Cyrano, who is naturally eloquent, also stands for sincerity and integrity of expression, an underlying theme of the play. In a speech to Roxane in his own voice, but shadowed in the shrubbery and disguised to her as Christian, he pleads against the demand for an eloquence that strains sincerity in the expression of love:

> C: Look once at the high stars that shine in heaven
> And put off artificiality!. . . .
> R: But . . . Poetry?
> C: Love hates that game of words!
> It is a crime to fence with life—I tell you,
> There comes one moment, once—and God help those
> Who pass that moment by!—when Beauty stands
> Looking into the soul with grave, sweet eyes

---

3. See Kraut, "Love De Re," for a defense of the Platonic option I do not consider: that the object of romantic love could be a quality or set of qualities. I would argue that the object of an emotion is restricted as to type by what could count as behavior expressive of that emotion. One cannot make love to a quality. As this argument can be made on grounds of what would be minimally necessary to distinguish an emotion such as love from other sorts of attitudes, I take it to support my general approach.

That sicken at pretty words!
(Act III)

The lesson of the speech is that those who fail at appropriate expression fail at love. Ironically, as this crucial act called "Roxane's Kiss" progresses, Cyrano insists that Christian perform the direct expressive act that the moment calls for: "Climb up, animal!" (Act III). And Roxane, who, throughout the play, demands expressive eloquence, performs conventional acts of expression that begin to give a character to her emotion that she cannot repudiate.

I propose to treat "Roxane's Kiss" as Roxane's first unsuccessful attempt at forming an emotion traceable to a failure at performing expressive acts that individuate a single appropriate object. To understand Roxane's failure at giving form to her feelings, I will give Roxane a certain preliminary authority, not about *whom* she loves, but about *when* she loves. Like Ryle, I will take her avowals as the best and most direct evidence that she has come to love.[4]

In "Roxane's Kiss," Cyrano speaks to Roxane from the dark, pretending that he is Christian, and Roxane, assuming that the speaker is Christian, is tremendously moved by the speech and the voice and claims she has come truly to love for the first time:

Yes, I do tremble . . . and I weep . . .
And I love you . . . and I am yours . . . and you
Have made me thus!
(Act III)

She kisses and marries Christian before the scene is out.

In Roxane's speech, and in the actions that follow, she undertakes or undergoes at least six distinguishable actions or behaviors, which I will list. I use the doubled term "response/feeling" as a way of indicating that there is no clear separation between these features in the formation of Roxane's love. As will becomes clear, an emotion such as love develops gradually through the very sorts of actions that Roxane undertakes:

1. Roxane undergoes a significant response (trembling and weeping).
2. She affirms that the cause of her response/feeling is apparent to her (the speaker).
3. She identifies the cause of her response/feeling (the speaker).
4. She identifies the object of her feeling (the speaker).

4. I characterize this authority as preliminary because it is defeasible. We can be mistaken in all sorts of ways about our emotions, and at this point, I wish to leave open the possibility that Roxane might be mistaken not only about whom she loves, but also about when or even whether she loves.

5. She identifies her feeling (love).
6. She engages in actions expressive of love (she avows her love, kisses, and marries).

I would like to point out that moments 4 and 5 take place coincidently in Roxane's avowal of her love. Roxane discriminates her feeling and its object through the action of her avowal. That is, it is through an action expressive of love that she performs acts of identification that are central to determining the intentional component of her emotional state.

Roxane has made a serious mistake at moment 2. The identity of the cause of her response is only partially apparent to her. She correctly identifies the cause of her response as the speaker, but she believes that the speaker is Christian when it is really Cyrano. It is Cyrano's speech and voice that have (in large part) caused her response, trembling, and weeping, which do not themselves require an object. But the further actions of Roxane's that are expressive of love do require an object, and in undertaking these actions, Roxane begins to determine whom she loves. She avows her love to the speaker, Cyrano, but kisses and marries the man whom she believes to be the speaker, namely, Christian. Roxane has identified an object for her love, but she has failed to establish one uniquely. She has begun to fix the object through actions that pick out two men, not one. Cyrano's words cue the audience to the object confusion that is the outcome to the scene: "Kissing my words/ My words, upon your lips!" (Act III).

The difficulty, at this point, is to say how Roxane's actions or expressions of love can be loving in the sense of being formative of her love without falling into locutions that suggest they are loving because they are revealing of her love. As John Dewey pointed out, the very phrase "expression of emotion" carries the misleading implication (to Dewey) that an emotion is formed prior to its expression (Dewey, "Theory of Emotions," 152). We then take the expression as evidence of the existence of the already formed emotion. We are especially inclined, I think, to do so in cases where the expressive action is an avowal that we may be tempted to interpret as a self-description. However, in agreeing that, when Roxane expresses her love, she is doing what gives us good evidence that she loves, we are not committed, outside of prejudice, to the view that she is revealing a prior state. Rather, she may be engaged in publicly interpretable behaviors that give us reason to attribute a psychological description to her—that she loves—precisely because they are formative of her love.[5] My aim is to establish that this approach offers a better understanding of

---

5. The contrast with "public" in this study is "epistemically private." See Chapter 5. Roxane may, of course, perform many publicly interpretable actions in socially private spaces.

Roxane's situation than can be gotten from a cognitive/perceptual analysis.

My preliminary obligation is to show that Roxane has behaved in such a way that her behavior itself can be clearly interpreted as emotionally expressive behavior. Roxane's behavior has consisted of trembling, weeping, avowing love, kissing, and marrying. All are conventional, albeit somewhat clichéd, ways of expressing love. On the assumption that Roxane is sincere, these behaviors have their expressive character in virtue of being embedded in well-defined social practices that are partly constitutive of romantic love.[6] Cyrano, himself, elaborates the significance of the kiss:

> And what is a kiss, when all is done?
> A promise given under seal—a vow
> Taken before the shrine of memory—
> A signature acknowledged—. . .
>
> (Act III)

Many of the passions are expressed in performances directed toward their objects—a kiss is such a performance. In kissing Christian, and by doing so in this particular situation and sincerely, Roxane is engaged in an action that is socially designated as expressive of love, and this is because it brings into being a certain state of affairs. She has thereby committed herself to Christian. Avowing love also is such an action, and this she has done to Cyrano. In offering this analysis of Roxane's expressive acts, I echo J. L. Austin's analysis of performative utterances: linguistic acts that, in felicitous circumstances, help bring about certain states of affairs. As a reminder, in Austin's account, if the circumstances are infelicitous, the act does not come off (Austin, "Performative Utterances," 237–41). I discuss at a later point whether Roxane can claim that her expressive actions were not felicitously performed.

Roxane does not simply kiss, marry, and avow love. These are general types of action, but their instances take particular objects. Therefore, a full description of an action socially expressive of love is "Roxane kissed Christian" or "Roxane avowed love to Cyrano." These action-descriptions specify not only a feeling, but also the object of the feeling. Because of the nature of love as a controlled social practice, this object is limited to

---

6. Some theorists (e.p., Jaggar, 135) suggest that romantic love is to be wholly understood in terms of conventional social practices, which we engage in much as actors playing roles. I do not accept this strong a social constructivist account of love, although I do go on to refer to it in the text as a controlled social practice. I mean by this that there are strong constraints on what will count as nondeviant love in a society, many having to do with whom one can love. These constraints inform our practice. See Chapter 5 for more general arguments against social constructivism.

type. Cyrano's assumption that Roxane will come to love Christian somewhat independently of how her emotion is caused depends on recognizing the importance of expression in fixing an object and believing that the expressive conventions of romantic love will lead to the decisive establishment of a unique object. However, it is Roxane's actions that establish or fail to establish whom that object is.

To generalize, what type of expressive behavior forms or individuates an emotion such as love may be established partly by the place of that behavior in practices conventionally associated with the emotion. However, a description of these practices does not, of course, fully individuate the specific behaviors, many of which are actions requiring objects. Some of these actions will have, as their object, an item with properties causally relevant in instigating the process of our response. Performing these actions fixes their objects. So a full account of the expressive behavior that helps form an emotion may involve a considerable number of actions: acts of identification, as well as performances that are culturally standard, or even required, for expressing particular feelings. Roxane has not failed to perform actions expressive of love, but she appears to have failed to perform actions that individuate a unique object. This leads to confusion as to whom she loves.

I wish particularly to stress the point that Roxane's mistaken beliefs or perceptions are, by themselves, an inadequate explanation of the confusion that begins to develop.[7] By the time "Roxane's Kiss" takes place, Roxane already has mistaken beliefs: that the writer of certain letters she has received is Christian (it is Cyrano) and that Christian is eloquent. These mistakes lead not to loving actions toward Cyrano, but rather to loving actions that individuate Christian. Up until "Roxane's Kiss," Roxane's appraisals and actions have both supported the same object for her love, Christian, even though some of her appraisals of Christian have been inaccurate. We can imagine that Roxane might have gone through her life happily loving Christian for qualities that he does not straightforwardly have, but which she believes that he has. This sort of situation, we suspect, occurs all the time. "Roxane's Kiss" offers only a slight variation on misperceptions already in place. Roxane now believes that the speaker is Christian (it is Cyrano) and still believes that Christian is eloquent. But Roxane's avowal to the speaker begins to implicate Cyrano as an object of her love. To display its lesson about the importance of expression, "Roxane's Kiss" adds action to a situation already characterized by mispercep-

---

7. In describing this situation as confused, I do not mean that Roxane, at this point, feels confusion as to whom she loves. I mean there really is confusion as to whom she loves, for the audience and, increasingly, from this point, for Christian, Cyrano, and finally Roxane.

tion. Insofar as misperceptions are important to the emotional confusion, it is because these misperceptions lead to actions taken toward two persons.[8]

Act IV of *Cyrano de Bergerac* offers Roxane a second chance at fixing a single object for her love and removes it by Christian's death. Tremendously moved by the letters that she believes Christian has written her every day from the front, she again is urged to action and travels to the front to tell Christian that now she believes she *truly* loves him, for she would continue to love him even if he were ugly. Roxane's avowed change from an immature to a mature love gives her the renewed possibility of locating a unique object and the audience the permission to accept the result.

It is, of course, Cyrano who has, again, written the letters. The dismissal of beauty as a feature necessary to sustaining Roxane's love appears to open the possibility that Roxane could come to individuate Cyrano as the sole appropriate object of her love, and Christian and Cyrano, recognizing this development, decide to tell Roxane of their deception. Before they can do so, however, Roxane is again moved to act. She avows her love anew ("It is yourself/I love now: your own self") and pledges it for an eternity ("Oh, my Christian, oh my king,— / . . . /It is the heart of me that kneels to you,/And will remain forever at your feet—"). Christian interprets the avowal as an expression of love *for Cyrano*, thinking that Roxane does not yet know that this is whom she loves. But Roxane's pledge is clearly a pledge of love *for Christian* to Christian. Before she discovers the true identity of the author of the letters, Christian dies, with Cyrano's last letter to Roxane by his heart. Roxane: "On his letter—blood . . . and tears." The tears are Cyrano's but the blood is Christian's. The scene repeats and intensifies the drama of failed unique individuation. Roxane takes no further action that could be interpreted as expressive of loving Cyrano, but goes into seclusion, further fixing Christian as the object of her love.

Fifteen years after Christian's death, and on the day Cyrano is mortally wounded, Roxane discovers that the cause of her feelings has not been fully apparent to her. Her options for saying what was true of her love, before and after discovery, reveal possibilities for further understanding the object directedness of her love. Let us designate t (before discovery)

---

8. A cognitivist might point out that in avowing love to the speaker, Roxane has appraised him as cherishable and this is a crucial misperception responsible for the resulting situation. I would respond that this likely appraisal does not cause her avowal but takes place through it. That expressive behavior often is our only ground for attributing an emotive appraisal seems even more reason to think that a model that discounts the importance of expressive behavior is inadequate.

as a time after Roxane has kissed and married Christian but before Christian dies, and t' (after discovery) as a time after Roxane discovers that Cyrano loves her and that Cyrano and Christian have deceived her, but before Cyrano dies. I will offer my analysis through an investigation of Roxane's response to her discovery.

In trying to clarify for herself the nature of her love, Roxane attempts to understand the sense in which her loving has been object directed. At t', Roxane has a maximum of four options of what to say about her love at t. She now understands, as well as she can, the causal account of her coming to love. She now knows, as well, that Cyrano loves her. She has the option of saying that at t she loved only Christian, she loved both men, she loved only Cyrano, or she did not love. None of these options is entirely satisfactory. All need to be assessed with reference to the actions Roxane has taken.

Roxane's first inclination, on evidence of her speech to Cyrano at t' is to deny her love for Christian and conclude that the soul she has loved has always been Cyrano. She tries explicitly to retell the causal story of her love so that she can finally individuate a single appropriate object for it:

> R: I understand everything now: The letters—
> That was you
> C. No!
> R. And the dear, foolish words—
> That was you . . .
> C. No!
> R. And the voice . . . in the dark . . .
> That was . . . you!
> C. On my honor—
> R. And . . . the Soul!—
> That was all you.
>
> (Act V)

Put somewhat fancifully, Roxane here is calling on the resources of the cognitive/perceptual model to attempt a redescription of the intentional component of her love. Roxane might argue that her appraisals of a soul as eloquent, however these appraisals have been expressed, have supported only her love of Cyrano; Cyrano is the real object of Roxane's love. But Roxane's actions preclude such redescriptions. The majority of Roxane's actions have fixed Christian, not Cyrano, as the object of her love, and she has pledged her love, eternally, to Christian just moments before his death. Cyrano interrupts Roxane's retelling to remind her that actions have consequences that cannot be undone:

Cyrano (holds the letter out to her): The blood
                                                    Was his.

It seems implausible that Roxane loves only Cyrano at *t*—she has mistaken too much of the cause of her feelings, and consequently Christian has been the object of much of her socially significant expressive action.

If Roxane cannot retell her love to make it true that she loved only Cyrano at *t*, might she then, at least, claim that she did love Cyrano at *t* and loved Christian as well? The momentum of her retelling races back toward the moment when she first avowed her love to Cyrano, and I have argued that she begins to fix Cyrano as an object through this avowal. But I suggest that Roxane has not yet done enough to make it clearly the case that she loves Cyrano at *t*. In particular, although we might interpret her avowal as, at the same time, an appraisal of the speaker of cherishable, Roxane does not yet know whom the speaker is. Cyrano has not yet, therefore, been made the object of the sort of practice of loving action that Roxane has undertaken toward Christian.

We are left with two options: that at *t*, Roxane loved only Christian, or that at *t*, Roxane did not love. Roxane's speech to Cyrano indicates her reluctance to affirm that it was only Christian that she loved at *t*. She recognizes that the eloquent words that have caused much of her response have been Cyrano's words in Cyrano's voice. Further, Cyrano has, at *t*, been the object of some of her loving action. It is not clear that she loved only Christian at *t*. Can Roxane claim then that at *t*, she did not yet love? This would involve denying she loved Christian at *t*, without attempting to replace him with Cyrano in her retrospective account.

I believe that Roxane could take the option of denying that she loved Christian at *t*, but realizing the importance of her own acts of expression toward Cyrano, does not take this option. Roxane's expressive actions toward Christian have been sincere and conventionally appropriate for love. However, these actions have been undertaken in circumstances of Roxane's being deliberately deceived about whose eloquence is motivating her to act. Deception might vitiate the force of her actions. I am suggesting that Roxane could, as an option to appealing to a cognitive/perceptual model, appeal to something like Austin's analysis of performative utterances, extending this analysis to expressive actions. She could claim that her expressive acts were not felicitously performed and, therefore, did not bring about a states of affairs in which she loved Christian at *t*. The deceptive circumstances, however, have grounded action taken toward both men. In denying that her actions have established her love for Christian, Roxane would risks the implication that her avowal to Cyrano has similarly lacked the performative force of initiating Cyrano as an object of love. In annulling the meaning of her response toward Christian, she would have little ground now for pleading her love to Cyrano in Act V.

In summary, Roxane's expressive actions are relevant to her t' understanding of t in the following ways. Her actions have implicated Cyrano as an object of her love and established Christian so decisively that she cannot redescribe her love to make it persuasive that she loved the man whose qualities have, in the main, caused her to engage in loving. She may, I believe, deny having loved at t. The grounds she could use to do so would leave expressive actions central to the formation of love, but set conditions for felicitous expressive actions. As her expressive actions have initiated Cyrano as an object of love, however, Roxane does not wish to claim that her avowal in Act III has been infelicitous. She therefore cannot claim that her expressive actions toward Christian have misfired. Thus, although Roxane is reluctant to affirm that she loved only Christian at t, the best she might be able to do is to say that she loved Christian at t, and maybe loved Cyrano just a little bit as well.

What Roxane can say at t' of her love at t' is, I think, more clear. The longer the period in which Roxane engages in loving action, the less it will be possible for her to claim that her expression had misfired, even given the deception that Christian and Cyrano have practiced. By Act V, at t', Roxane has nearly twenty years of her life at stake in loving action. Roxane, for love, has kissed, cried, married, gone to war, and worn widow's weeds for 15 years. She has declared and redeclared her love, and in doing so, has performed every type of identification and engaged in every social performance necessary to individuate the object of an emotion. Fortunately, the discovery at t' both gives Roxane reason to affirm the felicity of her expressive actions and places Cyrano as the potential object of an ongoing practice of loving action. The process of individuation that forms her loving is complete at t', and Roxane is able to give a description of her love. She has loved Christian through engaging in a temporally extended social practice. She has come clearly to love Cyrano when she finally identifies him as the appropriate object of yet further actions expressive of love. ("You shall not die! I love you!—"). By t' and with Roxane's final avowal, Roxane loves both men. It is Roxane's understanding that her appraisals have supported actions taken toward two men in a single process of loving that allows the play to reach resolution:

> I never loved but one man in my life,
> And I have lost him—twice. . . .

Roxane's description of the object of her love is, at the same time, a description of what she has done in loving, and of the consequences of those actions. Roxane's love has fixed two men as the single object of a temporally extended practice. But the actions through which Roxane has come to love—the kiss, the pledge, the various avowals—each conventionally guarantees faithfulness toward a unique individual. Roxane's love is not possible and Cyrano now dies.

In "Roxane's Choice," I have offered an example of a situation in which the object of an emotion is established, completing the formation of that emotion, partly through the expression of culturally significant actions that themselves require an object. What makes a particular object appropriate is (1) our identification of that object as having qualities that caused our initial significant response; and (2) our taking that object to be the appropriate object of further response. In this identification and in our subsequent actions, the object becomes established or formed as the object of that emotion. In other words, the causal history of our emotion and the object of that emotion are related through the need to take action involving a causally relevant item, and though the taking of that action. My analysis of *Cyrano* offers a sketch for the relation between the cause and object of an emotion that acknowledges the importance of the cause, but gives it its importance within an account of expression. I conclude that on some occasions, we must allow expressive action a role in determining the intentional component of an emotional state.

EMOTION AND OBJECT: COGNITIVE/PERCEPTUAL MODELS

A persistent intuition in theory of emotions is that the object of the emotion is somehow established by the causal conditions of the emotion. No one holds a simple view of the relationship between cause and object, but what underlies the view is clear in the foregoing analysis of *Cyrano*: some item or situation in the causal history of an emotion has a property sufficient to motivate that emotion, and that item or situation is the object of the emotion. Although I want, importantly, to account for feelings that do not have objects, to argue directly against a conflation of cause and object is important to the general objective of this study. If a feeling has an object by virtue of the fact that activities expressive of the feeling take an object directly and, indirectly, make it the object of the feeling, then we have located one relatively clear mechanism by which expressive activity gives the feeling its character. Accounts that deliver the object to the feeling as a component of its causal, and so antecedent, history, are an obstacle to the progress of my own.

I have identified a cognitive/perceptual model as the view that appraisals, beliefs, or perceptions both cause an emotion and establish its object or content. Cognitive/perceptual models separate what they take to be the cause of an emotion from what they take to be the expression of that emotion in behavior, giving priority to the former in establishing the intentional core of an emotion, and hence its appropriate description. The separation of cause from consequent behavior is clear in this passage from Rorty: "When we focus on their consequences on behavior, most emotions can also be described as motives. . . . But when we speak of a *psychological state* as a emotion . . . we focus on the ways we are affected by our appraisals, evaluative perceptions or descriptions" (Rorty, "Explaining Emotions," 105; emphasis mine).[9]

My case against cognitive/perceptual models has so far been a negative one. We sometimes, and for some emotions, need as thorough an understanding of the expressive dimension of emotional experience as we do of the cognitive dimension to adjudicate puzzles about the object of an emotion. In this section, I argue more directly that cognitive/perceptual models are inadequate to the task of individuating emotions.

To make a general case about the importance of expressive action I examine the theoretical machinery of de Sousa's "cognitive/epistemic model" for object acquisition. In this complex account, the challenge is to place emotion uniquely as a mental phenomenon by relating an evolutionary account that secures a special place for emotions as mental phenomena in the explanation of behavior—the very project at which Darwin and James failed. De Sousa's commitment is clear in the following passages: "the motivating role of emotions makes them part of our mental life. What makes emotions fully mental and specifically human relates to their capacity for certain sorts of intentionality" (80).[10] De Sousa also gives emotions a unique explanatory role in theory of behavior by developing a model where the evolutionary function of emotions is to mimic perception and thus make some beliefs, desires, decision procedures, and courses of action more salient for us than others. If the account succeeds, it avoids explanatory redundancy by explaining how emotions lead us to act on some primary reasons rather than others.

The awkward position of expressive behavior in de Sousa's account is evident in the crucial chapters that attempt to argue for the necessity of a

---

9. Similarly, de Sousa says that the behavior expressive of emotion "[does] not relate directly to the perceptual model" (120).

10. James's and Darwin's concentration on the actual expressive behavior as criterial evidence for the feeling, although it precisely fails to place emotions as unique mental phenomena, captures something that we want about the nature of the behavior as determining the nature of the emotion.

theory of emotions to a theory of behavior by developing the perceptual analogy. The tension first appears in de Sousa's taxonomy of objects where he considers the aim of an emotion: "Emotions also have objects in the sense of goals or *aims*. And although aims do not relate directly to the perceptual model, I shall, for completeness, include an emotion's aim in our classification of objects" (120). The aims that de Sousa has in mind are those "consisting in immediate expressive behavior," which, from an evolutionary point of view, "must have been essential to making them [the emotions] just what they are" (120). These aims thus act as "a constraint on the character of each specific emotion" (121), but seem not, in general, to be required for the occurrence of a emotion.

This lack of integration in de Sousa's account between a behavioral and mentalistic analysis of the nature of emotions occurs once again and, I think, most perspicuously in de Sousa's account of how we learn our emotional vocabulary:

> My hypothesis is this: We are made familiar with the vocabulary of emotion by association with *paradigm scenarios*. These are drawn first from our daily life as small children and later reinforced by the stories, art and culture to which we are exposed. . . . Paradigm scenarios involve two aspects: first, a situation-type providing the characteristic *objects* of the specific emotion-type . . . and second, a set of characteristic or "normal" *responses* to the situation, where normality is first a biological matter and then very quickly becomes a cultural one. It is in large part in virtue of the response component of the scenarios that emotions are commonly held to *motivate*. But this is, in a way, back-to-front: for the emotion often takes its name from the response disposition and is only afterwards assumed to cause it. (de Sousa, 182; emphasis in original)

I accept that something like de Sousa's account of paradigm scenarios must be roughly the right account of how we learn our emotional vocabulary. It is nearly always possible to give an initial description of the emotion you are trying to analyze in terms of an evoking situation:

> Anger may be defined as an impulse attended by pain, to a revenge that shall be evident, and caused by an obvious, unjustified, slight with respect to the individual or his friends. (Aristotle, *The Rhetoric*, 93)

> Shame can be characterized in a preliminary way as a species of psychic distress occasioned by a self or a state of the self apprehended as inferior, defective, or in some way diminished. (Bartky, "Shame and Gender," 85)

The social importance of an emotive situation is surely what has been in large part responsible for our extensive emotional vocabulary and for the social conventions governing expression within these situations. But, if the emotion takes its name from the response disposition, and if it is an acted-out drama through which we gain our emotion vocabulary, it is reasonable to suppose that, in most cases, a particular emotional episode is not formed prior to its expression or response.

There is one level of object description, a level I have so far not discussed, that points to the inadequacy of the causal formulation: the description of emotions as having targets. I preferred in "Roxane's Choice" to provide a basic schema for object formation before considering how these objects are further distinguished by type. I now argue, more generally, that accounting for targetlike objects of emotions essentially involves reference to expressive behavior. De Sousa's definition of a target is "a real object, typically an actual particular, to which the emotion relates. The target is that real object, if any, *at* which the emotion is directed" (116). But I cannot think of an alternative analysis of the "at" in this definition beyond saying that the grammatical object that follows it is an object of expressive action. I am prepared to offer a series of considerations for this alternate view that take the form of variations on a case.[11]

De Sousa, in his discussion of targets, offers a case of ill-formed emotion: Calvin is angry at the person who stole his bicycle, and mistakenly believes "of a specific person S that S stole his bicycle. Here again, the ascription would be modified by Calvin's discovery either that someone else stole it or that no one did" (115). De Sousa never specifies exactly what the ascription is that would be subject to modification. But taking S to be me (Sue), presumably it would be "Calvin is angry at Sue." What makes it true that I am the ostensible target of Calvin's anger? The epistemic grounds for ascribing to Calvin anger at me are, for example, his cursing me and yelling at me. These behaviors, it may be said, do not suffice for saying that his acting toward me in anger has *made* me the target of his anger. Consider, however, what we should say if Calvin does

11. Using grammatical indicators as an account of object directedness is so common that Nissenbaum makes special room for it as a quasi-theory (10). Tormey is certainly guilty, and his prepositional criterion is difficult even to formulate adequately. He gives a general account of an object as "whatever is designated by the prepositional object of a particular mental state or act of a person" (11–12). Because mental states arguably do not have prepositional phrases, Tormey points out that this formulation is elliptical for whatever the prepositional object is in a sentence used to ascribe a mental state to a person, but this practice still picks out the object of the emotion in terms of the linguistic role of the term that designates it. As such, this prepositional criterion for the intentionality of emotions does not provide, and in many cases substitutes for, any actual account of how mental states and processes get content.

direct all his anger behavior at me, but discovers that I am not the thief. Although his feelings may now change, can we modify the original ascription of Calvin as angry at me? I see no grounds for the ascription to be modified. Granted, after someone else confesses, Calvin may no longer be angry at me, but we cease being angry for all sorts of reasons, and surely it would be quite appropriate for Calvin to apologize to me for having been angry. In doing so, he would not thereby be apologizing for *having mistaken me for the target* of his anger, but rather for *having fixed me as the target* of his anger by *accusing me, shouting at me,* and so on.

More evidence for the necessity of referring to expressive action to explain target acquisition can be garnered by pursuing a traditional strategy for investigating issues of intentionality: determining whether the contexts of co-referring expressions are opaque or transparent. When emotions are ascribed in certain obvious ways, these ascriptions contain contexts that are opaque to co-referring expressions. When emotions, sometimes these very same emotions, are ascribed in another way, a way that obviously specifies a target, it is at least *not clear* that these contexts are opaque.

To modify de Sousa's example with an example,[12] now suppose that Calvin believes that I stole his bicycle, that I did in fact steal his bicycle, and that I have that day become his new colleague—a fact which he does not yet know. We have the following possible descriptions of Calvin's beliefs and feelings:

1. Calvin believes that Sue stole his bike.
   1a. Calvin believes that his new colleague stole his bike.
2. Calvin is angry that Sue stole his bike.
   2a. Calvin is angry that his new colleague stole his bike.
3. Calvin is angry at Sue for stealing his bike.
   3a. Calvin is angry at his new colleague for stealing his bike.

Although neither substitution of the co-referential expressions, into 1 to produce 1a, or into 2 to produce 2a, preserves truth, the same substitution in 3 to produce 3a arguably does preserve truth. There's no conclusive way to prove this assertion. However, it seems to me plausible. If we read a particular pair opaquely, there is the possibility of assigning each member of the pair a different truth value. If we read a pair transparently, this possibility does not exist. We are more likely to feel committed to the same truth values for 3 and 3a than we are for the statements in the other two pairs. The account of object formation in "Roxane's Choice" at least offers an explanation of this difference. Object directedness generally in-

12. Thanks to Debbi Brown for this example.

volves the person in that emotional state in some *act of identification or reference*, which is why ascriptions of emotional states carry the problems of intentionality. But the objects are identified as the objects of expressive *actions*, and thus the ascriptions carry implications that are partly opaque and partly transparent. The descriptions contain, to borrow a designation of Daniel Dennett's, *mongrel contexts* (Dennett, *Content and Consciousness*). When object directedness is analyzed in terms of actual actions:

4. Calvin shouted at Sue.
4a. Calvin shouted at his new colleague.

the substitution of co-referring expressions to produce 4a clearly does preserve the truth of 4, and thus we see why we are inclined to read 3 and 3a transparently. The more the ascriptions carry the implications of action, that is the more they are written as target ascriptions, the more the transparency of the action contexts begins to dominate the opacity of the identification contexts in our assessments of these ascriptions. On a cognitive/perceptual account of object acquisition, the opacity should be a clear feature of 3 and 3a. But we are ambivalent about 3. We are unclear about whether we should treat it like 2 or 4.

Because the cognitive/perceptual view is committed to an emotions being fully formed prior to its expression, a response from a cognitive/perceptual theorist might be that it's Calvin's belief that Sue stole his bicycle that fixes Sue as the target of his anger, *and not his actions*. This response does not explain our intuitions about the partly transparent or mongrel contexts of 3 and 3a. The belief contexts of 1 and 1a are clearly opaque. The mongrel contexts of 3 and 3a are not clearly opaque. Furthermore, beliefs are typically picked out or attributed by their suitability for explaining action. They are then often thought to play a part in the cause of this action, but the essential point here is only that there has to be some relevant action that makes this belief attribution appropriate. Otherwise, what are we trying to explain by attributing a belief? Finally, suppose, then, all of the following, which includes an attribution to Calvin of some sort of angry behavior: (a) Calvin is exhibiting anger behavior; (b) Calvin is angry that his bike was stolen; (c) Calvin believes that Sue stole his bike. The conjunction of (a) to (c) still is insufficient to generate the further proposition that Calvin is angry at Sue. Calvin might even be angry that I stole his bike and not be angry at me. He might be angry at the person who encouraged me to steal his bike, thinking only that I am too susceptible to influence. The opacity of 2 and 2a indicate a level of description where we cannot infer target directed action. I conclude my discussion of emotion and object by elaborating on this point.

What would motivate our differential selection of 2 or 3 as the appropriate description of Calvin's anger? Both are complete emotion descriptions: both include specification of an object. Descriptions of form 2 involve a *propositional object*, and this type of object comes in for some very uncertain discussion in the literature. Rorty defines a target as an object extensionally "described and identified" (Rorty, "Explaining Emotions," 107), but many instances of emotions, and some types of emotion, do not have targets. De Sousa, in his brief discussion of propositional objects, tentatively fixes a base notion of a propositional object, by considering cases where the emotion does not have a target. He proposes that if an emotion "has a purely propositional object, it consists in an attitude appropriate to some fact, proposition, event or situation type that has the property instantiating the formal object of that emotion" (139).

Neither Rorty nor de Sousa consider at any length a case where an emotion could be described as having a double object, one of which takes a propositional form and one of which takes a target form. Calvin might be both angry that I stole his bike or angry about my having stolen his bike, and also angry at me. On the other hand, Calvin might be angry that I stole his bike and be angry at someone else for having encouraged me to do so. Finally, Calvin might simply be angry that I stole his bike.

To take up cases of object doubling is useful for seeing how objects are formed. Language is one of our primary resources for expressing emotion. Roxane, for example, began to determine Cyrano as an object of her love through an avowal. Cases where an emotion takes both a propositional object and a target allow us to consider the variety of ways in which emotions can be avowed.

Emotion ascriptions that can display a doubling of objects, where one object may typically be stated either propositionally or causally (e.g., (1) "I am angry that she did that" or "Her doing that angered me") and the other object is a target (e.g., (2) "I am angry at her.") have an interesting feature. Target statements (2) entail object statements (1), but not the reverse. If you are angry at me, there will be an appropriate type (1) statement whether or not you know it, but if you are angry about what I did, there may be no appropriate type (2) statement. You don't have to be angry at someone to be angry about something, but if you are angry at someone then you are angry about something, whether or not you know what it is.

What accounts for this asymmetry? You may become angry in situations where there is no particular item in that situation that could be the appropriate object of action expressive of that anger. You may be angry that your bike was stolen and know that I stole your bike, but also think that I am easily influenced by friends and should not be taken to task. The avowal of your anger, however, will still fix a situation as an object, and the corresponding description will explain behavior consequent on, or in response to, the situation.

If de Sousa is right, and I think he is, that emotions are learned in paradigm scenarios involving a characteristic evoking situation, I suggest that response to some instantiation of a situation-type, or some response to a situation-type itself (as in the case of hope, for example) is a part of the process of forming an emotion on any particular occasion. How we further describe this response—and, through it, the objects of emotions—is determined by what could count as action expressive of that emotion. Some emotions, love for instance, must have targets: the action expressive of love can only be taken toward real particulars. Other emotions, anger for instance, might on occasion have targets, but might, on other occasions, have only propositional objects. I can be so angry that my bike was stolen that I never buy another bike without locating any culprit at whom to be angry. This does not mean that emotions that take only propositional objects, by the nature of the emotion or the occasion, will not involve expressive action that forms or gives character to the emotion. In the next section, I elaborate how, on all emotive occasions, cause and response collaborate in forming that emotion.

THE ASSOCIATIONAL NATURE OF EMOTIONAL RESPONSE

A cognitive/perceptual model of emotions has seemed attractive to theorists for two reasons. First, the model purports to ground the role of emotions in theory of behavior by explaining how emotions have content and thus can rationalize our actions. Second, in cases of emotional confusion, the model offers the further possibility of arguing that emotional behavior can be understood as well organized by examining the emotion's causal history. Through an investigation of this history, we can sometimes redescribe the intentional component of a particular emotional state and thereby see the emotional response as more intelligible than previously. I have argued that these accounts do not succeed in explaining the content of emotional states.

We require an account of emotion and object that elaborates the importance of the history of an emotion in determining the emotion's nature while accounting for the importance of this history within a theory of emotional expression. I have adopted Ronald de Sousa's account of paradigm scenarios as the situation types that are of historical importance in emotional response. In this final section, I suggest that John Dewey's theory of emotional attitudes indicates how we might proceed with an account that integrates history with expression. Regrettably, Dewey's theory of emotions is little known. Originally published in 1894, "A Theory of Emotion" was not reprinted during the author's lifetime. A consequence of the view I develop is that we no longer need have so many gnawing concerns about object and/or target confusions. You are, barring some exceptional explanation, angry at the person who's at the end of your fist and in love with the person to whom you are making love. I find this a relatively plausible and politically appealing view to argue.

I propose that accounts of object directedness that deliver the object via the history of the emotion seem more plausible than they are because of our sense that the object of an emotion, be it a situation or a target, gains its suitability as an object through its association with a situation type, or paradigm scenario. This may lead us to believe that the particular response to a particular object is a post facto acting out of an emotion, and not the formation of one. Indeed, as illustrated in this passage from Patricia Cornwell's *Post-Mortem*, we often feel we could only make sense of a person's response through access to that person's paradigm scenarios:

> "What am I supposed to do? Agree and look as incompetent as he is?"
> "So it's a simple case of professional jealousy," he said with a shrug. "It happens."
> "I don't know *what* it is. How the hell do you explain these things? Half of what people do and feel doesn't make a damn bit of sense. For all I know, I could remind him of his mother."
> My anger was mounting with fresh intensity and I realized by the expression on his face that I was glaring at him.
> "Hey," he objected, raising his hand, "don't be pissed at me. I didn't do anything."
> "You were there this afternoon, weren't you?" (128)

We also lack an adequate vocabulary for describing the *process* element of emotional experience without falling into locutions that imply that an emotion is individuated prior to response. At a certain level of description, it is not easy to state how the view that an emotion motivates a response is wrong. Roxane's developing feelings indeed motivate expressive action that further characterize these feelings. If we understand a situation type partly through the property vocabulary of emotions, we can see how responsive behavior or expression is necessary to the formation of an emotional experience by being a necessary part of recognizing a property. When an emotion is a response to a situation in virtue of that situation's resemblance to a person's paradigm scenarios for the emotion,[13] I will say that the response has an *associational character.*

It is not clear how committed de Sousa is to an account of emotions that locates emotional response as an *effect* of emotions. From his description of an aim as putting constraints on the character of an emotion, it is evident that he wants a complex account that incorporates both a situation type and a characteristic set of responses into a core description of an emotional experience. I suggest that the bridge between these is an account of the properties that we learn to recognize or predicate in the scenarios in which we learn our emotion vocabulary.

Without using all of de Sousa's terminology, in a case, say, of love gone right, the real object at which the emotion is directed must have a real property that motivates the emotion. Supposing that Cyrano had been a story of love where no one's nose got in the way, Roxane might have simply come to love Cyrano by virtue of his eloquence. That is, occasions involving his eloquence might have caused her love. This would be an intelligible story if, in a way we can understand, Roxane values the quality of eloquence in her lovers, and we might describe this by saying that Roxane finds either that quality or the people who have it cherishable. Because love, by its practice, requires a person as object, I think that only the latter formulation is accurate.

Cyrano's first-order property of being eloquent supports his second-order property of being cherishable (or cherishable for Roxane). As I understand de Sousa's account, the second-order level of properties—being cherishable, threatening, offensive, and so on—are *observer-relative* properties that we recognize in emotional situations and that, furthermore, ground the intelligibility of our response. When we argue within the constraints of the perceptual analogy, however, the response itself becomes irrelevant to the individuation of the emotion. The perceptual analogy halts at perception. However, there may be something about the further examination of these properties that allows us to integrate a richer notion of response into the core description of an emotion, a notion of response that contributes to object directedness in the way I have tried to display and thus ties emotion to behavior through an emoter who necessarily acts in the world.

Properties such as being threatening, cherishable, or offensive have obvious characteristics: (1) they are emergent; (2) they are observer relative; and (3) like the properties associated with taste, there is wide personal

13. I take it that people will have a great many different paradigm scenarios for each different emotion type.

and cultural variation in the application of these properties (whom one finds cherishable enough to love, for example) while these predications remain comprehensible and acceptable to others who would not make the same predications. Despite this wide variation in application, these properties still activate a critical vocabulary underlain by some notion of correctness. To borrow an old example from George Pitcher, fluffy white lambs are not threatening, whatever my idiosyncratic response to them.

De Sousa accepts the characteristics of emotive properties that I have described. He uses a standard definition of emergence: "A property is *emergent* if it could not be deduced from the lower level properties on the basis of which it is explained" (32) and argues that the observer-relativity of emotive properties does not compromise the objectivity of our response. Our response is in fact rendered objective by the resemblance of the evoking situation to the paradigm scenarios that also, in large degree, account for the personal and cultural variation in our emotional appraisals.

All that we need to do to integrate response more fully into our account of emotions is to elaborate the ways in which emotive properties such as being threatening are observer-relative. What seems plausible is that a minimal condition of my finding a situation threatening, of the property of something's being threatening emerging for me, is that I have the response learned in or adumbrated by my paradigm scenarios for fear. Otherwise, although I might well understand why someone else might find something threatening, and might even agree that a certain situation type is generally threatening, *being threatening* is not a property that would emerge for me on that occasion. We might suppose that my finding something threatening involves my running (or at least having the impulse to run), and what's more my *running from that object.* On this suggestion, my predicating "threatening" of that bear involves a response that fixes the bear as the object of my fear through my response.

There is an troubling aspect, however, to using emotive properties to make an emotional experience intelligible through its history while also incorporating the response into the core description of an emotion. Our responses evidently change with time and experience. How am I to explain this while holding that the recognition of the properties involves, as a condition for its objectivity and success, the response that fixed it as an emergent property in my experience? If the emergence for me of an emotive property (such as threatening) depends on my responding in a certain way (I run from that spider) when I begin to respond differently (I beat that spider to death), what grounds do we have for thinking that this response is related to the same emergent property?

As an example of changing response, many women become acquainted in adolescence with a paradigm scenario that I will call "recognition anxiety" and that involves the sense of being ignored on precisely those occasions when you are trying to assert yourself in ways that might not accord with traditional gender expectations. The initial responses that characterize this anxiety might be attempts to meet gender expectations. You grow your hair and throw like a girl. What starts out as an attempt, in the face of this anxiety, to conform, however, frequently changes to a growing insistence on not conforming. Feeling this same anxiety at 30, you get your hair cut even shorter. But how is this response still recognizable as characterizing recognition anxiety?

Failure to need response in the *formation* of an emotion would commit us to a view of an emotion's having been formed or individuated prior to its expression. What I require is some account of response-dependent recognition of evaluative properties that can accommodate changing response. This case is easier to make if the change in response is gradual and intelligible. John Dewey's account of emotional habits offers a promising model of such change.

De Sousa is concerned about the back-to-front feature of an emotion's motivating a response when the response appears to partly determine the character of the emotion. The former appears to require that the emotion occur prior to the response, whereas the latter holds the response responsible for the emotion. It is precisely this feature of emotional *description* that bothers Dewey.[14] Dewey's account, like de Sousa's, attempts to reconcile the features of situation and response in characterizing emotions, but Dewey attempts to do so by explaining the object-directedness of emotions as a feature of the response that necessitates a double level of understanding of our descriptions of emotional experience. Dewey maps these levels onto different phases of our experience. As these phases take place coincidently, I prefer to explain the account in terms of a double level of understanding.

Dewey's theory of emotions reactivates Darwin's notion of habit. The account depends on the idea that we give sense to our experience prereflectively through our changing responses: habituated responses to our environment, acquired by prior activity, provide resources, in a form we take for granted as useful, for our responses to future resembling situations. Victor Kesterbaum, in a study of Dewey's theory of habit provides this brief summary: "Habits reflect and record the outcomes of an individ-

14. Dewey is a strict evolutionist and was bothered by the inadequacies of Darwin's and James's accounts. To give an explanation of emotional expression by saying that this expression is caused by emotions is not to give an evolutionary account of the expression; the appeal to emotions is idle unless they are given some account in which the movements expressive of emotion are themselves useful as movement.

ual's experiences; they provide the resources, in the form of taken for granted meanings, for his future experiences" (3).

Dewey's way of accounting for the unique evolutionary place of emotions is to point to the nonstatic nature of our environment, its resembling, but always changing, situations. Because the elements of action are ordered by the habitual response, a changing environment will create disappointed expectations if our habits are not gradually modified to keep up with these changes. The tension of adjusting our habits to a continually changing environment is what Dewey calls "emotional seizure."[15]

As an example of emotional seizure, in explaining grief, Dewey says that "actions surge forward to some stimulus or phase of a situation; . . . the factor necessary to co-ordinate all the rising discharges is gone . . . the expectation or kinaesthetic image is thrown back on itself," and this breakdown is the experience of grief (Dewey, "Theory of Emotion," 159). Early in "In Memoriam," Tennyson returns to Hallam's house, and, because of the familiar situation, there is the nearly breathless expectation for the greeting touch of Hallam's hand:

> Dark house, by which once more I stand
> Here in the long unlovely street,
> Doors, where my heart was used to beat
> So quickly, waiting for a hand,

The abrupt severing of this expectation by the thought of Hallam's permanent absence:

> A hand that can be clasp'd no more—

leaves Tennyson with no resources through which to complete the experience of visiting Hallam's house (Tennyson, 249). The failure to adjust a habit that has supplied purpose and direction to his action leaves Tennyson paralyzed with grief. Tennyson's grieving is a process of gradually adjusting habit. This is marked in the poem by his final joyful visit to Hallam's house many years later.

Finally, with respect to the object of an emotion, the stimulus does not exist *as object* until the adjustment of the habit is under way. Here is Dewey's description of object acquisition:

15. Amélie Rorty's account is very much like Dewey's, but focuses on the possible pathology of leading this sort of life (our tendency to not modify habit, but, instead, seek out situations that will reinforce habit). For this reason, and for her lack of attention to expression, I prefer Dewey's account. Expression clearly is the focus.

There is one phase of the activity that constitutes the bear as object; there is another which would attack it, or run away from it, or stand one's ground before it. This makes it impossible to describe any emotion without using dual terms—one for the Affect itself, and one for the object "at," "toward" or "on account of which" it is. (Dewey, "Theory of Emotion," 182–83)

To clarify Dewey's somewhat obscure account of object acquisition, let us take a simple description of an emotional experience: "I was frightened of the bear." This is the type of description that appears to be cause/ object ambiguous (is the bear the cause of my fear, the object of my fear, or both?).

Dewey thinks there is a necessary ambiguity in the description "I was frightened of the bear," a description that contains the bear as both object and cause of my fear. The ambiguity, he maintains, is a consequence of the fact that there are two levels of description going on. Qua object of my emotion, the bear does not explain my response; it becomes the object because of my response to it—I run from it. Qua cause, it does explain my response, but only when taken together with the history of the habit of my responses. Only because I habitually run in resembling situations does the object of my behavior become the cause that makes my behavior intelligible. Establishing the object of an experience and establishing its cause are reciprocal processes where my response is what makes both features of the description possible. At the point where I have modified habit to accommodate a resembling situation my emotional experience is complete.

Darwin's use of habit was, in the end, inadequate to an account of emotional expression because it was divorced from an account of a creature that learns through experience. For creatures like us, at least some of this learning involves conscious deliberation, and much more of it can be intellectualized in retrospect. What is important about Dewey's account is that this retrospective summary carries information about the *history* of a person, not just a description of an isolated response. We can, with Dewey's account, maintain our interest in how emotions often are intelligible only through an understanding of a person's complex history in certain situations. We also can locate the present object of an emotional experience through a response, although the analysis of *Cyrano* shows that this remains a complex undertaking.

Dewey argues for a doubled level of understanding of the descriptions of emotional experience. These levels illuminate how the object of an emotion is formed through action, while that emotional experience must nevertheless be described in a way that makes that object appear to be the cause. Dewey's account offers a way of understanding the process of emo-

tional experience that makes our sometimes ambiguous cause/object for-
mulations of this experience ("I was frightened by the face at the window") a necessary part of our emotional descriptions. In summary, I argue
that the motivational structure of my emotions is secured by my involvement in situations that are of a type, while the changing particulars that
instantiate this type lead to changing responses, fixing new objects and
targets in new situations.

By treating de Sousa's paradigm scenarios as situation types to which we
respond through habit that: (1) is activated by associational property
emergence; and (2) is modified as we learn through experience, several
features of an expressive theory of affect are satisfied. Our response to
various situations is associational, dynamic, and always relevant to the description of the experience, for it is our response to a stimulus, described
in the context of evolving habit that forms our experience.

This chapter has had a single argumentative theme: our acts of expression
contribute to the individuation of instances of classic emotions by establishing the objects (or targets) for these emotions.

The force of this chapter has been to suggest that there is nothing
about the fact that emotions have objects that prevent their being a species of feeling. I hold that the emotions do have unity as a psychological
category, but that this is an explanatory unity that only can be located by
first broadening the category of affect to include all feelings and then
giving an account of the category. In this chapter I have also highlighted
the notion of expressive opportunities and of emotional change. The acceptance of any view of emotional habit, such as the one that Dewey for-
mulates and I endorse, raises questions of what the real possibilities are
for emotional change. To change emotionally, we appear to need situations to work through, and some history of success. In Chapter 4 I offer
an account of affect as an explanatory category. I also begin to analyze the
circumstances that condition our expressive successes and failures.

IV

A MODEL FOR AFFECTIVE MEANING

If you still believe that shame is a feeling inside you and that you principally announce the presence of that feeling when you say "I am ashamed," then you might for consistency's sake interpret "I am sorry" in the same way. You would then assume that the man is merely telling you how he feels, so that you could perfectly well reply, "Enough is enough! First you kick me, and then you give me an account of your internal life."

—Frithjof Bergmann, "A Monologue on the Emotions"

COLLABORATIVE INDIVIDUATION

What must I do and what must you do for either myself or you to attribute an affective state to me? Particularly what must we both do, when this state is not a classic emotion? In Chapters 2 and 3, I have been advancing the suggestion that feelings are not individuated prior to their expression, although the phenomenon of concealment, discussed in Chapter 2, must be accommodated. I return to the phenomenon of concealment in Chapter 6. I have yet to give an account, however, of how feelings are individuated through their expression. Such an account is the task of the present chapter. I will argue that their individuation is collaborative.

In Chapter 3, I suggested that some questions of how we individuate feelings, specifically, questions of how emotions acquire objects, could be resolved if we understand expressive action as the modification of habit to meet changing circumstances. But modifying habit also is how I succeed in riding a bicycle over unfamiliar roads. The account in Chapter 3 not only was restricted to the classic emotions but also consciously assumed that we have no trouble in recognizing certain behavior as expressive of affect. It was precisely the comfort of this assumption as a resting place that created problems for the theories discussed at the start of this study.

Darwin, James, and Ryle assumed that we have no trouble in recognizing behavior as expressive of feeling and particular patterns of behavior as expressive of particular feelings. Their dependence on this assumption left them unable to give an account of affect as a category of explanation and of the individuation of any particular feeling. When we add free-style feelings to classic emotions, the problem magnifies exponentially. I have always liked the anarchic flavor of this statement by Frithjof Bergmann: "Let me start with a simple but powerful fact. Emotions are very complex. They are subtle and terribly hard to describe, and there are hundreds and perhaps thousands of varieties of them" (3).

In this chapter, I propose an account of the individuation of feelings that can accommodate the uniqueness of feelings while suggesting how emotion categories arise. This account is modeled on Donald Davidson's account of the individuation of propositional states. Davidson's account is *externalist,* that is, the account argues a version of the more general view that the individuation of a subject's psychological states cannot be accomplished by reference to the condition of that person alone, but must make reference to the person's environment. Davidson's particular externalist account not only allows for, but requires, the presence of expressive behavior for the individuation of psychological states. My use of his model does not, however, solve the problem of how we recognize this behavior as *expressive of feeling.* I argue that this recognition can be understood only through an account of our explanatory purposes when we use the category of affect. I offer the proposal that our interest in affect, as both expressers and interpreters, is an interest in personal or autobiographical significance.

My account of the individuation of affect assumes that expression generally is a communicative activity and that a model for communicative success is a reasonable place to look for the formal conditions for the successful individuation of feeling. Although I also assume that communicative activity is broader than that picked out by the intent to communicate, I believe that our expressions of feeling are, for the most part, intended communications. I begin my account of how affective states are individuated with some initial investigation of the concept of individuation. In particular, we must attend to the ways in which individuation often is a collaborative achievement, especially in communicative circumstances.

The concept of individuation may be analyzed into two processes: (1) forming something as an individual; and (2) recognizing an individual. I propose to refer to these aspects of individuation as simply "formation" and "recognition." It is natural to think of formation of an individual as prior to, and a condition of, recognizing that individual. Indeed, many times these are separate processes, and recognition simply means identifying what has been formed separate and prior to the circumstances in which it might be identified. I do not have to create you to pick you out in a police lineup.

Despite our inclination to think of individuals as formed before they can be recognized or identified, recognition or identification often is a part of the process of formation. Arguably, there are limiting cases where the two processes collapse, that is, cases where individuals are formed purely through our recognitional capacities. Hume's theory of causation might be such a case. Recognizing one event as of a type reliably correlated with a later event type makes the first event a cause. This limiting case is important. It offers an actual account of the formation of individuals (particular causes) through an account of recognition. If our affective behavior is *not* like this, however, and certainly there is every reason to believe it is *not* like this, then theorists such as Ryle substitute an ability to recognize for an account of how what is recognized develops as an individual. For an account of the individuation of affective states, then, we must examine more closely the possible relations between acts of formation and acts of recognition. I am particularly interested in these relations for circumstances that require more than one person for individuation.

In circumstances that require collaborative individuation, I will use *articulation* as central to the notion of formation. I define articulation as performing the appropriate acts (in both type and number) to give something the form by which it may be recognized. To form a token of the word *cat* so that someone will recognize it, may depend on drawing the right number of lines, connected at the right points, with the right amount of space between interconnected groups of lines, and so on. Neither C/-\ T nor CA   T might do. Along with the core notion of articulation, there are several other features of formation that are of interest.

Formation requires a *medium* in or through which we form the individual. Preformed particulars—rubber balls or sheets of aluminum siding—are formed of a material through a process. When we form an individual, I propose to refer to the combination of the material and process as our medium. When we have a choice of media—printing, writing, or using a computer, for example, to form a token of *cat*—I propose to refer to these media as our *resources*, a term I used in my discussion of expression in Chapter 2. I highlight it here because in circumstances of collaborative individuation we need to assume that our interpreters are familiar with our resources. But when we express our feelings, our resources are remarkably diverse: gesture, avowal, involuntary response, action, metaphor, aesthetic creation, or even just pointing to the things that catch our attention. What's more, none of these resources seems privileged in allowing the formation of feeling. Charles Taylor referred to "trying to get" as a natural expression of wanting. Although facial expression has had, from

Darwin onward, an important theoretical place in theories of affective expression, our aesthetic and everyday activities testify to lives of feeling that are subtle, complex, and embodied and articulated through multiple media.

Finally, to switch to the recognition aspect of collaborative individuation, I shall say that collaborative individuation requires recognition or *uptake*, a feature that can best be described by considering cases. To elaborate the possible relations of recognition to individuation, consider the following examples.

If I say the word *cat* to a person who does not understand English, I will not have succeeded in forming the word *cat* so that it can be recognized as a word of English by that person. I will not have succeeded at securing collaborative individuation, even though there may be nothing more I can do. There are, however, three different kinds of cases where formation is not adequate for collaborative individuation. In the first, although I have failed in local circumstances at securing collaborative individuation, I may have succeeded in forming an individual as evidenced by the possibility that someone else, who is familiar with the medium of formation, can recognize that individual. If an English speaker later recognizes my word *cat*, collaborative individuation with my Egyptian friend may have failed, but I have succeeded in forming the word *cat*.

The second case is a limit on the first: on some occasions only we can recognize the individuals that we have formed. People who must decipher their handwriting for us are people who have not succeeded in communicating through writing, although they have succeeded in forming words, as evidenced by their own ability later to read what they have written. Another very ordinary case of when we do not depend on the response of others, and, indeed, when it would ruin the fun if we did so, is when a group of people try to persuade each other of the different things we can see in the shape of a cloud. This also is, perhaps, another instance of forming individuals through our recognitional capacities. The aesthetic theories considered in Chapter 2 are all committed to this limiting case as one that will mark the success of having individuated or objectified a feeling.

Third, there is, however, a quite separate kind of case of the relation between formation and recognition that can be identified best by its denial of the limiting case I have just offered and that marks success at formation through response. There may be cases where our success at formation (and not just our success at collaborative individuation) depends on other people's recognitional capacities and where our own recognitional capacities are not sufficient to guarantee this success. We might think of the clown who makes figures for children out of balloons while the children call out the names "dog," "duck," "bunny," "cowboy." She will keep manipulating the balloons until she secures the appropriate response *from the children*. If our achievement at forming individuals depends on *other people's* recognitional capacities, and not just our own, I refer to the necessity of, or uptake, not just for collaborative individuation but also for actual formation. This is not to suggest that the clown with the balloons could not practice at home, where her own recognitional capacities will determine when she has formed an individual. What will count as *forming* an individual may depend on social context. I will offer the example of a party game, as an elaboration of this case.

Finally, there is no requirement, even in cases where uptake is necessary to formation, that what is formed persist as an enduring individual. This means that there is no requirement that we be able to reidentify an individual as a condition of an individual's having been formed. I may erase the token *cat* immediately. If recognition is necessary to the success of the formation of balloon animals, this recognition seems to depend on no more than the immediate *shared response* of the children to the shapes the clown has created.

Describing the complexities of the relation between formation and recognition displays the possible complexities of the collaborative individuation of feelings and also raises central political and moral questions about the conditions for the successful expression of feeling. How much do I have to do and how much do you have to do for me successfully to form my feelings? How much authority do I maintain over this process? The following example illustrates the importance of these concerns.

Not long ago, I played Pictionary. You are given a word in a category (the categories include Object, Action, and Difficult), and, using a felt-tipped pen on a washable board, you are given one minute to draw something that allows your team to guess your word. You have a *medium* and a mission involving *formation* as a *subordinate act of individuation*. Your team wins the right to roll the dice when someone on your team forms the verbal token of your word; this is the higher-level objective, and in itself it constitutes a case of forming an individual. It is no part of this game that you should be able to draw at all well or most people would not be able to play Pictionary.

Obviously at the level of forming an individual on the drawing board, formation is highly dependent on recognition. Pictionary thus highlights *uptake* in interesting ways. Members of my team, who, through their activities, were familiar with certain items, had less trouble recognizing my confetti and skipping rope. In addition, the people who knew *me* better were more successful at recognizing what I was attempting to articulate. With players I didn't know well, I began to pay more attention to personal style. A woman from Nova Scotia started out many drawings with a boat. After a few turns, I recognized her boat so quickly I became impatient for the further discriminatory acts that would be useful in helping me to recognize her drawing. Individuals existed only momentarily on the board and would have been recognized only within the context of the game. Uptake in collaborative individuation was facilitated by either overlapping biographies, personal knowledge, or increasing familiarity with a person's resources, in this case, their style within a medium.

Recognition in the form of a certain verbal response was the sole criterion for successful collaborative individuation, and it was unnecessary that this recognition even be a matter of widely shared response. A Pictionary individual is established after a single appropriate instance of response. Finally, I can, in Pictionary, attempt to draw a duck when my word is *rabbit* and if someone gives the verbal response of "rabbit," what I have attempted to form makes no difference whatsoever to what I am taken to have formed. The game in a social context in which I have little authority over what counts as articulation that is adequate for forming an individual. In forming Pictionary individuals, I lack authority over the meaning and success of my own acts of expression.

In Pictionary, I have deliberately offered a situation of collaborative individuation where participants have a firm mutual grasp of highly constraining conventions. There is no doubt about when a Pictionary individual has been established, and there is no doubt about what that individual is. One instance of appropriate uptake (where what is appropriate is fixed by the rules of the game and what is written on a small card) is sufficient to secure individuation. When we move outside these highly constraining conventions, collaborative individuation may be necessary for the success of a certain communicative act, even though the possibility that the collaboration might be successful may seem to crumple. I conclude this general discussion of the relation between formation and individuation by contrasting expressing a feeling to forming a Pictionary individual.

In "A Theory of Emotion," John Dewey gives a wonderful description of the expressive complexity of a simple gesture—the impotent shrug:

> The raising of the brows is the act of retrospect, of surveying the ground to see if anything could have been done; the pursing of the lips, the element of tentative rejection (doubt); the raising of the shoulders, the act of throwing a burden off . . . the holding out of the hand, palm up, the attitude of asking or taking. To my introspection the *quale* of the emotion agrees entirely; it is a feeling of "I don't see how I could possibly have done anything else, so far as I am concerned, but I'm willing to hear what you have to offer." (Dewey, "A Theory of Emotion," 167)

Suppose that failing, once again, to draw a Pictionary individual that my team can recognize, I turn around and give a Dewey shrug to a teammate. That person shrugs back ("I don't see how you could possibly have done anything else either") and smiles sympathetically. I have obviously succeeded in expressing my impotence at being unable to draw. But suppose I give this same shrug and my teammate says, "Look, if you hate the game that much we'll all quit playing." Have I failed to communicate my feeling of impotence at being unable to draw or have I instead communicated my frustration or even contempt for Pictionary? It is not at all clear to me that I will be myself confident of the feeling I have formed.

The example seems to me authentic enough. I might go home and actually worry about whether I had, in shrugging, perhaps inadvertently, but sincerely, expressed my contempt for Pictionary. But it is difficult to understand how your response on this occasion should confuse mine to the extent that I'm no longer sure what I was attempting to convey by my shrug. Granting that identification is necessary to individuation, and granting that appropriate response is necessary to successful communication, why isn't this a case where I can identify what I was trying to express but have failed to communicate it successfully? Why isn't it like the first or second cat case? Why, in other terms, don't I simply summarize this case as follows: I was attempting to express a feeling of impotence that you mistook for contempt, but I know I was expressing impotence and other people would have recognized it as impotence. You misinterpreted me, and I can be as confident of this as I would be if I had said "pass me the felt pen," and you had handed me a chip with dip. Of course, I might be this confident about my shrug, but, still, there is a significant difference between the cases. In fairly simple cases of linguistic communication, I ordinarily have confidence in what I said and what I mean. In cases of Pictionary individuation, I have no authority over what the meaning of what I have drawn, but the conventions of the game that place this authority with others allow me the same confidence in achieving individuation. In fairly simple cases of affective communication, someone's response can make me unsure of what I have expressed, and, therefore, of what I feel.

Moreover, in cases where interpreter response makes me unsure of what I feel, the nature of my feelings will become more indeterminate. I wish to argue against a merely epistemological role for uptake in the case described.[1] Here is the epistemological alternative: the interpreter's perhaps willful reading of my shrug as an expression of contempt makes me unsure of whether I feel impotence or whether I feel contempt. His re-

---

1. Karen Jones has pointed out my need to argue directly against this alternative.

sponse may have the power to confuse me about what I feel or to prevent my knowing or being sure of what I feel. Nevertheless, there is some truth of the matter about what I feel, independently of both my shrug and the response that confuses me. I simply lack privileged access as to what my real feelings are. I may really feel impotence even while wondering whether I really feel contempt.

Against this epistemological reading, I would first stress that my claim is a limited one. The response to the shrug is likely to make it less clearly true that I straightforwardly feel impotence. I do not claim that the response is likely to make it more true that I feel contempt. I am persuaded of the ontological reading by Stuart Hampshire's "Sincerity and Single-mindedness." Hampshire's argument is that we discriminate our own states of mind partly through reference to the occasions that cause them and the description under which we view an occasion partly determines the content of that state of mind. One's thought of one's state of mind "as having a certain cause, and therefore being of a certain kind, is one of the factors which determines what [the] state of mind actually is" (Hampshire, "Sincerity," 237). In cases where we would argue that a subject is in error about his own sincere self-description: "He cannot, so to put it, be merely, or wholly wrong: if he is in some way confused about his state of mind, or self-deceived, then his state of mind must be a complex and confused one" (Hampshire, "Sincerity," 237).

One of Hampshire's examples involves the difference between belief and hope. If Harry says that he believes that p is true and you think for good reasons that Harry is self-deceived, that he merely hopes that p is true, it would, nevertheless, be misleading to describe his state of mind as the "hope that p is true." Undoubtedly, there is something about Harry's behavior that you think is better explained by describing his state of mind as one of hope; however, as long as Harry believes that he believes that p is true, you will not adequately account for all of his behavior without acknowledging the complexity of his mental state. You would be leaving out something essential, "namely, that the subject takes what is really his hope that p to be a belief that p, and that he is ready, or disposed, to assert that p in the relevant circumstances" (Hampshire, "Sincerity," 238). In the same way, if I doubt, or am confused, about whether I behaved badly enough to be ashamed of myself, it would be misleading to describe my attitude as simply one of shame.

I am not, in the Pictionary example, interested in the case where I remain confident that I expressed Pictionary impotence, even when you thought I was expressing Pictionary contempt. I am interested in the very common case where the response to an expression begins to make the subject uncertain about what he or she feels. This uncertainty has repercussions for how the subject actually feels. If I become uncertain as to whether I feel impotence or contempt, my affective state itself becomes a more confused one.

In Chapter 3, I argued that our appraisals of objects and situations do not deliver our emotions and feelings, fully formed, individuated, and independent of our acts of expression. In the remaining sections of this chapter, I offer a view of how expression and interpretation help establish or confuse the determination of the very occasions to which we respond. I thus accept Hampshire's arguments that confusion in the Pictionary case will have both ontological and epistemological ramifications, but with an emendation. It is the collaborative nature of individuating feeling that accounts for the indeterminacies and confusions with which many occasions are viewed.

TRIANGULATION AND AFFECTIVE MEANING

It is difficult to analyze the conditions for successful expression of affect, and I am first attempting to try to locate, with some precision, the nature of these difficulties. I propose to pursue, for some distance, an analogy with belief, to show how conditions for successful affective expression might be more difficult to satisfy than similar conditions for the successful expression of a simple belief through language. I argue that we can locate differences and difficulties at the level of fairly well-accepted conditions for what makes an expression meaningful, explaining the lack of confidence we often have about our own affective meanings. Two important assumptions underlie the usefulness of such a comparison: (1) although my feelings cannot always be said to have a clear propositional content, when I express a feeling, I am nevertheless attempting to communicate a kind of meaning. I am attempting to communicate the significance or importance to me of some occasion. I will have more to say, presently, about personal significance, but I leave this now as an intuitive explanation of what I am trying to do in expressing a feeling. (2) Some accounts of the conditions that make determinate linguistic meaning possible can be understood as also setting the possibilities for the determinate meaning of behavior that is not linguistic (a shrug, for example). I chose a particular discussion of meaning, Donald Davidson's, partly because of the applicability of his model to nonlinguistic behavior.

It is a widely accepted view that the determination of linguistic meaning only is possible through the standards of objectivity that arise interpersonally through the ordinary success of linguistic communication. The importance of people who understand me (widely and generally, although not necessarily on any particular occasion) in establishing the meaning of what I say derives from Wittgenstein's private language argument. Generally, this argument is summarized by using the notion of correctness. If there is no way, in principle, for me to distinguish whether I have used a word correctly or incorrectly, then what I have said does not have a determinable meaning, and only publicly accessible language, language that can be understood, can give rise to standards of correctness. In its basic form, the argument that I cannot use a language that no one else could understand has to do with isolating the conditions under which an expression of mine can be said to be meaningful, can be said to have a meaning. A central project for philosophy of language is to use an account of the conditions of ordinary linguistic competence to give an account of linguistic meaning. I am particularly interested in Donald Davidson's notion of triangulation as a simplified model of the conditions of linguistic competence for its emphasis on the necessity of shared differential response to common stimuli. I propose to adopt triangulation as a model for viewing the structure of affective communication.[2]

Davidson's view is, I believe, much more useful than has been recognized for theorists who are interested in the political dimensions of being meaningful to others. As a preliminary clarification, it is the fact that we can have *shared differential* responses to common stimuli (what we share is that they are differential responses) without those being shared responses (responses of the same type) that allows the view to ground rather than depend on conventions, to explain rather than assume them. To make the notion of shared differential responses a bit clearer, if, whenever we come to a fence, I go under it and you go over it, we have shared differential responses to fences.

I find Davidson's externalist account a useful model for the following reasons: (1) feelings and emotions have been philosophically isolated and often have not benefited from being a part of central debates in philosophy of mind. (2) Affect has been difficult to handle because of the particularity of our affective responses, and Davidson's view offers resources that can accommodate this particularity. (3) To redescribe my commitment to the importance of expressive behavior from within an explicitly externalist perspective highlights the complexities of how we interpret this behavior and who has authority over the outcome of this process.

To make explicit the conditions necessary to understanding each other's

2. The model of triangulation is first used by Davidson in "Rational Animals" and is developed in "The Conditions of Thought," "Epistemology Externalized," and "Three Varieties of Knowledge." I find the account clearer and more detailed in later articles, particularly "Three Varieties of Knowledge." When I offer Davidson's defense of his own view, I take it from this article.

utterances, Davidson generally uses a simplified situation involving an interpreter's ability to understand a single expression of a speaker. I use, from "Epistemology Externalized," the example of a speaker's uttering of "raton" whenever a mouse appears. Davidson's project is to understand what makes the interpretation of this utterance possible without the assumption that the speaker and interpreter share either particular linguistic conventions, or even conventions about the kinds of meanings the speaker is trying to express, whether or not, for instance the speaker is trying to express a perceptual belief or a feeling. We are entitled to assume that the speaker is sincere, that he or she is not trying to deceive the interpreter.

As a Davidsonian interpreter of a speaker's use of "raton," you notice a systematic difference in the speaker's utterance pattern. Whenever a certain stimulus appears (you call it a mouse), the speaker utters "raton," but does not utter "raton" in the absence of this stimulus. After a while you conclude that, for that speaker, "raton" means mouse. You may be wrong, of course, and you may have to abandon this conclusion for a new hypothesis in the light of more evidence, where anything that speaker says or does will count as evidence. But whatever the complications, one keeps making the same point: the minimal condition that must be satisfied for "raton" to be interpretable, and hence meaningful, is that you notice a pattern to the speaker's responses. But you can respond to her responses in this way (that is, respond by noticing a pattern to her responses rather than taking them to be erratic) only because you yourself have similarly differential responses to similar stimuli. You look at the same rodent and think "mouse" every time she says "raton." And what makes your words meaningful is the possibility of interpretation when you are the speaker. More than one person's differential response to similar stimuli grounds the possibility of determinate meaning through the possibility of mutual interpretation. Davidson refers to this as *triangulation*. I respond to a stimulus (the mouse) and to your response to the stimulus (the utterance of "raton"). You respond to a stimulus and to my response to that stimulus:

> It takes two points of view to give a location to the cause of a thought, and thus to define its content. We may think of it as a form of triangulation: each of two persons is reacting differentially to sensory stimuli streaming in from a certain direction. If we project the incoming lines outward, their intersection is the common cause. If the two people now note each other's reactions . . . each can correlate these observed reactions with his or her stimuli from the world. The common cause can now determine the contents of an utterance and a thought. (Davidson, "Three Varieties of Knowledge," 159–60)

The speaker's utterance "raton" and your utterance "mouse" have the same content or meaning. They each refer to that creature which causes the shared differential responses. Davidson grants that "[o]bviously the matter is subtle and complicated" ("Epistemology Externalized," 3), and I am interested, of course, in the basic complications that are likely to arise in this model, for the communication of affective significance.

A comprehensive defense of the necessity of shared differential responses to shared environmental features as a condition for determining meaning is beyond the scope of this study. I need to depend, however, on its plausibility to examine the fate of this condition in circumstances where we are trying to convey affective meaning. I first give Davidson's own defense of his view from "Three Varieties of Knowledge." This description of triangulation is offered after posing the questions of why an interpersonal standard should be an objective standard and why we need communication to establish this standard:

> All creatures classify objects and aspects of the world in the sense that they treat some stimuli as more alike than others. The objective criterion of such classification is similarity of response. . . . The criterion on the basis of which a creature can be said to be treating stimuli as similar, as belonging to a class, is the similarity of the creature's responses to those stimuli; but what is the criterion of similarity of the responses? *This* criterion cannot be derived from the creature's responses; it can only come from the responses of an observer to the responses of the creature. And it is only when an observer consciously correlates the responses of another creature with objects and events in the observer's world that there is any basis for saying the creature is responding to those objects or events (rather than any other source of the creature's stimuli). . . . For until the triangle is completed connecting two creatures, and each creature with common features of the world, there can be no answer to the question whether a creature, in discriminating between stimuli, is discriminating between stimuli at the sensory surfaces or somewhere further out, or further in. Without this sharing of reactions to common stimuli, thought and speech would have no particular content—that is no content at all. ("Three Varieties," 159; emphasis in original)

For my purposes, the plausibility of the shared response condition derives from two fundamental considerations. First, we need some account of how concepts of whatever sort we are interested in arise. When Helen Fay Nissenbaum, in *Emotion and Focus*, states that "[i]t is reasonable to ask how one determines that a pattern of interactions represents a particular emotion" (107), she responds to her own question by appealing to the "conceptual content" of the emotion. My concern in this chapter is with a more fundamental kind of answer to this same question. Second, to interpret a stimulus as information rather than noise, there must be some structure accessible to the interpreter in which that stimulus counts as information.

In "Expression and Communication," Gombrich uses the story of Theseus' expedition against the Minotaur as an eloquent illustration of the necessity of structure to our ability to receive stimuli as information:

> When Theseus' father, Aegeus, scanned the sea for the returning expedition . . . he thought of the pre-arranged code according to which a white sail would mean success, a black one defeat. Theseus, having lost Ariadne on Naxos, forgot to hoist the white sail and his father drowned himself. . . . [N]othing Theseus could have done at that distance could have conveyed to his father his state of mind which was indeed plunged in gloom, but for entirely unforeseen reasons. The sail could only function as a signal "operating on the alternatives forming the recipient's doubt." (Gombrich, 61)

Aegeus was operating with a certain structure, in this case a prearranged code, where only one kind of stimulus would count as information about the success of the mission. Gombrich concludes his article with a lesson for expressionist theories of art: "understanding the language of emotions is much . . . like any other understanding. It presupposes a knowledge of the language and therefore a grasp of alternatives" (62).

In trying to isolate the conditions that must be met for us to be interpretable creatures for each other, we are precisely not allowed to assume that we already share, in advance, the understanding of form or conventional structure that allows signals to be meaningful; we are not allowed to assume, for instance, that we share a language. Thus the structure or pattern of alternatives through which I can make sense of your utterances as information could be established only by what I respond to in structured or patterned ways.

My argument at this point has the form of a negative challenge. If communicating how you feel is the attempt to make clear or convey meaning, we have no reason, in cases of affective communication, for rejecting the basic conditions for the possibility of some piece of behavior of mine being meaningful. It is thus appropriate to pursue an analogy with the kind of simple case of linguistically expressed perceptual belief that Davidson uses to demonstrate triangulation.

Davidson's account of the conditions of interpretation that ground the possibility of a piece of behavior's having a meaning involve, in summary: (1) at least two people in a shared environment of objects or events; (2) attuned responses to features of this shared environment; and, (3) responses to each other's responses to the features of this environment. Let us first try triangulation on an example with a slight complication. Suppose a German friend drops by during our game of Pictionary. We do not know whether or not she knows the conventions of the game, but she does stand up and shout "boot" every time the woman from Nova Scotia draws a boat and at no other time. We might suppose, by the end of the evening, that "boot" means boat in German and that knowledge would not depend on any prior knowledge of German. On the other hand, we might equally well suppose that "boot" means "Oh, for God's sake, get on with it!" or some other expression of impatience. I wish to draw two conclusions from this variation. First, our interpretation will be structured by what we are responding to in that environment while noticing the pattern of her responses. We would not, for instance, assume "boot" meant "Please pass me a chip with dip." Second, if we interpret her expression as one of impatience, we may well have successfully individuated a case of affective significance, demonstrating, I think, the relevance of the model of triangulation to cases of affective communication. I now return to Dewey's shrug, suggesting we view it within the model of the speaker's uttering of "raton."

Because conditions (1) to (3) reliably obtain for a world of shared objects, we can continue to have confidence in what we meant on those occasions when we are misinterpreted, for communication about these objects succeeds most of the time. To make a somewhat artificial separation, we are reinforced in both our responses and our ways of expressing ourselves through the success of communication. The foundational role of a physical object vocabulary is evident in Davidson's model—and for good reason. That we classify similar stimuli in similar ways for this dimension of our public world seems undeniable and a forceful guarantee of the possibility of objectivity for these classifications.

If, however, during an affective interchange, I shrug, and after your response to this shrug, lack confidence about whether I have expressed impotence or contempt, and further, if this is a common sort of situation, then there is something about the communication of affect that makes the possibility of fulfilling the basic conditions for the determination of meaning (1) to (3) more difficult. As the social occasion provides a shared environment of objects and events (condition 1), and the case of the shrug is a case of your responding to my responses within this shared environment (condition 3), the difficulties must lie in (2): the necessity of attuned responses. I suggest there are two separate difficulties with meeting this condition.

The first difficulty with meeting (2) is that, when our shared environment is one of events and occasions as well as objects, we may view these events or occasions in different ways. To put the point somewhat artificially, we may each view an occasion under more than one description, and our descriptions may overlap in some cases but not in others. Thus there is a problem with establishing the common cause that determines the meaning of our responses. The second difficulty with meeting (2) is that, if the type of meaning we are trying to communicate is that of the personal importance of a shared occasion, the responses of others to our responses may become a part of the significance of that occasion.

The difficulties for meeting the conditions for determining meaning apply to the case of the shrug in the following ways. We are sharing the occasion of playing the party game of Pictionary. We both view it under this description, and we are responding to each other's responses to this occasion. But this occasion will undoubtedly have a different significance for me from the one it has for you, and we will accordingly view it differently. I may view it as (1) an occasion on which my participation has been coerced; and (2) as an occasion on which I'm likely to feel stupid because I can't draw. You may view it as, (1) an occasion that you have initiated knowing full well that some people are feeling coerced into playing; and (2) an occasion that you enjoy because you like to draw. When I shrug, is this piece of behavior, as interpretable in meaning, a response to my coerced participation in a party game or to my inability to draw? To employ an inevitably overdetermined description of my action—I send out a response to my inability to draw. Your response to my response to a stimulus picks out, as this stimulus, my coerced participation in a party game. This is one way that you view the occasion, and *the* way that you view it *qua* occasion to which I am responding. However, I also view Pictionary as a matter of coerced participation. I would accept this description as one description of the occasion if you offered it to me. We both view the occasion as coercive. The model of triangulation does not locate a stimulus under a single stable description, and I become confused about the meaning of my own response.[3] I followed Hampshire in arguing that, if I am confused about my feelings, those feelings are themselves confused. The model of triangulation allows us to see Hampshire's point that this confusion will likely involve a problem in fixing the cause of my feelings. On this model, the problem with fixing the cause takes place within a context of interpretation.

---

3. As Quine wrote in *Word and Object*: "One frequently hears it urged that deep differences of language carry with them ultimate differences in the way one thinks, or looks upon the world. I would urge that what is most generally involved is indeterminacy of correlation. There is less basis of comparison—less sense in saying what is good translation and what is bad—the farther we get away from sentences with visibly direct conditioning to non-verbal stimuli and the farther we get off home ground" (77–78).

Second, if we share an occasion that is in some way significant to me, both your responses to that occasion and your responses to my responses are a part of that occasion and may become a part of the significance of that occasion to me. There is no stable standpoint of interpretation. You may become a part of the stimulus to my responses in ways that you obviously do not become a part of a rat or a wildflower, or physical events such as a light being on or off or a telephone ringing. Occasions are very loosely individuated both temporally and descriptively. Sometimes the bounds of occasions are socially fixed. A wedding is an occasion that brings into being a particular kind of relation, and the wedding is over when the recessional has finished and the church is emptied. But even with relatively well-defined occasions, how these occasions are individuated, described, and temporally bounded can have much to do with their meaning to those present.

Instability at one apex of the triangle produces instability at the others. But this means not that we just can't *tell* which of two or more alternative meanings a person's utterance or gesture has, but that there may be no clear truth to the matter. This is the affective analog to the indeterminacy of translation,[4] and we have already encountered it, under a different description in Chapter 3: does Roxane love Christian, or does Roxane love Cyrano? The mistake is to suppose, for most of the play, that there is a truth of the matter here. Even though Roxane may have *thought* that the occasions to which she responded with expressive behavior were clearer and simpler than they really were, those thoughts are not enough to provide a fact of the matter about her feelings. Roxane is at one apex of the triangle. As an audience, our responses to her responses to the occasions provided by the play put us at another apex of the triangle. At the third apex are the qualities and actions of sometimes Christian and sometimes Cyrano. The instability at the third apex produces instability in our responses to Roxane's expressive behavior, which leaves her feelings themselves unformed for most of the play. Alternatively, if we as an audience are rooting for Cyrano, we are likely to respond to Cyrano's eloquence and Roxane's responses to Cyrano's eloquence so as to conclude that she loved Cyrano from the start. There is, however, no way to settle this issue during the play's progress, and this, of course, raises the question of whether Roxane gets to settle the issue at the end of the play, and if she does, what grounds her authority to do so.

The feature of indeterminacy seems potentially far more pervasive and threatening to affective meanings than it is to our talk about medium-size physical objects. First, the occasions to which we respond with expressive

4. See Quine's *Word and Object* (especially chap. 2) for the classic presentation of this view.

behavior are responded to in ways that implicate more of our histories and biographies (see Chapter 3), as well as what is of present importance to us. The occasion to which we respond is far less likely to be the occasion to which an interpreter "triangulates" our response. Though our sensory apparatus shares much with the sensory apparatus of our interpreters, our biographies share much less with their biographies. Where our biographies significantly diverge from the biographies of others, there will only be an objective matter of fact about what we feel to the extent that our responses to the occasion secure sufficient uptake to fix the significance of that occasion.

We do of course find people with whom our biographies overlap and to whom we successfully communicate our feelings. The importance of this is not limited to the occasion on which we have successfully communicated our feelings. Its importance spreads to those occasion where we are not understood. If people have understood us previously, we can use the existence of those people to form an apex of the triangle on occasions where we are fail to communicate affective meaning. If I continue to shrug impotently, or start to shrug indifferently, this is because I will have been understood often enough in the past that I have confidence in my own affective meanings, as my German friend may have confidence in her meanings. This clarity or confidence contributes to affective meaning. How much of this confidence I have is a matter of luck in having found people who share my responses or who share my expressive idiolect.

We also have several strategies for trying to get people to view occasions under the same descriptions we view them. That these strategies are so persuasive a part of our actual practice in expressing how we feel, I take to be strong informal support for the view I am defending. All of these strategies have to do with making the description of the occasion explicit. The Plath example in Chapter 1 specifies the occasion ("The Cut"), we make appeal to emotion categories that bring with them a description under which to view an occasion ("offensive," "threatening"), we have an extensive feeling vocabulary that simply offers an occasion under a description "homesick," "insulted," "bored," and so on, and we try to get other people to see an occasion the way we do by finding, in their past, a similar occasion. Finally, we sometimes add authority to our description of an occasion by pointing to others who might view the occasion in the way we view it. It was the feeling "Mangaliso Sobukwe used to tell us about" (Tlali, 91) None of these strategies guarantees that we will secure adequate uptake to our expression.

In affective communication, very often there is no stable point of triangulation that determines affective significance. Yet my attempts to express my feelings, to engage in an act of communication seem founded on the possibility that others will understand me, that is, that they will understand the significance of the occasion to me, that I can bring them to understand, or that they may try to do so. I have suggested that affective communication is an attempt to convey the personal significance of some occasion. I now argue that understanding personal significance also is the role of affect as a category of explanation.

AFFECT AND EXPLANATION

What is it to recognize behavior as expressive of feeling when we try to give an account of this at the most general level possible? We cannot settle issues of authority and address our obligations as interpreters without first understanding what we are trying to do when we invoke the category of affect.

In Chapter 2, I argued that expression is the activity that individuates psychological states. If expression is the activity of individuating feeling, we cannot suppose that those feelings are already individuated in trying to give an account of expression. As a parallel to this problem: affect is a category of psychological explanation. We cannot assume this category in our explanations of behavior, explaining behavior from within this category, and in this way hope to give an account of it. This assumption was precisely the mistake that Darwin, James, and Ryle made by depending on our prior abilities to recognize patterns of behavior *as expressive of affect* in trying to give an account of affect. However, this is a very natural mistake to make when we deal with the issue of affective recognition by considering examples of it. For to recognize any particular behavior as affective behavior is to assume the relevance of the category of affective explanation. In Darwin and Ryle this tendency leads to the explanatory redundancy of the category. The problem of assuming the relevance of a category is quite general in explaining action, but its relevance to theory of affect has not been noticed. I shall offer Davidson's general description of this problem only after offering a case that makes clear its relevance to affect.

We must assume that behavior is expressing feelings in order to recognize it as expressing feelings, and there are reasons why we sometimes make this assumption. I intend to display this point by generating the sort of case for emotions that philosophers standardly use to defend *externalism,* the view that the existence and content of a mental state depend on the relation of the subject of that state to her or his environment. Externalist arguments usually are generated by a particular kind of thought experiment: "Consider a pair of subjects whose internal properties are supposed the same but whose external environments are different. Now ask whether this is consistent with supposing that the two subjects' mental states are the same. The externalist claims that it is not consistent—the mind varies with variations in the environment" (McGinn, 1). The value of this type of thought experiment to my account is that it helps us see where and how our explanations of people's behavior diverge in order to raise the question of *why* we would move to an affective level of explanation in one case but not in another.

I will use the familiar strategy of talking about psychological states in the *narrow* and *wide* sense. A psychological state is "narrow" if its ascription does not presuppose "the existence of any individual other than the subject to whom that state is ascribed" (Putnam, 220). It is "wide" if its ascription does presuppose such an individual. I also use the familiar case of jealousy, an appealing example for externalists, as an example where the standard case always is a psychological state in the wide sense: "So, for example, '*x*'s *jealousy of y*' is a schema for expressions which denote psychological states in the wide sense since such expressions presuppose the existence, not only of the *x*s who are in the states, but also of the *y*s who are its objects" (Fodor, 244).

Consider the following case:[5] Two identical twins, Stanley and Darren, are separated shortly after birth on a trip home from the Johns Hopkins Medical Centre, where a research staff has implanted a matching device in the head of each twin. When one device is activated, the second twin will come to be in exactly the same neurophysiological state as the activated twin. Stanley falls out of the car and is sympathetically adopted by wolves. He has no language and has never been in contact with another person. Darren suffers a similarly clichéd fate. He is raised in suburbia, becomes a stockbroker, and marries.

One afternoon, Darren is on his way to the train and spies his wife having an intimate drink with another woman. He flies into a fit of jealousy, bangs his head against the wall at his naivete, flings his briefcase through the window at his wife's companion, and runs from the scene. Because Darren has accidentally activated the matching device by banging his head, Stanley, hunting in the woods with a stone, goes into a neurophysiological state identical to Darren's from the time of the head banging. He flings his stone, turns, and runs west.

The standard externalist question is whether Stanley and Darren are in the same psychological state. If we accept, for the standard case, that jealousy requires the existence of people of whom we are jealous, Stanley is obviously not in the same psychological state as Darren. Stanley is not

5. This case was worked out in conversation with Rockney Jacobsen.

jealous because he has never even met another person. Then we may say that, although, in some sense, Stanley, in behaving like Darren, is behaving as a jealous person would behave, Stanley is obviously not expressing jealousy because Stanley is not jealous. This makes it look as though the cause of Darren's jealous behavior is Darren's jealousy. But the interesting feature of this case is that the *behavior* of the two men, as well as their psychological states, can be either narrowly or widely described.

Darren *flings* his briefcase *at* y and *runs from* the scene. Stanley *flings* a rock, *turns*, and *runs* west. There are three levels of description of Stanley's and Darren's behavior, and only at the third level, the widest level of description, are the two men behaving differently: (1) there is a narrow level of description, a level that makes no reference to anything other than the consequences of the identical neurophysiological states of each man, where Darren and Stanley are moving in identical ways—they are performing all the same bodily movements.[6] (2) There is a second level of description, which is slightly wider. Both Darren and Stanley can be described as flinging an object, turning, and running. At this level, we are describing bodily movements as behavior, but this behavior is again not described in such a way that we can make out any difference between what Darren does and what Stanley does. The behavior is not so described as to be expressive of any particular psychological state.

If, at two levels of description, Darren and Stanley can be seen as acting in the same way, what then makes it reasonable to attribute jealousy to Darren and not to Stanley? What evidence would we normally offer to others, or to Darren, to substantiate the claim that Darren is jealous? In normal cases, we would offer Darren's behavior as evidence, but there is nothing in these descriptions of behavior that would provide others, or Darren, with reason to believe he was jealous. There is, however, a third and wider level of description of Darren's behavior that it would be appropriate to offer as evidence, and this is a level of description where his behavior seems quite different from Stanley's: (3) to describe Darren's behavior in such a way that it is complex enough to be evidence for his jealousy, we must pick out this same behavior (i.e., the behavior we have already described in (1) and (2)), in terms of some of its relational characteristics. For example, Darren *flings* his briefcase at the woman drinking

6. The type identity of Darren and Stanley's neurophysiological states and of their bodily motions would certainly have the consequence that, in one very sense, they *feel* the same way: they undergo the same bodily sensations, have the same kinesthetic and proprioceptive experiences. But because Darren does, and Stanley does not, feel jealousy, it follows, contra James, that the affective state cannot be identified with the complex of bodily sensations that they share.

with his wife (or *flings* it *at* his *rival*), or Darren *runs from* the cafe (or *flees the scene of his humiliation*).

To give a description of Darren's behavior that is the appropriate level of description to support an attribution of jealousy is to give a wide or externalist description of his behavior in order to support the attribution of a wide psychological state. This is not to deny that the evidence we have for thinking that our third-level ascriptions are true depends on our recognizing that the lower levels of description apply. The motion of Darren's hand may be evidence that he is throwing, and the lie of his face may be part of the evidence that he is throwing his briefcase *at* the women. All this and more may be evidence that he is expressing rage or jealousy. But only at the third level of description is the behavior widely enough described to license any inference to jealousy. We are not inclined to give a correspondingly wide description of Stanley's behavior.

To attribute jealousy to Darren, we have given an obviously intentional level of description to his behavior, and this is obvious in two ways: (1) The verbs, or verb-preposition combinations, that we pick to describe Darren's movements have intentional implications. We *flee* or *run from* something because we want to get away from it. We are not inclined to describe Stanley's behavior using verbs with intentional implications, although it would be possible for us to do so. If Stanley's rock hit a tree, we are not inclined to say, in the case described, that he *flung* his rock *at* a tree, rather than that he flung a rock and it happened to strike a tree. (2) The features of Darren's environment which he reacts to can be described in extremely rich ways. To speak about "his rival" or "the scene of his humiliation" is to describe certain environmental items as we would take them to be implicated in someone's jealousy, and we use these descriptions to attribute jealousy to Darren. We might not use these descriptions to try to persuade Darren that he was jealous. This would be a pragmatic choice ("You must have had some reason for throwing your briefcase at her. Are you sure you don't think of her as a rival?" But we would think to ourselves: "He was obviously fleeing the scene of his humiliation.")

I have attempted to make out the claim that it is our third level of description of Darren's behavior by which we individuate it as jealous behavior. What justifies this further level of description? And what further justifies our picking this level of description as the level *from which* we move to an attribution of jealousy, rather than the more basic levels of description offered in (1) and (2)? The issue here is that we seem to be assuming jealousy to recognize Darren's behavior as jealous behavior.

In "Problems in the Explanation of Action," Donald Davidson argues that the assumption of a relevant category of explanation will always be involved in our attempts to explain behavior and that the necessity of this assumption is what makes explanation of action only weakly explanatory. Davidson is interested in causal explanations of intentional action through the specification of the belief/desire pair, or the intention, that caused the action. The key feature to understanding the "weakness" of such explanations is that the cause of the action is itself picked out by its suitability for causing *that particular action*. In other words, we have already assumed the appropriate description of the action in picking out its cause.

Thus, as a final option for justifying divergent descriptions of Darren's and Stanley's behavior, we might suppose that we could advert to a causal level of explanation, but because the specification of the cause depends on the level of the description of the behavior, this strategy simply repeats the assumption of an appropriate description at a slightly different level. This problem translates to the present example in the following way: at at least one level of causal description—a level that corresponds to the initial level of behavioral description, Stanley's and Darren's behavior has the same type of cause, their respective neurophysiological conditions at that time. When I or when the people at Johns Hopkins describe Darren's behavior narrowly (Level 1), this reflects our respective explanatory interests. I am interested in a philosophical discussion of the individuation of behavior; they are interested in whether, after a certain age, identical twins can come to be in exactly the same neurophysiological states. These explanatory purposes will lead us to pick out not only the behavior but also the *cause* of the behavior at a level that matches these interests. I point out that at a certain level of description Darren's and Stanley's behaviors have the same type of cause: their respective neurophysiological states. The team at Johns Hopkins will point out that a certain type of neurophysiological state causes identical movements as evidence for the matched state.

Suppose then that we attempt to identify a cause in a way that is appropriate to Darren's behavior, such that this cause explains Darren's behavior when that behavior is described in ways that make it expressive of jealousy. We might suggest that Darren's behavior has been caused by his perception of his wife's infidelity. But Darren's perception of his wife's infidelity also is a part of the causal history of Stanley's behavior, and we are without some further account of why it is more appropriate to offer Darren's perception of his wife's infidelity as the cause of Darren's behavior than it is to offer this same perception as the cause of Stanley's behavior; once again these behaviors have the same cause, and we have no license to move to a special level of description of Darren's behavior.

We might propose that, insofar as Darren's assessments of his wife's actions are a part of the causal environment of Stanley's behavior, they have only a *remote* relation to this behavior, where these same assessments have a *direct* relation to Darren's behavior. This fact, by itself, cannot explain why Darren's behavior is appropriately described as expressing jealousy, whereas Stanley's is not. Causes of jealousy can be near (a sighting) or remote (receiving a letter or hearing a rumor at third hand). In the claim that the cause of Stanley's behavior, as now identified, is too remote or indirect for his behavior to count as expressive of jealousy, the vague notions of remoteness and indirectness explain nothing. In the example constructed, the decision must go the other way around: the causal chain leading from the infidelity, via radio transmissions, to Stanley's behavior, must be too remote or indirect for it to produce a state of jealousy because, evidently, Stanley is not jealous. And the decision that Stanley is not jealous is made as part of the same set of decisions, all of which come together: the decision that, although his stone struck the tree, he did not throw it at the tree, the decision that, although he ran west, he did not run from anything, the decision that, although the tree was before his eyes, he did not see it as a rival. In conclusion, it is only the divergence in the level of description of behavior—Darren is behaving jealously or expressing jealousy but Stanley is not—that licenses our postulation of different causes of behavior. We pick the cause to fit the level of description of behavior if we want citing that cause to explain the behavior.

Finally, when we give the cause of an intentional action, we often specify an intention: Bass's intention to cross over the swamp caused him to attempt to cross over the swamp. In the same way, when we give the cause of affective behavior, we often specify an affective state: Darren's feelings of jealousy caused him to act jealously. When we understand the role of our explanatory purposes or aims in explaining behavior, this specification of an affective state as the cause of behavior does not oblige or even encourage us to grant that affective states can be formed independently of acts of expression. If we can provide *various* levels of description for the *causes* of behavior and for the behavior caused, but succeed only in providing an *explanation* of the behavior under a certain description by matching it up with a cause under a certain description, then we must inevitably select the description both of the cause and the behavior to fit each other. When we have the right fit, the cause explains the behavior. So what we really need to be asking is: What do we want from explanations of behavior in terms of affective descriptions, whether these descriptions take place at the level of describing the behavior or describing the cause in the appropriate way, to explain this behavior?

The lesson of this example is that to give a philosophical account of the conditions under which we recognize affective behavior, we must move back from particular cases that assume the appropriateness of a certain level of explanation. We must offer some account of why we interpret Darren's behavior, but not Stanley's behavior, as expressive of jealousy in a way that does not already assume that jealousy is the appropriate level of explanation. As any particular explanation will always depend on our explanatory interests or assumptions, we must give a general account of ascriptions of affect as an explanatory psychological category, and one that does not take up the space already occupied by belief/desire explanations of action.

My proposal is that the category of affective explanation is the category of explaining behavior through what we take to be the personal or autobiographical significance of that behavior for its subject.[7] When people express a feeling, they are trying to make clear the meaning or significance of something in the context of how they view their lives. When we identify, recognize, or respond to behavior as expressive of feeling, we are attempting to understand or interpret how something is significant for a particular person. Stanley's behavior either has no particular autobiographical significance or none that we can understand. We interpret Darren's behavior as expressing the significance of what he just saw for his life because we take Darren's wife's behavior to be very important to Darren's view of his own life. We, in general, understand, or think we understand, the significance to people of occasions of infidelity.

There certainly are problems in trying to give an analysis of a person's sense of herself or her point of view on her own life. These problems are especially manifest in accounts such as the one I have offered, where the interpretation of our behavior by others plays such an important role in determining the significance of our behavior to us. Nevertheless, there is an underlying idea that is both simple and plausible. It can be illustrated by briefly considering a case offered by Nissenbaum (106–7). Discussing Julia's envy of Pamela as a complex interaction pattern involving the two, Nissenbaum lists nine types of events that might be part of the pattern (Julia gives poor evaluations of Pamela at work, and so on), all of which involve both Julia and Pamela or Julia's thought and fantasies about Pamela. If we started to add items to the list, such as: Julia jogs after work, or Julia now eats more jujubes than previously, would these be part of the pattern of Julia's envy? We could not know without knowing more about how Julia views her life.

---

7. Other directed emotions, such as sympathy, might seem to be an exception to this. See Scheman's treatment in "On Sympathy" for an example of expressive failure. I believe that other directed emotions, such as sympathy, can be incorporated into the model I have argued for. Briefly, to interpret someone as sympathetic to you, you need to understand your importance to them.

Many recent treatments of the emotions, and especially of particular emotions, note, in some fashion, the importance of the idea of narrative to this category of psychological interpretation.[8] These accounts rarely specify a particular type of narrative. The general difficulty with using narrative as a model for the explanation of behavior is that, without the incorporating of other sorts of explanations into the narrative, the story could evolve in any way. Narratives do not give us the power to explain what has happened or to predict what will happen next independently of other kinds of explanations embedded in the narrative. There are other serious problems, I think, with the current use of narrative in psychological explanation. Meaning and intelligibility can come to be associated too much with linguistic activity and too little with other forms of behavior. I suggest that the advantage of considering a narrative model of explanation, in the present context, however, is that it presses us to reflect on the idea of a point of view.

Specifying *autobiographical* significance as the specific type of narrative interest is, I think, plausible as a general thesis about the role of affective explanation. It makes clear why affective explanation has a role that is distinct from belief/desire explanation and that is supplementary. Darren performs two actions: flinging a briefcase at his rival and fleeing the scene of his humiliation. The resources of belief/desire explanation would require two different explanations, one for each action. By understanding the importance to Darren of what he has witnessed and using this to guide our explanatory purposes, we can systematize more of Darren's behavior under a single explanation.

I do not mean to imply that explanatory simplicity is a good in itself when we try to understand people. People are complex. The point is that an adequate understanding of behavior often requires that we see how different events and behaviors are related in a way not easily possible using belief/desire explanation. To return to the example of the Introduction, it is through understanding the deep ambivalence of Muriel's "white-master's-well-fed-dog feeling" that we make sense of events in the story that, taken singly, would be explained by different desires. Muriel's actions indicate the desire to resign from Metropolitan Radio and the desire to stay. An affective level of explanation does not deny the reality of these conflicted desires. Rather, it lets us see how the desires and the actions they give rise to are related.

Belief/desire explanations also oblige us to predicate holistically of an

---

8. See Rorty ("The Historicity of Psychological Attitudes"); Sarbin ("Emotion and Act"); and Calhoun ("Subjectivity and Emotion"). See Morton for a different approach to the unity of the category of affect resting on its use in explaining an individual.

agent the set of beliefs and desires that make a particular action comprehensible to us. To return to a case offered in Chapter I, where Bass drives
his car off a board road into a swamp, we would likely explain his action
in taking the board road by specifying his desire to get to a certain place
plus beliefs that the road went to that place, that the road was passable,
and so on. But some of the beliefs we might predicate of Bass to rationalize his behavior, the belief that the road was passable, for example, would
not fit well with the fact that Bass has wrecked so many cars. When we
interpret his behavior within our understanding of the importance to Bass
of discovering oil, when we interpret it as an expression of this passion for
discovering oil, we can make sense of this incident and many others without attributing implausible beliefs to Bass. For very likely, he didn't care
whether the road was passable: "When you're going to or from a well, you
can't dally. You can't let anything stop you. The earth and the well are
bigger than you are but you have to try and hold your own against them
anyway" (Bass, 23).

Finally, autobiographical significance also allows us to understand some
of the complexities of the role of recognition or uptake in the individuation of what we have expressed. Other people's responses to what we do
are sometimes very important to us. When my teammate accuses me of
having expressed Pictionary contempt, the occasion and its shrug take on
a certain significance to me through the response they elicit. Part of the
significance of that occasion involves other people, and responses of mine
have part of their significance through the responses of other people to
them. Ryle distinguished sharply between first- and third-person points of
the view on the psychological, worried that if we allow a first-person point
of view or allow the ordinary meaning of our language of feeling to capture this point of view, we would be endorsing notions of psychological
privacy and the privileged access through introspection to the nature of
these states. I argued at the time that we need not hold that a person
knows special things about herself in special ways to allow the importance
of her having a point of view on her life to our attempt to understand her.
In this chapter, I also have argued that this personal standpoint is not in
any way inured from the interpretive practices of others.

Taking into account (1) the necessity of interpretation to determining
affective significance; (2) the difficulties in affective interpretation; and
(3) affect as the communication and interpretation of personal significance, we now have a useful and flexible model for understanding expressive success and failure. I end this section with an example of each.

Case 1. The model nonmysteriously accounts for the often seamless
communication of affective significance. It also accounts for the development of feelings between people, where this development does not re-

quire invoking emotion categories. Feelings often develop by coming to share expressive idiolects themselves developed through shared differential responses. As two young women falling in love, Annie and Liza, in Nancy Garden's *Annie on My Mind*, do not have access to a conventional language of love or to socially sanctioned romantic behaviors. It is their willingness to respond to each other's responses as important that grounds the possibility of establishing the mutual significance of their encounters.

The girls first meet in the Metropolitan Museum of Art and, in the Hall of Arms and Armor, Annie draws an imaginary sword and cries "*En garde!* Stand and fight or I'll run you through*" (Garden, 11). Although Liza is embarrassed, she responds to the significance of the occasion to Annie by drawing a sword as well. They do battle in front of two enthusiastic small boys: "Annie and I caught each other's eyes and I realized we were making a silent agreement to fight on till the death for the benefit of our audience. The trouble was, I wasn't sure how we were going to signal each other which one of us was going to die and when" (Garden, 12). Liza later shows Annie the Temple of Dendur and Annie tries to respond to its importance to Liza: "This room seems like you." She smiled. "Bright and clear. Not somber like me and the choir screen" (Garden, 14). This meeting is the start of their friendship.

Later in the novel, when Liza and Annie begin to struggle with their desire for each other, sure of neither its meaning nor its mutuality, they can come to see that they share desire only through referring to this background of shared encounters. Annie says to Liza: "[W]e're like the temple and the choir screen as I thought the day I met you, only then I was guessing. You—you really are like the temple—light—you go happily on without really noticing, and I'm dark, like the choir screen, like the room it's in. I feel too much and want too much, I guess" (Garden, 120). Liza responds: "'It's not true . . . that I want to ignore it. And I'm not going on happily not noticing.' I stopped, feeling Annie take my hand, and realized my fists were clenched. 'It scares me too, Annie,' I managed to say" (Garden, 121). When we see the creation of affective significance as public and involving shared differential responses to a common environment, we can see the importance of developing shared expressive idiolects and styles to the formation of this significance. It is, on the other hand, difficult to understand how Liza's and Annie's affection develops without understanding their shared differential responses to what each sees as personally significant to the other.

Case 2. Often participants do not share an understanding of the significance of an occasion. This can lead to serious cases of expressive failure. The very features that facilitate affective interpretation (an understanding of a person's biography, style, point of view, and so on) may make a person highly manipulable when significance clashes, and a culture legitimates only one interpretation of the interaction. Date rape often seems to be such a case. In "Date Rape: A Feminist Analysis," Lois Pineau analyzes a legal situation where "the very things that make it reasonable for *him* to believe that the defendant [sic] consented are often the very things that incline the court to believe that she consented. What is often missing is . . . an account of what is reasonable from *her* standpoint" (219; emphasis in original).

Pineau presents a scenario where a woman's expressive actions, her actions that express distaste, reluctance, or resistance are interpreted by a man to suit the significance of the occasion to him. Her expressions of resistance are interpreted as either unfairly thwarting: "I wouldn't take no for an answer. I think it had something to do with my acceptance of rejection. I had low self-esteem and not much self-confidence and when I was rejected for something which I considered to be rightly mine, I became angry and went ahead anyway" (Pineau, 219–20) or as teasing: "She resists, voicing her disinclination. He alternates between telling her how desirable she is and taking a hostile stance, charging her with misleading him, accusing her of wanting him, and being coy . . . all the time engaging in rather aggressive body contact" (Pineau, 223). What's more, the woman is expected to interpret and respond to the man's expressive actions through the significance of the occasion to him: "He uses the myth of 'so hard to control' male desire as a rhetorical tactic, telling her how frustrated she will leave him" (Pineau, 223).

Pineau concludes from her analysis of such encounters that the woman knows she did not want to have sex with her date. On the model I have defended, in at least some cases, a woman may be confused about the extent to which she did not want sex. Clarity may depend on previous encounters where resistance has been taken seriously from the women's point of view or at least on her ability to imagine such encounters. But one of the descriptions under which the women may herself view the situation is the unfair thwarting of important male desire. In situations of date rape, women may become unsure of the extent to which their actions are or have been misleading and of what motives have resulted in the encounter. Pineau, herself, acknowledges that "we have a situation in which women are vulnerable to the most exploitive tactics at the hands of men who are well known to them" (Pineau, 221), and the resources of triangulation allow us to see how that manipulation is taking place on an affective level.

Pineau develops a communicative model of consent—one that stresses continual uptake to each other's responses:

Just as communicative conversationalists are concerned with more than di-
dactic content, persons engaged in communicative sexuality will be concerned with more than achieving coitus. They will be sensitive to the
responses of their partners. They will, like good conversationalists, be intuitive, sympathetic, and charitable. Intuition will help them interpret their
partner's responses: sympathy will enable them to share what their partner
is feeling; charity will enable them to care. . . . Their concern with fostering
the desire of the other must involve an ongoing state of alertness in interpreting her responses. (236)

Pineau envisions a model of consent where two people's responses to
each other's responses will eventually clarify to both the descriptions under which the occasion is being viewed. They will be able to assess
whether the occasion is viewed by both as one of mutual desire. Once
again, triangulation displays the dynamics of the kind of encounter
Pineau advocates. My students have been reluctant, however, to endorse
Pineau's model fully. Although they like its spirit, they doubt that they
have sufficient competence at articulating the significance of sexual occasions to be equally authoritative in this sexual conversation.

AFFECT AND EXTERNALISM

The complex proposal I have defended is this: we form our feelings
through acts of expression and, in doing so, attempt to make clear to
others, or even just to ourselves, the personal significance of some occasion or set of occasions of our lives. This is to defend an externalist account of feelings, and I should briefly mark the relation of this account to
the externalist accounts of belief that now dominate the treatment of that
explanatory category in philosophy of mind.

The basic condition that externalism places on the existence of a mental state is that this existence requires, for its account, some account of
the relation of the subject to her or his environment. A standard way to
define externalism is by a statement of what the view claims is not possible. Externalists claim that the content of a mental state that individuates
that state (for instance, what a belief is about individuates that belief)
cannot be determined solely by reference to, or examination of, internal
features of the person who has the mental state. As the internal features
of a person must, for an externalist, be specified independently of that
person's environment, I shall take all possible relevant internal features to
be the total neurophysiological state of a person. I have argued, in my

discussion of Darren and Stanley, that feelings cannot be identified as the internal states of a person.

Externalism is a commitment to specifying the content of mental states, thereby specifying at least some of the conditions for their individuation, through making reference to features of a subject's environment, and this environment will be a shared environment.[9] Thus the kinds of conditions that externalism places on the existence of a mental state in general are conditions that should facilitate the recognition of that state. The focus of much externalist discussion about the conditions for psychological attribution centers on a particular sort of mental state: a belief or thought about a physical object or substance. Donald Davidson's externalism about belief, for instance, grounded in the causal relation between a subject and her or his environment, has the following simplified outline: we are reliably caused to think about cows (for example) in the presence of cows. This is evidenced by our disposition to say: "Oh look, there's a cow!" (for example) in the presence of cows, but not in the presence of chickens. The reliable causal interaction between a person and their environment is what makes it true that the above utterance is an expression of belief about cows and not about chickens. Thus, to fix the content of the expressed belief through an account of what has caused it, we need to make reference to cows: "[In] the simplest cases words and thoughts refer to what causes them" (Davidson, "Epistemology Externalized," 194).

These discussions explore the ways that certain environmental features, physical objects or substances, figure prominently in the identification of our mental states. The importance of how we pick out the relevant environmental items for an externalist account is not always apparent, for any single version of externalism, considered in isolation, will contain some commitment as to how we identify these items. With the externalist account of belief first proposed by Hilary Putnam, and now held in various forms by many philosophers, the individuation of a belief about a physical object or substance depends on our subordinate abilities to recognize the relevant environmental item. Davidson, however, rejects Putnam's theory that some substances are to be picked out by their physical constitution— water, by the arrangement of H_2O, for example: "While I agree, as I have said above, that the usual cause of my word determines what it means, I do not see why sameness of micro-structure is necessarily the relevant similarity that determines the reference of my word 'water.'" ("Epistemology Externalized," 196). The dispute indicates that how we should pick out

---

9. Colin McGinn suggests that externalism "is best construed about as a thesis about the *individuation* of mental states: a thesis, that is, about the existence and identity conditions of mental states. It places conditions on the existence of a mental state in a possible situation, and tells us what kinds of change preserve the identity of a mental state" (McGinn, 3).

the relevant items is no insignificant part of the debate about the details of an externalist strategy.

Davidson's counterproposal to Putnam depends on our shared recognitional capacities, and I have adapted this part of Davidson's view to my account of feelings. What I wish to highlight at this point is that individuating a mental state through an externalist strategy requires prior successful individuation of the relevant environmental features. How we perform these prior identifications is an issue that must be addressed in any particular externalist theory of any particular category of mental states.

Feelings are not propositional attitudes about physical objects. The types of behavior through which they are expressed are various, and no type of behavior plays the central role that language plays in the discrimination of belief. Not all of us respond in much the same way to shared environmental features or occasions; furthermore, we use our environment creatively to form our response. Donald Davidson encapsulates his commitment to externalism about beliefs by saying, "Somewhere along the line . . . we must come to the direct exposures that anchor thought and language to the world" ("Epistemology Externalized," 195). I respond that the metaphor of anchoring is not appropriate to externalism about feelings. I have committed myself to what, in a person's environment, is most relevant to the existence and recognition of their affective states— their behavior within this environment. This is where the individuation of feeling must focus, so many feelings have no objects. The assumption that we share response is what makes it possible to engage in a creative attempt to make clear to others and ourselves the personal significance of what we encounter. However, the element of personal significance that underlies affective expression, and the remarkably varied and creative use we make of our environment as a medium for communicating this significance, has the consequence that applying the resources of externalism to affective states gives us no systemic security that we understand the feelings of others or that they understand ours.

My proposal has been that the expression of feeling is the attempt to form the personal meaning or significance of some experience or occasion. Expressionist theorists are right to say that we should attempt to understand feelings as unique individuals, as the kind of significance something has in my life will differ from the significance that that same sort of experience or occasion might have in yours. If this account is roughly right, it raises the interesting question, not of why we have a category of feeling, but of why some of these feelings are grouped under emotion concepts. I have offered some explanation for this.

The account also shows the difficulties that mobilizing a externalist strategy for the analysis of feelings displays for the success of affective communication. We cannot always assume a broad community of reliably similar responses to particular occasions. When expression is communicative, successful collaborative individuation is complex and may actually prevent my making clear, even to myself, the significance of my experience. Chapters 5 and 6 attempt to follow out some of the more obvious political ramifications of this account of expression of feelings for both emotional feelings and free-style feelings.

V

FREEDOM OF EXPRESSION

*Feminism, Externalism, and
Social Constructivism*

> The idea that I am the way I am no matter what anyone else
> thinks is not politically neutral. To take this position is to stifle
> the possibility of particular sorts of political change. But it's also
> to blind ourselves to the truth that we are in many deep and im-
> portant ways what others take or at least allow us to be. . . . The
> alternative is not "a clear space in which to get your head to-
> gether" but a hidden political framework that pretends not to be
> one and hence is spared the bother (and the risk) of argument.
> —Naomi Scheman, "Anger and the Politics of Naming"

If what we feel is, by and large, what we express, then people
can control our feelings by controlling our modes of expression.
There is no such thing as a protected private life of feeling. That
people can control our feelings through controlling our modes
of expression is a straightforward consequence of the view I have argued
for, and this consequence directs us toward an ethics of interpreting the
personal. In this chapter and the next, I begin to develop this ethics. I am
concerned to defend maximum freedom of expression in ways I will explain as I proceed.

One of the most obvious ways in which our feelings are controlled
through their expression is by the power of interpreters to view the occasions of our lives and respond to our expressive acts. In this chapter, I
examine a particular kind of interpretive power, predictably, given my interest in free-style feelings, how our expressions of feeling are interpreted
and our feelings understood by being placed under generic emotion concepts.

Understanding feelings through broad classifications is a pervasive part
of our actual social practice of attempting to understand how people feel.
It is not, for instance, a redescription of this practice for the purpose of
giving a theory of affective interpretation. I grant that it also is to some
extent a necessary practice. I have, in fact, suggested two uses of emotion

categories that I think are not adequately recognized. Using these categories allows for a great deal more of people's behavior to count as organized behavior than is covered by the category of intentional explanation. Second, these categories carry ways to view a situation reflected in the extensive property vocabulary associated with the classic emotions: offensive, threatening, and so on. Reference to these categories is thus a powerful expressive resource that can be used by both expressers and interpreters to determine affective meaning. When we say we are very angry at what we have witnessed or ashamed of what we have done, we invoke a shared understanding of a concept in the hope that it will lead others to figure and respond to situations in ways that reflect the significance to us of those situations.

Such invocations are common in public discourse. In the *Halifax Mail Star* (May 14, 1997), a doctor wishes to protest the very public arrest for murder of a colleague who had euthanized a terminally ill patient. He describes the arrest as "an example of the excessive use of power," as "intimidation of the defendant and harassment and victimization." He describes himself as "an outraged citizen . . . who also happens to be a physician." Through his use of the language of anger, injury, and injustice, he invites other citizens to share outrage while at the same time establishing his authority to affect our understanding of the situation and our sense of its significance. He claims, as a physician, to "have a . . . recognition of the disruption this engendered in the health-care system."

I do not, then, want to deny the power and utility of expressions of affect that use emotion concepts. However, because the classic emotion concepts form that part of our feeling vocabulary where personal significance is most closely entangled with social significance and moral norms, these concepts may have a limited expressive and interpretive use. I am concerned, especially, that interpreting others within the narrow range of categories set by emotion types will restrict the range of affective significance that can be determined and the significance to people of their own lives. We often bypass restrictive interpretive tendencies in practice, but not always, and certainly theory affects practice. Sometimes affect is unambiguously expressed through the language of classic emotions. Outside of these cases, I argue that understanding people's feelings through emotion categories should not be promoted as any kind of comprehensive theory of affective meaning. To defend the view that our only way of understanding how we or others feel, our only way of determining affective meaning, is by categorizing these feelings under emotion concepts, is, I think, just wrong and seems plausible only because of the false view or assumption of set patterns of social behavior associated with these concepts, an assumption I hope by now to have rendered implausible. Viewing emotional categorization as our access to affective meanings also is an increasingly popular theory of the emotions known as "social constructivism." I wish to distinguish my own view of externalized affect from social constructivism.

EXTERNALISM AND SOCIAL CONSTRUCTIVISM

In Chapter 4, I argued that the expression of feeling is the articulation of the personal significance of an occasion, often in communicative situations. I defended an account of feelings in which behavior is publicly individuated by hypothesizing its relation to an occasion that may be viewed under different descriptions by the people involved in a collaborative act of individuation. The response of others, then, can make a difference to the feeling formed in several ways, most notably, perhaps, by becoming a part of the occasions to which we are responding. Of course the view of the situation that motivates their response also may become part of the now broader occasion to which we are responding. Affective interactions quickly become extremely complex and are a breeding ground for indeterminacy, insecurity, and abuse of power, and there is no way of simplifying our practices to rid them of these complications. Nevertheless, attention to the range of resources that we can use in our expressive activities, and the use of interpretability as the sole condition on the formation of meanings also directs our understanding to the potential creativity and sophistication of people's affective lives. I remind the reader of features of the view defended because I do not wish the externalism consequent on the public individuation of behavior to be confused with a certain prevalent theory of the emotions, called social constructivism, which is, itself, a type of externalism.

Social constructivism is an increasingly endorsed account of the emotions that has wide interdisciplinary support. I base my assessments of social constructivist theory of emotions on the articles in Rom Harré's anthology and on articles by Naomi Scheman and Alison Jaggar that investigate the possible feminist uses of social constructivism. I hold that there are reasons to be cautious of social constructivism as a theory of how affective meaning is determined. Social constructivists deny that affective significance is a private matter that can be determined independently of the social or moral norms of a given local culture. The positive way of stating the view (from most of its presentations) is that *affective meaning is social meaning*, where social meaning involves moral norms or social rules:

It turns out that the dominant contribution to the way that aspect of our lives unfolds comes from the local social world, by way of its linguistic practices and moral judgements in the course of which emotional qualities are defined. (Harré, 5)

The most important feature of moral development involves the acquisition of the social norms and rules that provide the component responses with their meaning and co-ordination. (Averill, 105)

The consequence of this approach is summarized and endorsed by Jaggar: "The emotions that we experience reflect prevailing forms of social life. . . . This is not to say that group emotions historically precede or are logically prior to the emotions of individuals; it is to say that individual experience is simultaneously social experience." (157–58). Jaggar uses as an illustration of the individual as social an analogy with linguistic meaning, where words both constitute a language and are meaningful because of their place in a language, where language is understood as a rule-governed system (Jaggar, 173, note 10).

Social constructivism for the emotions has been fundamentally a research methodology and one meant to be adequate to the task of uncovering the meaning of any affective experience within a given culture. Regrettably, like the theories presented in Chapter 1, the theory limits its attention to the classic emotions where social norms are most likely to be involved. As a kind of emotional anthropology, social constructivism depends on marked conventional behavior, linguistic evidence (labels and properties), and well-established emotion types (whose presence, absence, or variations can be noted in other cultures) as basic research tools. The use of these tools establishes the paradigm cases of affective meaning within social constructivist theories, and these will be cases where significance is widely shared and gives rise to social conventions. In other words, a social constructivist methodology is most likely to locate classic emotion types for a society. In the following passage from Harré, free-style feelings are degraded to life's little problems, and the dismissal seems contemptuous.

There are about *four hundred words* for emotion in English, and there are many words in other languages that seem to pick out something like emotions for which there are no English equivalents. . . . In this work, we will be dealing in detail with about a dozen emotions only. *But our aim is exemplification, not salience to life's little problems or completeness in the scientific sense. Much remains to be done and what we offer here is a lead and an example.* (6; emphasis mine)

I question the necessity of an additional kind of meaning, *social meaning*, as necessary or sufficient to determine affective meaning. In the remainder of this section, I indicate the confusion on which I take the view to rest and consider whether social constructivists have a positive account of social meaning. In the following section, I comment more broadly on the politics of emotional categorization as a way of interpreting people's expressions of feelings and argue for a strong supplementary practice faithful to the hermeneutic principles that triangulation suggests.

In Chapter 4, I argued that to understand affective experience as meaningful requires an understanding of the communicative and interpretive circumstances, individual and political, in which such meaning is created. Social constructivism is not an innocuous theory about the public nature of meaning. In its attempt to respond to a privacy that I, too, agree is incompatible with possibilities for meaningfulness, social constructivists confuse the private, in the sense of epistemologically private, with the legitimately personal.

In daily discourse, we move easily and legitimately between talking of the private and/or personal on the one hand, and the public and/or social on the other. In theories of mind and meaning, the members of each pair need to be carefully distinguished. Davidson, for example, has a theory of semantic meaning in which private meaning is dismissed in favor of public meaning. However, he rejects the idea that public meaning depends on or is determined by shared conventions or rules. Semantic meaning is public in the sense that my words must be interpretable by others, but personal in the sense that those others (their conventions and rules) do not determine what my words mean (Davidson, "Communication and Convention"). I follow Davidson and others in putting the distinctions in the following way:

1. Public meaning: meaning accessible (knowable, interpretable) to others
2. Social meaning: meaning determined by shared rules, conventions, norms, and so on.
3. Private meaning: meaning inaccessible to others
4. Personal meaning: meaning not determined by shared rules, conventions, norms, and so on.

Social constructivists collapse (1) and (2) and suppose thereby that if my meaning is accessible to others, then those others determine (by their norms, etc.) what my meaning is. They likewise collapse (3) and (4) and so suppose that if my meaning is not determined by social rules and norms it must be inaccessible to others. But by distinguishing (1) from (2) and (3) from (4), we can suppose that affective meaning is public, accessible to interpretation by others, while being personal and as such not determined by the rules or conventions of those others.

I offer as a useful example the relatively widespread and familiar experience of "Sunday melancholy" (Rorty, "Explaining Emotions"). When I express Sunday melancholy, I am expressing something of personal significance, and its significance is publicly determinable. It is not epistemologically private; nevertheless, it is not determined by rules or conventions. It's just not society's business if I suffer from Sunday melancholy and there are no societal norms that specifically govern the expression of Sunday melancholy. This does not, of course, mean that it is *nobody's* business if I suffer Sunday melancholy. It might be the business of the person I live with. Nor is it the case that we don't have general social norms for behavior on Sundays: don't call others before 10:00 in the morning, for example. These norms, however, govern activities as activities one might perform on a Sunday for a variety of reasons, and give us no special insight into the meaning of Sunday melancholy. Sunday melancholy is not private, but it is personal; it is public, but it is not social, as these have been described.

I have said that social constructivist theories confuse the epistemologically private with the legitimately personal. The confusion or conflation of private and personal is evidenced in Jaggar's criticism of cognitivist theories of emotion:

> most cognitivist accounts explain emotion as having two "components": an affective or feeling component and a cognition that supposedly interprets or identifies the feeling. Such accounts, therefore, unwittingly perpetuate the positivist distinction between the shared, public, objective world of verifiable calculations, observations, and facts and the individual, private, subjective world of idiosyncratic feelings and sensations. This sharp distinction breaks any conceptual links between our feelings and the "external" world. (156)

Reducing the legitimately personal to the unsharable private rides, in this passage, on the back of a prior reduction of feeling to sensation. Subsuming the personal to the private removes such legitimately personal experiences as Sunday melancholy from their rightful place in a shared, public world. Without the personal, all that is left of the public world is the social world that involves norms, rules, and institutions, hence Jaggar's conclusion, referred to earlier, that in cases of emotional experience individual experience is *social* experience. My identifying a confusion of the epistemically private with the personal, the account of meaning offered in Chapter 4, and the example of Sunday melancholy are meant to challenge the legitimacy of invoking a notion of social meaning, at least for feelings such as Sunday melancholy. To move back to the externalist view with which I am most sympathetic, as Akeel Bilgrami writes:

> It would be a mistake to think that the only way to repudiate the conception of meaning as private and purely inner is to . . . raise the importance of the social, conventional elements in solving for an agent's meaning. . . . At most it needs an agent and someone to discover and attribute meanings and beliefs to her. This can be done quite independently of the discoverer looking to the social and linguistic norms of yet others. (196–97)

To make quite clear, for a theory of affective meaning, the parallel challenge to Bilgrami's assessment of the role of social conventions in determining linguistic meaning, suppose we stay as a house guest with Kris Kristofferson for a number of months. Kristofferson wrote a Country and Western anthem to Sunday melancholy entitled "Sunday Morning Coming Down." Let's suppose that on Sundays, and only then, Kristofferson's behavior is expressive in ways described by the song's lyrics. He has beer for breakfast, wears a dirty shirt, wanders around without purpose, watches children sadly, and pulls out old photos and letters.

Interpreting Kristofferson's Sunday melancholy may well depend, for some interpreters, on a shared world of events, or shared biographies, involving church on Sunday mornings, family dinners, and the loss of traditions, loved ones, and opportunities as we age. The interpretation may, however, for particular imaginative interpreters, depend only on some experiences of community and loss and their ability to use these experiences to find the pattern to Kristofferson's responses. But the interpretation can then be explained by an account of similar responses to shared stimuli. Our ability to recognize Kristofferson's feeling as Sunday melancholy, whether or not we can label that feeling, shows the public nature of his feeling—it is not epistemically private. The fact that what Kristofferson feels is Sunday melancholy is determined by the behavior he engages in on the occasions in which he engages in it, by his background biography, and by the fact that he is interpretable. There is no need or use here to appeal to rules or norms.

A possible response to the claim that there is no need to appeal to norms is that church or shared Sunday dinners are social conventions and these conventions have had an biographical role in determining the nature of Kristofferson's feelings. This is an important point. We can make room for social conventions in the interpretation of meaning on any particular occasion without assigning these conventions a general role in theory of meaning. Crudely sketched, on Davidson's theory of semantic meaning, meaning partly depends on cause or occasion of utterance, not on rules. This claim is not limited by the fact that sometimes the cause is or involves rules. Suppose, for example, that the meaning of the word *rule* is fixed by its regular utterance in the presence of rules. Here, it is because rules serve as causes that they give the word *rule* its meaning. Likewise, on my account of affective meaning, meaning partly depends on cause or occasion, not, as the social constructivists would have it, on rules. And this claim is not limited by the fact that sometimes the cause or occasion involves social norms, conventions, or rules.[1]

I emphasize that my main objection to social constructivism is the restrictions it places on the possibilities of affective interpretation by its commitment to social or moral norms as the major determinant of the meaning of any of our affective experiences. I have argued, however, that, given the general explanatory unity of affect as a category of personal significance, emotions form the subset of that category where the significance of the occasion is both widely enough shared and of sufficient social concern to give rise, in many cases, to conventions governing the way we ought to view occasions and how we ought to express the significance of those occasions. Do we then need, at least for classic emotions, an account of social meaning to supplement the account of affective meaning offered in Chapter 4? And does social constructivist theory offer such an account?

In regard to the second question, the two most common offers of the theory are that to engage in an emotion is to undertake a social role (see Averill and Sarbin) or that the idea of rules can be applied to emotional experience (see Harré and Averill). I do not find the notion of social role helpful. I may express any classic emotion quite idiosyncratically and secure uptake through people's understanding of the nature of the occasion and my expressive idiolect. I present a grief poem in the appendix to this chapter where grief is expressed through political pageantry. I may also perform any social role insincerely. I may perform as a grief-actor, for example, and because of my insincerity, not be expressing grief.

Rules also do not seem promising. Averill, the main proponent of this approach, although granting that the use of rule in emotion theory may be somewhat metaphorical, argues that there are constitutive rules for emotion concepts. He uses, as an example, that we cannot be proud of the stars: "to be proud of something, the existence of which is not connected with the self even remotely or by association, violates are of the

---

1. To illustrate, for a classic emotion, how conventions may be involved on one occasion, but not another, we need only think of two different occasions of anger, one, where I back my car into a cement block for the third time on a single day, the other, where I am publicly insulted by a person clearly inferior in status to myself.

constitutive rules of this emotion" (106). I see no reason that we should accept this example. I do not find it beyond imagination that someone should feel star pride, however inappropriately or even inexplicably. What I mean here is that a person's behavior, responses, or expressions might best be interpreted in this way. I grant we might argue with a person who expresses, explicitly, star pride about whether his or her response is pride or, more appropriately, wonder. But we would then be suggesting either that the person is using the wrong term for the response, or that a response of pride is inappropriate. Averill's other categories of rules result in my emotion's being subject to certain sorts of criticism—"you've grieved too long," for example—but do not compromise the description of the emotion. Although Roxane's love for two men may have fallen outside of the conventions governing romantic love that her culture endorses, hence Cyrano's death, we conclude as interpreters of her expressive acts that she did love both men.

Evidently, for emotions, conventions will play a role in determining significance on many particular occasions. My emotional responses will be shaped and limited by a history of earlier occasions in which I was interpreted in certain ways rather than others and in which I was taught what I should feel through response to my expressions and correction of my behaviors. To understand how I am responding to or viewing an occasion often requires interpreter familiarity with such conventions governing emotional expression as may have given shape to my response. However, to look for the meaning of my response as affective meaning, to take this stance as an interpreter, is to try and understand the significance to me of certain occasions, and for those occasions involving emotions and conventions, an interpreter will require an understanding of how I see myself in respect to particular social norms or rules. No set of rules, conventions, or descriptions can substitute for these acts of interpretation and give meaning, by themselves, to my expressive responses.

I find it, in fact, difficult to know what is meant by social meaning other than the very strong claim that something is defined by its place within an institution or a set of convention-governed community practices. If I, for example, without a sanctioning official position and with predeliberation kill someone, it is murder quite independently of why I did it or whether I prefer the description justice, euthanasia, or revenge. How that act is to be interpreted is encoded in a set of laws and determined through a formal and regulated interpretive practice where the authority to say what my act means rests with official others whose task is to uphold a certain set of restrictions on behavior. But that such an example should be appropriate for illustrating how our own motives for or understanding of what we are doing or have done can be clearly overridden by institutionalized social descriptions of an act brings up the question of whether the emotions could, in general, be anything like this. If we accept the account of affective explanation I have offered, they cannot. In cases of override, one is no longer trying to understand a situation from the subject's point of view. I have argued that we have a discourse of feeling precisely to acknowledge the subject's point of view.

Sometimes my interests, and the interests of many people in a society, oppose the present rules, norms, and conventions of that society.[2] Social constructivism appears to restrict political practice to wresting control of existing categories, and I will have more to say about this in a moment. My interest here is a final comment on the possibilities of social constructivism as a theory of affective meaning. As such a theory would leave very serious gaps for categories of widely shared significance outside of or in opposition to conventions, or it would distort our understanding of people by referencing, in our understanding of their behavior, categories not widely shared but promoted by conventions.

As an example of probable distortion, the fact that women reputedly feel less jealousy in cases of infidelity than men is taken by Dorothy Dinnerstein in *The Mermaid and the Minotaur* as grounds for considerable speculation about the psychological lives of women—why it is that they don't mind sharing men. But if it is the case, let's just suppose, that jealousy serves the needs of people who have property rights over their partners, and women have not had these property rights, why suppose that their failure to feel jealousy indicates anything other than the inapplicability of that concept to many women's experience? Why should it be assumed that because a woman does not regard a man as her exclusive property she regards him as potentially shared property instead and that what we need is a psychological theory that explains that interesting fact about women?

Linda Kaufmann's *Ways of Desire* and Lawrence Lipking's *Abandoned Women and the Poetic Tradition* investigate a certain type of expression that occurs cross-culturally and through the history of the poetic tradition— women expressing their feelings of abandonment to the men who have seduced them and then left them. The occasion is very specifically characterized. These women express themselves in voices that will not secure uptake—this is part of what characterizes the genre—and these expressions display abandonment in two senses. Abandoned and marginalized

---

2. Scheman suggests that "psychological predicates (such as "is angry") . . . pick out socially significant patterns, ways of organizing feeling and behavior in accordance with particular social needs" ("Anger and the Politics of Naming," 179). The question arises of whose needs are served by our present emotion categories, that is, who has the political power to have their needs converted into social norms.

in their societies, the women lament and accuse with abandonment. These types of occasions are so universal that Lipking claims that many men have written some of their finest poems in the voices of abandoned women, and occasionally even suppressed these poems. But we have no classic emotion called "abandonment." The voices of abandoned women are a challenge to social norms.

Finally, I would like to offer an example that is a case of the absence of an emotion concept, the AIDS demonstration poem "Yellow Kitchen Gloves," by Michael Lynch. As the poem is very long, I include it as an appendix to this study. It is a powerful expression of the feeling of political action through the threatened or terrorized body.[3] This is a serious cross-cultural feeling for which we have no special emotion concept. The poem also is an excellent example of how a classic emotion, grief, can be expressed through a highly personal pattern that is indisputably publicly accessible, and yet depends on none of the conventions that typically facilitate the expression of grief.

Social constructivism as a comprehensive account of *affective meaning* limits our emotional repertoire to what society has an interest in; but society does not have a legitimate interest in everything that I do or feel, and I object to some of the things my society values. The consequence of the confusion between the private and the personal is a deeply restrictive and conservative view of affect that allows people very few affective states and allows only those that are legitimized by the norms of the society or culture of which they are members. Thus, insofar as people interpret my expressive acts, and hence my feelings, within these legitimized categories, when interpretive situations allow them this power, they are exercising a strong influence over my affective life through these restrictions.

CONSTRAINTS ON INTERPRETERS

The view of affect externalized that I have defended—that other people's responses may become part of the occasion to which I am responding—is nearly always a part of the ordinary life of affect and is not always a negative feature of the ordinary life of affect. People can see things about our lives that we cannot. Their responses to us can be of great value. Nevertheless, we enter a danger zone in cases where interpreters clearly have more power over the description of the occasion, and over the determination of the meaning of my response than I myself have. People become increasingly vulnerable to a loss of power over their affective meanings as

3. The pervasiveness of this feeling in the poem was pointed out to me by Denise Blais.

they have less real power to determine how the occasions of their lives are viewed. This may be a problem for the minimalist position I have been defending about emotional characterization.

I have argued that social constructivism is not a viable theory of how affective meaning is determined. It does not yet follow from this critique that we should expand our interpretive practices. We might have strong pragmatic reasons for restricting our practices, on many occasions, to the limited categories offered by emotion types. We may have special reasons for doing so depending on our political situation. I now broaden the political base of my argument against social constructivist approaches to interpretation by considering a case of interpretation within an emotion category, offered by Naomi Scheman as an exploration of the uses of social constructivism to feminist theory. I am still inclined, on balance, to argue that social constructivism, as an approach that guides interpretation, is antithetical to the role of affect as an explanatory category. This is an argument for constraints on interpreters. I argue for an alternative or strongly supplementary interpretive practice that I claim is implicit in our use of affect as an explanatory category. This is the practice of trying to understand people as if they were autobiographers.

A strong political consideration for a practice of interpretation that operates through categorization and naming is offered by Naomi Scheman in "Anger and the Politics of Naming." Scheman regards the political consequences of the myth of private knowledge of feelings as a powerful reason to investigate the resources of social constructivism and offers a deliberately challenging and explicitly political use of interpretive power in the following example of how the interpretation of a woman's anger might take place: Alice joins a consciousness-raising group and through interaction with this group becomes aware of having felt, at various times with her family, depressed, pressured, harried, snappish, moody, and guilty about all of this:

> We must distinguish here among the reality, the legitimacy, and the justifiability of feelings. One can acknowledge the reality of an emotion while believing that it is in some way illegitimate. And to acknowledge that one's feelings are legitimate—sincere, not self-deceptive—is not necessarily to take those feelings to be justifiable. They may, no matter how deeply or fully felt, be irrational, unfounded, needlessly self- or other-destructive.
>
> It is likely that the other women in the group will urge Alice to acknowledge the reality of her depression and guilt, *but to deny the legitimacy of those feelings.* This denial amounts to the claim that she is feeling something that she is unable to face. The guilt and depression are a response to and a cover for those other feelings, notably feelings of anger. Alice is urged to

recognize her anger as legitimate and justifiable in this situation. (177; emphasis mine)

We can obviously interpret Alice's case in a quite ordinary way consistent with the externalism I have been defending. The formation of the significance of an occasion (especially when that occasion is something as cosmic as one's family life) may remain continuous, unsettled, and subject to changing and multiple determinations. The response of the women in the consciousness-raising group to Alice's responses to her family life are a part of the significance to Alice of an ongoing part of her life. However, Scheman's description incorporates a disturbing element, which I have highlighted, the denial of the legitimacy of some of Alice's feelings, as necessary to establish the legitimacy of her anger.

Obviously, the women in the group view Alice's situation as being in some way an offense to Alice. However, insofar as they share expressive biographies with Alice, or alternatively, are good or imaginative interpreters after whatever fashion, they recognize her expressions of feeling as expression of guilt, depression, and so on. This is what allows them to sympathize with and affirm the reality of Alice's feelings. The women encourage Alice to avow anger because they believe that, if she comes to see her situation as offensive, she will change it. Likely Alice shares with these women a similar cultural understanding of anger and may come to understand why being angry would be a legitimate response to her situation.

However, to encourage Alice to *recognize* her anger, the women deny the legitimacy of Alice's guilt and depression. In this denial, they are claiming that Alice, in feeling depressed or guilty, is either insincere or self-deceived. This seems like an extraordinarily strong conclusion for them to draw, and a dangerous one given that the people in the group may well have more power than Alice to determine the description of the occasion. The women in the group have, in effect, made themselves Alice's affective biographers. This, for Scheman, may be an inevitable consequence of expressing ourselves that we need to face more clear-headedly and more politically.

I take the political considerations to be the following: (1) people have considerable power over our feeling through their acts of interpretation. (2) Those who already occupy positions of social power will interpret our feelings through emotion categories that serve *their* needs and interests. We should recognize both (1) and (2). We do not recognize these facts because they are mystified to us by the political promise of privacy and authority about what we feel. Once we do recognize these facts, we may then be forced into a position where our best political option is to gain control of the categories through which we are interpreted and to change

the meaning of certain emotion concepts through our revisionary participation in practices associated with these categories. As women, guilty, harried, depressed and irritable, we may with good reason declare that this
pattern can be called women's anger, and by appropriating this category
begin to organize through the power that anger offers. Our expressions of
affect will be interpreted socially, and what Alice can best do is put herself
in a position where this interpretation is to her maximum advantage.

The women may change the significance of the occasion to Alice by
encouraging her to avow her feelings as a classic emotion—anger. However, as Alice has already avowed depression, guilt, feeling harried, and
being moody, we might wonder why they would bother to do this. Scheman challenges that it is appropriate to call the pattern of behavior and
response to the occasion anger, that this pattern corresponds to a socially
meaningful pattern of behavior and response that we can now call anger
(woman's anger). Scheman thus wants us to contemplate that it's appropriate for the women in the consciousness-raising group to decide that
Alice is angry independently of Alice's willingness to avow anger and,
what's more, to decide that Alice already was angry at a time when she
would have absolutely denied that she was angry, that is, at a time when
she joined the group:

> I may think, and you may disagree, that you are angry at me, or in love with
> me, but afraid to admit it even to yourself. . . .
> Now why do you get to do the settling? What is wrong with my taking you to
> be some way you don't take yourself? (Scheman, "Anger and the Politics of
> Naming," 180)

Scheman concludes that we need to "explore the possibility of allowing
our emotions to be fully and openly social constructions, rather than
needing, as we do now, to acquire and keep to ourselves the final authority about them" (181).

There is nothing, thus far, in the externalism that I have defended that
easily answers Scheman on this case. I have defended the view that expressive behavior is and must be publicly interpretable. I have proposed that
what marks off, in part, the classic emotions as a category of affect is that
the nature of the occasion and the possible responses such an occasion
might elicit are such as to make personal significance a matter of public
concern and control. Evidently, the possibility of women becoming angry
now is a matter of political concern on all sides. Assuming a culturally
homogeneous group for this example, we share ways of referring to the
occasion/response and our shared vocabularies reflect the presence of

standards of correct assessment and appropriate response. And Scheman's suggestion that women's family guilt, frustration, and depression may appropriately be called women's anger, seems very plausible. Finally, nothing I have said about what I take to be the inadequacies of social constructivism as a theory of meaning deals with the ideological use of the myth of epistemic privacy or the best political strategies for countering it.

To illustrate this political concern, let's suppose that Alice appeals her case. I take it that precisely part of Scheman's point is: to whom will Alice make this appeal? Scheman sees the case as involving the ideological myths of privileged access and first-person authority that allow us to believe that we have an authoritative position with respect to the determination of our affective meanings. As we do not have this authoritative position—Scheman and I agree on this point—it can make a great deal of difference who our interpreters are. I thus agree that there will certainly be no such thing as evaluating Alice's appeal without acting as interpreters to her feelings, now partly in response to the consciousness-raising situation that Scheman has described (e.g., "Just who do those women think they are, anyway?").

Nevertheless, it seems to me that the important point here is not whom Alice can find as her best interpreters, but what the responsibilities of those interpreters are, whoever they turn out to be, and in the case presented, I think, once again, that supposing that the category of affect is fully occupied by the classic emotions can do damage to interpreters' choices. Alice has within the setting of the group, secured uptake that has allowed her to determine her affective meanings. She feels moody, harried, guilty, occasionally irritable, and depressed. The challenge to the women in the consciousness-raising group as interpreters is: Is there a justification for going beyond this interpretation?

Scheman suggests that part of what makes anger a legitimate interpretation is that, given the emerging legitimacy of women's anger, Alice's response will have a natural future as anger. We can call Alice's response "anger" today because of what we can predict about its future transformations. But this, as a general prediction about women in Alice's circumstances, tells us nothing about Alice, not even that Alice will eventually avow anger. Scheman predicts that if Alice does avow anger, she will then start to organize her behavior around that anger, but we have to add that, even if this is true, Alice will start to organize around anger in whatever way Alice organizes around anger. The problem of a social constructivist appeal to a special sort of social meaning is evident at this point. If the "patterns" of anger can be instantiated in an indefinite variety of ways by different individuals, there is no sense in which anger is one pattern. It does not stretch plausibility, for instance, to suppose that Alice might have had an expressive upbringing that licenses expressing guilt or depression, but encourages concealing anger. It might further be the case that Alice, through a long history of expressing useless guilt, is about ready to wash her hands of situations that make her feel guilty, but is impotent toward her own anger. Alice's organization around her anger may be to keep her house spotless, never yell at anyone again, and grind her teeth at night. Thus whether or not Alice is successfully encouraged to avow anger, whether the women in the conscious-raising group have interpreted her so as to further her interests seems open to question. I suggested that what is unique about the role of affective explanation is that: (1) one person is not replaceable by another; and (2) affective explanation systematizes more behavior as organized behavior than other explanations. Is Alice a replaceable member of the consciousness-raising group when they call her angry? If so, her interpreters will have defaulted on (1). But (2) depends on (1). Affective explanation only systematizes behavior as well as it does because many things that one person does are connected actions and experiences of that particular life.

The question I am focusing on is not why the women in the conscious-ness-raising group would want to encourage Alice to be angry—I take it this is clear enough: they believe the development of women's anger will facilitate political change—but why they take themselves to be justified in moving to this further level of interpretation. A good part of the answer is found in Scheman's claim that, if it is not catagorized under an emotion concept, Alice's feelings remain uninterpreted. Scheman uses "feeling" ambiguously to stand variously for things such as physiological surges, pangs, waves and for well-conceptualized emotions. But Alice's feeling harried or guilty falls into neither of these categories.

There appear to be at least two distinguishable ways in which the women in the consciousness-raising group are exercising their power as interpreters. One is by categorizing Alice's various responses under a classic emotion concept. The other is by denying that Alice gets to decide whether she is angry or not. These, however, are deeply related to social constructivist views of interpretation. The by-now familiar restriction of affect to the classic emotions, combined with two additional premises (that the meaning of these patterns is given socially and that in expressing ourselves we are attempting to discover how we feel) has the consequence that how we feel is to be determined by matching our behavior and response as closely as possible to a pattern that is either preexistent or being newly legitimized by people who have the power to do so. Thus the placement of Alice's expressive acts and feeling under a classic emotion concept and the denial of the relevance of Alice's possible unwillingness to avow anger to a description of what her feelings are are closely connected features of the case.

Part of what seems dubious political practice is that the women do not stop by telling Alice that she has the right to be angry or that they would angry, or even that they are angry listening to her, but rather they tell her that she is angry and therefore is not guilty or depressed. All this can do is to continue to mystify to Alice the ways in which affective meaning actually gets determined. If Alice has come to feel depressed and guilty through the collaborative individuation of affective meaning in her interactions with her family, she is not self-deceived in responding to the real power people have had over her affective life in the past. Finally, the more we accept the theory that we are discovering rather than determining how we feel and the more we accept categorization, the more likely we are to experience the world through these categories.

I have argued that the women in the consciousness-raising group have an obligation not to go beyond what would count as a legitimate pattern from Alice's point of view in their present task as interpreters. I would like to be able to argue, as Davidson does for linguistic meaning in "Epistemology Externalized," that you cannot simply *make me mean* by your interpretation, that you cannot determine affective significance for me through an interpretation of my acts of expression. However, if you have sufficient power over the nature of the occasion to limit my freedom of expression in very strong ways and deprive me of my point of view, you have determined the affective significance of the occasion, although this significance may not correspond to your interpretation. In "On Psychological Oppression" Bartky offers the classic example of the wolf whistle:

It is a fine spring day, and with an utter lack of self-consciousness, I am bouncing down the street. Suddenly I hear men's voices. Catcalls and whistles fill the air. The noises are clearly sexual in intent and they are meant for me; they come from across the street. I freeze. As Sartre would say, I have been petrified by the gaze of the Other. My face flushes and my motions become stiff and self-conscious. The body which only a moment before I inhabited with ease now floods my consciousness. I have been made into an object. While it is true that for these men I am nothing but, let us say, a "nice piece of ass," there is more involved in this encounter than their mere fragmented perception of me. They could, after all, have enjoyed me in silence. Blissfully unaware, breasts bouncing, eyes on the birds in the trees, I could have passed by without having been turned to stone. But I must be *made* to know that I am a "nice piece of ass": I must be made to see myself as they see me. There is an element of compulsion in this encounter, in this being-made-to-be-aware of one's own flesh; like being made to apologize, it is humiliating. (27; emphasis in original)

I do not concede, in general, that in a case such as the one Bartky presents, the men have succeeded in turning her walk into an expression of humiliated sexuality simply by their uptake, but she can no longer bounce freely down the street, and thus certainly the men have had power in determining the significance of that occasion for her.

Bartky no doubt has options for how to respond to a wolf whistle, but they are severely limited by the real power these men have had over the significance of her walking. The best she can do is adopt some attitude of defiance, and her ability to do this may well depend on her having secured uptake for previous acts of defiance. If you have sufficient power over the nature of an occasion and the ways in which I can realistically view it, the best I may be able to do is express an attitude toward this power. In the same way, in the example from Chapter 4 the date rapist does not have the power to make the occasion one of mutual desire or freely given consent. He does, however, have the socially sanctioned power to deprive his victim of her point of view both at that time and later in a court of law.

That the indeterminacy of affective significance gives the people who interpret affective significance power over its determination brings up questions of whether we can argue that constraints be placed on this interpretative power by using the account of affect I defended. I have argued this case only for the friendly interpreters of the consciousness-raising group, and I acknowledge, in the face of an example such as Bartky's, that the argument must itself be normative. I mean by this both that I cannot argue that these constraints are already an integral part of our practices, I must argue that we should observe such constraints and also that there are, then, normative considerations that should move us to adopt such constraints.[4] I believe that there often are such considerations

---

4. To argue that our actual practices contain normative dimensions that we can argumentatively exploit is not an uncommon philosophical strategy. In *Spheres of Justice*, for example, Michael Walzer argues that the meaning we have already given to social goods ought to determine the principles of their distribution. In "Epistemology Externalized" Donald Davidson argues that the conditions on linguistic interpretation allow people to use words as unconventionally and idiosyncratically as they like as long as they remain interpretable. My argument may look like a far stronger use of the same methodology, but it is simply a more explicit one. Both Walzer and Davidson make, at points, very strong assumptions about the egalitarian nature of our practices that make their theories look more simply like arguments for greater consistency in our practice or consistency in matching our theories to our actual practice. Walzer, for instance, speaks as if women have contributed equally to the social meaning of goods and thus argues that health care should go to the sick without attention

as I will try to persuasively illustrate in the next section. I acknowledge, however, that ideally the interpretive strategies we undertake always need to be sensitive to the power configurations of particular affective interactions. Although the women in the consciousness-raising group should, I have argued, be more deferential toward Alice, and the wolf-whistling men toward Bartky, Bartky, it seems to me, is under no obligation to try to understand the point of view of the wolf-whistling men.

Nevertheless, that there are more feelings on heaven and earth than are discussed in most people's philosophies, along with the role of affect as a category of explanation that deals with personal significance, does seem to allow us to argue for an alternative practice of understanding people's affective lives in a way that tries as far as possible to eschew categorization of these feelings under emotion concepts, or, at the very least, understands the limitations of this categorization and the risks of this categorization given our power as interpreters. I wish now to bolster this normative appeal first by what seems to me a powerful consideration.

If I'm feeling piqued, buoyant, expectant, homesick, or harried, or at least three hundred other ways that I can discriminate in English, there is no property vocabulary that brings with it standards of correctness. This raises the question of whether we have a social practice (as one supposes we must have, given *all* this vocabulary) that incorporates shared vocabularies and shared responses, but does not bring with it standards of correctness or objectivity; what's more, a social practice that allows us to understand a passion for discovering oil, the feeling of weird sinking hilarity, Sunday melancholy, the voices of abandoned women, and the feeling of political action through the terrorized body.

There is I believe a common misconception in philosophy that a shared vocabulary always brings with it standards of correctness:

> [A]nything which can properly be called conceptual thinking can occur only within a framework of conceptual thinking in terms of which it can be criticized, supported, refuted, in short, evaluated. To be able to think is to be able to measure one's thoughts by standards of correctness, of relevance, of evidence. In this sense a diversified conceptual framework is a whole which, however sketchy, is prior to its parts. (Sellars, 6)

---

to how women have had so little control over the meaning of the ways they've been classified as sick or well that this prescription will continue to ignore their needs. Davidson rejects a certain kind of externalism, where people in power have control over our linguistic meanings, in part because he believes it is antithetical to our actual practice. I have argued in Chapter 4 that this is not always the case. A great deal of power goes into determining whether "no" means no or whether this response truly is more indeterminate in meaning. Thus the appeal to our explanatory practices to argue for constraints on interpreters must be in part a normative appeal.

The interesting question is whether we have room within this holistic conceptual framework for practices that do not require standards of correctness or whether every part of this framework is subject to these conditions. The assumption that the latter is the case prevents, from the start, an attempt to locate an alternative practice. An alternative way of putting this challenge is that, if philosophy is the critique of our evaluative discourse in general, part of the project of knowing one's way around the philosophical countryside may be to look for unmarked locations and practices where standards of correctness do not apply.

The absence of developed concepts for many feelings, labeled and unlabeled, need indicate nothing about their importance. They may, as with abandonment, be missing for political reasons. Second, they may not have a place in a social practice that involves intersubjective checks on correctness. It may be the case that some, but not all, of our affective interactions establish categories that ought to be subject to this kind of control.

I suggested that an affective property vocabulary arises out of shared responses when those who share the response have some stake in making notions of correctness applicable. This makes possible in a community a critical discourse for talking about people's feelings. We must take seriously the idea that there also are concerns and responses which such a critical discourse would undermine, and so where there is a reason that the notions of correctness, truth, falsity, and so on are not to be allowed a grip. Our extensive aesthetic vocabulary offers something close to this: here the expression of feeling is given more rein, and the complex diversity and idiosyncracy of feelings are acknowledged by critical practice. Free-style feeling is the attempt to give form to what is personally significant, using as our medium whatever expressive resources are available to us—even to those of us who are not artists. The attempt to understand a person fully must include an attempt to understand his or her free-style feelings, which are not essentially private, but often are idiosyncratic.

In the next two sections, I argue in greater detail that giving up social constructivism as a theory of affective meaning allows one to develop interpretive practices that are more deferential when this is appropriate and that also provide the space for new and politically significant affective meanings to gain voice.

Moral Deference

I have said that one of the most appealing features of the model of triangulation for an account of affective meaning is that we do not have to share each other's responses to interpret them such that they are formed or individuated through their expression. In Chapter 2, I also agreed with traditional expressivist theories that the response to a unique and un-categorized feeling, one that would fall outside of socially constructed meanings, is an important political possibility. Being able to interpret a feeling we do not share to facilitate the creation of affective significance is critical to what Laurence Thomas refers to as moral deference. I agree with Thomas that moral deference often is the appropriate attitude toward others and affirm with him that we need to create new models of interpretation that call attention to the possibility of this attitude.

Thomas has formulated the notion of moral deference to oppose the idea that we can, through good will and effort, come to understand by imaginatively sharing the affective experiences of others who belong to social categories systematically subject to social injustice. We cannot imagine our way into how the significance of their present experience is configured through structures of memory, expectation, and prior affective significance, and it is arrogance to think that we could do this. It often is arrogance, even when we ourselves belong to oppressed social categories. If I do not belong to a category that has been subject to colonization, I have a limited potential to grasp imaginatively what this would be like.

> Now the knowledge that someone belongs to a diminished social category group does not, in and of itself, give one insight into the subjective imprimatur of that individual's experiences of and memories stemming from the hostile misfortunes tied to the category to which the person belongs. If so, then a very pressing question is: how is it possible to be morally responsive in the appropriate way to those belonging to a diminished social category if one does not belong to that category? (Thomas, 237–38)

Thomas sketches an answer to his own question that gives us certain obligations as interpreters. We must "have a presumption in favor of the person's account of her experiences" (244), and we must aim for an ideal point of interpretation where the person could trust us to tell her story so as to "render salient what was salient for her in the way that it was salient for her" (245). For Thomas, this notion of being a sufficiently respectful interpreter that someone could trust us to bear witness for them is the ideal, however rarely achievable, that should guide our interpretive practice when we engage with those in devalued social categories. I am not sure that I agree entirely with Thomas's description of this interpretive ideal as it suggests that significance can be verbally articulated, but I propose we can be aided in modeling the kinds of respective interpretive practices that interest Thomas by understanding the determination of affective meaning through the model of triangulation I have presented.

In 1995 Patricia Monture-Angus, a Mohawk writer, professor, mother, lawyer, and activist published a collection of writings entitled *Thunder in My Soul: A Mohawk Woman Speaks.* In the "First Words" of the book, and in a lecture I attended at Queen's University, also called "Thunder in My Soul," Monture-Angus explained the title. I quote from the book:

> The Thunders are very important spirit beings to many First Nations people. Every winter they go away, and I miss them very much. Nearing the end of winter, I always find myself impatiently waiting for the return of the Thunder Beings. We know that spring is truly here when the Thunders return. These spirit people are tricksters. They tease us—just try talking to them sometime. . . . They have always been a source of both strength and inspiration to me. It is not a sad thing to me that there is thunder in my soul.
>
> The image of thunder is also a response to some of the labelling I have experienced in my travels in the non-Indian world. I have travelled this country from coast to coast more times than I can count. Much of this travelling has involved the conference circuit, including the participation at many "feminist" conferences. One of the experiences I have of this circuit is being called "angry." This labelling, and it is a form of silencing, always amazes me because I am not an angry woman. Calling someone angry has a lot of negative connotations. I suppose I have at least a million reasons to be angry when I reflect upon the history of oppression, racism, and colonialism that my people and every other First Nation in this territory have survived. I have struggled very hard to grow through this anger of my youth, and thunder is the image I have replaced anger with. (Monture-Angus, 1)

Monture-Angus is highly articulate. There is no possibility this time for a respectful interpreter of bringing the feeling under the nearest applicable emotion concept, "anger" for it is precisely anger that is being disavowed. We are, as interpreters, meant to understand this disavowal through responding to her responses to occasions of silencing. Some of these occasions were related in her talk and there are many more related in her book.

We also are meant to interpret Monture-Angus's disavowal of anger in a certain way. I had first interpreted Monture-Angus as denying anger, but this now seems wrong to me: "What I have to understand since that time . . . is the responsibility to be empowering and not merely reactionary. The experience of racism is one that is done to us. We react to racism. Even our pain and anger are reactions" (Monture-Angus, 29). If being angry is reactive, having to deny anger seems to me even more so. Monture-Angus's disavowal of anger takes place through its replacement with something empowering. I did not understand, during the talk, the importance or force of this empowering replacement of anger as what constitutes its disavowal, and coming to realize this through reading the book has led me to prefer the word *disavowal* to *denial.*

To see how replacing anger with thunder is empowering, an interpreter needs to respond to Monture-Angus's responses to thunder, and I did, on her visit to Queen's, begin to have some understanding of the significance of the thunder as an resource that expresses a positive power. The day after the talk, at an informal women's studies tea, the women in the room started to speak about their love of thunder, about going out into storms without permission, about siblings who had been scared of the thunder, and Monture-Angus told me that after the first thunder storm of spring, flowers would double their height. Although I am intimidated by thunder, I have always loved wild flowers, and this coming spring will look forward to the thunder to see if the wild flowers have grown. To try to understand the importance of thunder use self-consciously an aspect of my own experience, my love of wild flowers, rather than to look for what Monture-Angus and I might share: "I do not share with my colleagues a common view of the world. Nor do I share with them a common personal history." (Monture-Angus, 60). In Davidson's model we are free and encouraged to bring with us to situations of interpretation whatever might facilitate our understanding. Misinterpretation always is a risk. Nevertheless, my own access, however limited, to the power of thunder does allow me to image "thunder in my soul" in a way that I can understand how unlike anger it might be: "Sometimes it is a quiet rumbling. Other times it rolls over me with such force that I am immobilized" (Monture-Angus, 68). I get no sense that to be immobilized by thunder, to have it roll over one, leaves one weaker rather than stronger, and this seems quite unlike being paralyzed by anger.

The first four articles of *Thunder in My Soul: A Mohawk Woman Speaks* are a growing self-portrait of Flint Woman, where each article reflects on the previous one. Monture-Angus is attempting to articulate the significance of occasions of silencing in the developing context of how she views her life. It is throughout the telling of Flint Woman's story, a practice of autobiography, that Monture-Angus moves from expressing anger to expressing thunder in her soul. We must understand the concept of anger to understand her response, but it is not the conventions, norms, and rules of anger that give her response meaning. In the fourth and completing article to "Flint Woman Speaks," "Flint Woman: Surviving the Contradictions of Academia," Monture-Angus comments on the use of "anger" in the previous Flint Woman pieces: "I hesitate to use that imagery of anger because it is so full of someone else's negative assumptions about my own personal culpability for my anger. Trying to name what I was truly feeling helped lead me to the conclusion that English is a fully inadequate language for the expression of my experiences. English is the language of my colonization" (Monture- Angus, 68) Like Bass, Monture-Angus grapples with the limitations and possibilities of her own expressive resources, the limitations of English and the importance to First Nations of the practice of naming, and this, too, is part of the significance that she is trying to express.

The language of anger is not the language that expresses for Monture-Angus, the significance of racist encounters. In "Anger and Insubordination" Elizabeth Spelman has analyzed anger as encoding a complex network of attitudes, beliefs, rights of judgment over others, and assumptions of authority. Thus anger expressed by social "subordinates" toward "dominants" often is an act of insubordination. But in white Western culture, anger also is the language that responds to the violations of rights. I realized in going back to Marilyn Frye's "A Note on Anger" how difficult it is to elucidate the meaning of anger without the background imagery of rights, and especially property rights. This background imagery is striking in Frye precisely because she wants a sense of right that is more aligned with respect than with a narrow notion of rights:

> Anger implies a claim to domain—a claim that one is a being whose purposes and activities require and create a web of objects, spaces, attitudes and interests that is worthy of respect, and that the topic of this anger is a matter rightly within that web. You walk off with my hammer and I angrily demand that you bring it back. Implicitly, I claim that my project is worthy, that I am within my rights to be doing it, that the web of connections it weaves rightly encompasses that hammer. (Frye, 87)

Monture-Angus, however, does not understand her relations to others as primarily mediated by rights:

> When I went to law school, I learned all about rights. It was rights, rights, rights all the time. Do you know what kind of rights you have? My Elders taught me that I have only one. Do you know what that one right is? It is the right to live as a Mohawk woman because that is the way the Creator made me. That is the only right I have. After that, I have a series of responsibilities, as a Mohawk woman, because that is how I was made. (Monture-Angus, 87)

As soon as I point out to most people, "HEY, that's racist," it is distancing. You become defensive. Perhaps you blame me for calling you names or maybe you distance yourself by calling me angry. I feel guilty as I had never intended to hurt you. That is not my way. I have the responsibility to be kind. Kindness is one of my original responsibilities. The power to define my own experience is then taken away from me because racism is a bad word! (Monture-Angus, 38)

That afternoon and now as I read the book, I am only one of many interpreters of "thunder in my soul." This does not mean I can take the affective significance of occasions of silencing or potential silencing to be formed and stable independently of my efforts at respectful interpretation. The significance of occasions that have led to the development of this expressive response involves many different kinds of encounters with racist silencing, and the character of Monture-Angus's response develops historically as she moves through interpretive communities, some supportive, some dismissive, and many very mixed. My attendance at the lecture and tea and my reading of the book mean I am a member of some of these interpretive communities and may aid in Monture-Angus's articulation of significance. I may contribute to the clarity and definiteness, for example, with which she may express this significance on subsequent occasions. Alternately, my response can intentionally or unintentionally confuse or undermine her expressive projects.

I do not find social constructivism a helpful view of interpretation in attempting to understand what Monture-Angus expresses. Although we must come to understand the concept of anger to see what occasions she is responding to, it is not the concept of anger that gives meaning to her response. To try to get her to view her response as anger would be an act of arrogance rather than deference. And although Monture-Angus speaks as a Mohawk woman, as a member of a First Nation, there is no indication from her writings that "thunder in my soul" is a well-conceptualized response within the Mohawk Nation. Finally, because there is no well-conceptualized feeling called "thunder in my soul" and I must eschew the use of categorization to interpret it, there is little room to argue that Monture-Angus is correct or incorrect in applying this concept to her responses to certain circumstances. Someone could attempt to argue this I suppose. Any creative attempt to express significance can always be met with the response of "No, that's not how you feel." Crudely put, this is a certain move in the game of interpreting affect. But as a response it raises the question of the whether the interpreter really is interested in understanding what is of significance to the person expressing their feelings.

Thomas limits the applicability of his notion of moral deference to responses to individuals who are members of devalued social categories. I believe the idea has wider relevance in how we understand others, but I would stop well short of recommending moral deference as a preferred interpretive response to other's expressions of affect. Understanding feelings via the hermeneutic strategies that triangulation suggests might seem to require a stance that is always deferential in Thomas's sense, but it does not. Understanding others is, on Thomas's account of moral deference, elaborated through the moral objectives of gaining trust or being fit to bear witness. One may, however, be interested in discovering how someone feels only for the purpose of trying to alter or sometimes manipulate their view of a situation, and sometimes this is an appropriate response. Although the model of interpretation I have provided is meant to allow for moral deference, it does not require it.

In addition, understanding is not always the kind of response or uptake that helps secure the individuation of feelings. In undertaking this writing I have searched for affective meanings that are labeled—such as weird sinking hilarity, Sunday melancholy, or thunder in my soul. This may not only make free-style feelings look more occasional than they are, but also inadvertently suggest that language is the privileged resource for both expression and interpretation. I do not take this to be the case. What counts as appropriate uptake is not just or even usually the kind of understanding that could lead to reporting. It often is some other response. What counts as a range of uptake or response that helps secure individuation depends on what significance is being expressed. Finally, there often are good reasons for resisting the response that might count as the kind of uptake that gives a feeling life or definition. I was recently on the examining committee for a thesis written by Sharon Wohlgemut entitled "The Shame of It All," a wonderfully detailed study of the expressions of gender harassment that women high school teachers endure from their male students. The teachers whose stories are given in the study do attempt to see what is salient for those students from the perspective of those students to come to an understanding of hostility that they need to negotiate. On the other hand, insofar as the significance being expressed by the students is successfully formed only as a public meaning by securing defensive or shamed responses from the teachers, these responses are resisted.

OUTLAW EMOTIONS AND INTERPRETIVE COMMUNITIES

Scheman's investigation of social constructivism is subordinate to understanding the political dimensions of interpretation within a Wittgensteinian approach to philosophy of mind, one that makes interpretation central to meaning. In understanding that it is our comprehensibility to others that grounds our meaningfulness, we can begin to strategize around the necessity of interpretation. We can begin to see the importance of exercising some control over who our affective interpreters are, and with them, we can claim meanings for our experience that have been forbidden to us. I agree with much of what Scheman has to say. But an important issue for my account is the extent to which a theory needs to construct a social edifice of norms, conventions, rules, roles, conceptualizations, and like-minded others, in order to understand how meanings not previously available to some people come to be formed. I have tried to minimize that role of this edifice in a general theory of affective meaning. I have preferred the model of triangulation because, although it allows for the categorization of responses as one interpretive strategy, it also leaves room for the development of new meanings. I would like to emphasize the importance of this point by returning briefly to Jaggar's account.

In "Love and Knowledge: Emotions in Feminist Epistemology," Alison Jaggar introduces the useful idea of "outlaw emotions," which provide new and sometimes oppositional perspectives on dominant ideologies. "Thunder in my soul" is, I would think, a kind of exemplar Jaggar has in mind. Yet, because of Jaggar's commitment to social constructivism, it is difficult to see how such an emotion could be formed. For Jaggar, emotions are socially constructed in a number of ways through essentially involving judgments that depend on socially constructed ways of viewing the world. These judgments, which define our limited range of emotion categories, can be accurate or inaccurate, the resulting emotions appropriate or inappropriate. Because emotional judgments are socially constructed ways of viewing reality: "The emotions that we experience reflect prevailing forms of social life" (Jaggar, 157).

Conventionally inappropriate emotions are possible, and these "outlaw emotions" are epistemically critical to developing new perspectives. This is the central theme of Jaggar's account. However, as meaning requires a complex social edifice of conventions and conceptualizations, the question arises of where support for the new meanings is to be found. Outlaw emotions cannot be, for Jaggar, the expressive undertaking of an individual. In the following passage the idea of individual significance is linked to the notion of the pre-social in ways that undermine it as a possibility: "it is inconceivable that betrayal or indeed any distinctively human emotion could be experienced by a solitary individual in some hypothetical presocial state of nature" (Jaggar, 158). Outlaw emotions require instead, on Jaggar's account, the support of an oppositional "subculture," characterized itself by shared norms, perceptions, or values (Jaggar, 166). Using Jaggar's phrasing, the emotions we feel, even when they are "outlaw," reflect forms of social life, if not the social life of a dominant culture, then the social life of an alternative culture. Jaggar's model for an oppositional subculture is a feminist community, whose members might feel a distinctively feminist anger or feminist pride. These emotions would be reflective of feminist norms and values, and encouraging of feminist projects and investigations, all in opposition to dominant values.

Jaggar's account is an affirmation of why we need theories that allow for the creation of affective meanings that are new and potentially liberatory. The challenge is to leave room for these meanings to emerge. I question whether the notion of oppositional subcultures serves this purpose. It first of all does not seem to me to be either a good description or an acceptable self-designation for many groups or peoples colonized or oppressed by a dominant culture, First Nations, for example. Second, that I must belong to and reflect the values of an oppositional subculture to express outlaw emotions potentially restricts possibilities for expressing personal significance as is it reflective of the pattern I make of my life and experiences. Jaggar's account does not easily allow us to make sense of "thunder in my soul."[5] Finally, oppositional subcultures as made possible by Jaggar's view appear not to challenge dominant emotional categories, but rather seem merely challenge what counts as an appropriate occasion for making a judgment associated with a conventional emotion category:

> For example, anger becomes feminist anger when it involves the perception that the persistent importuning endured by one woman is a single instance of a widespread pattern of sexual harassment, and pride becomes feminist pride when it is evoked by realizing that a certain person's achievement was possible only because that individual overcame specifically gendered obstacles to success. (Jaggar, 166–67)

This, to me, is an indication that the idea does not go far to explaining the formation of new meanings.

I would like to emphasize that I do not doubt the existence and development of distinctive interpretive communities where significance is widely shared and often in opposition, and sometimes reflective opposition, to dominant social norms. Furthermore, shared significance affirmed in a community of interpreters can give rise to new categories of affect and to social norms and conventions further governing how situations are to be viewed and what counts as appropriate modes of expression and response. We would not now have the concepts of sexual or gender harassment if the significance of certain occasions had not been

---

5. I agree here with Ann Ferguson: "those concerned with culture building will tend to fall into the pitfalls of Identity politics. That is, they will emphasize the importance of symbolic unity in oppositional lifestyles, rituals, social practices, that is, of agreement of all values of the relevant oppositional community, on [*sic*] order to validate an alternative way of living to the dominant culture" (82).

widely shared; these concepts mark systemic interactions that have depended, for their conceptualization, on shared significance.[6] The importance of interpretive communities to affective meanings varies greatly, however, with the sorts of significance people might want to express and who can respond to this significance, and the existence of an interpretive community where meaning is shared cannot, in general, underwrite a theory of affective meaning.

At present, expressions of gay sexual sociability are theorized by gay men as expressions of attitudes and possibilities in opposition to the norms, values, perceptions, and practices of heterosexual love. Leo Bersani in *Homos*, for example, wants to suggest ways "in which sentiments and conduct we might wish to associate with love can emerge as a resistance, in the Foucauldian sense, to the violence and avidity for power inherent in all intimate negotiations between human beings" (Bersani, 108). And Frank Browning in *The Culture of Desire* offers an investigation both skeptical and optimistic of the ways in which gay sexual sociability might form part of the basis for a grouping of people that requires or deserves the quite substantive designation of "culture."

What's more, Bersani and Browning have, at points, an interest in the same sort of activities as expressive. Bersani finds in literary descriptions of the ambiguous knowing not knowing of the stranger one cruises the potential for a type "community in which relations would no longer be held hostage to demands for intimate knowledge of the other" (Bersani, 151), taking lovers out of history. This idea is oppositional to the norms of heterosexual sex: "Our culture tells us to think of sex as the ultimate privacy, as that intimate knowledge of the other on which the familial cell is built. Enjoy the rapture that will never be made public, that will also (though this is not said) keep you safely, docilely out of the public realm, that will make you content to allow others to make history while you perfect the oval of a merely copulative or familial intimacy" (Bersani, 165–66).

But the kind of encounter that interests Bersani expresses quite a different relation to history, on at least on some occasions, for Browning. Encountering a David in a park, no words exchanged except a name, lets loose to his fantasy a gallery of past Davids: "All these Davids of mind and memory press in on the present tissues of the David before me. They will not leave us free of our pasts." On this occasion Browning wishes to be taken out of history into desire "a desire that imagines no past, no future, no knowing that the mind can mediate" (Browning, 77).

---

6. Interestingly, once conventions develop that give a *social meaning*, as they seem to have, to harassing actions, the significance of the occasion to the participants, that is, the affective dimension of harassment, becomes of less importance in characterizing the interaction.

Bersani and Browning share an interest in what expressions of "queer" desire might mean, a sense of the social value of raising these questions, and an understanding of the importance of helping develop a community where the meaning of gay sexual expression can find articulation. However, their interpretations of the same sorts of expressive practices do not always agree, and any interpretation remains highly contestable by the participants of these practices.

As an oppositional subculture, the gay urban "culture of desire" has arisen gradually and without affective categories that are already articulated. Bersani and Browning take on a project of articulation, and their interpretations remain both adoptable and contestable by the individuals who engage in the sexual practices they find diversely expressive. The affective meanings that interest these authors are developed through expressive and interpretive practices within and outside the gay urban community and are a matter of speculation, debate, disagreement, self-reflection, and political strategizing. It is these kind of processes that we need to understand in discussing the importance of many outlaw emotions and to place the role of interpretive communities in a theory of affect. We will understand these processes only if our theory of affective meaning does not already assume that these communities are in place and controlling the meanings that are reflective of their values.

Jaggar's appeal to the notion of culture to explain the possibility of meaning is a consequence of the social constructivism she cautiously endorses. This is the space of possibility that social constructivism, as a theory of meaning and interpretation, seems to offer to her for the establishment of new meanings. I believe Jaggar's use of this apparatus is antithetical in spirit to her idea of outlaw emotions. I prefer the possibilities of Davidson's account of interpretation: "it takes two to triangulate. Two, or, of course, more" (Davidson, "Three Varieties of Knowledge" 160). I would add, and sometimes only two.

I wish to reemphasize the main point of this chapter. We do not need another account of meaning called "social meaning" to understand the formation of affective significance. We need to understand, in much greater detail, the power people already can exercise over what we mean on any occasion by their willingness or ability to interpret us on those occasions. A theory of meaning that depends on conventional categories grounding the determination of meaning will have its force on particular occasions of interpretation by limiting how we can be understood.

VI

BEING DISMISSED

The Politics of Emotional Expression

It was my experience that when confronted with a feminist
complaint that I did not agree with (typically because I did not
understand it) I attempted to disprove the validity of the complaint. . . . I would contend that offense required two conditions:
one being an event of potential offense and the other being a
sensitivity to the event. This, in fact, seems to be true. My argument was made faulty, however, through a belief that women (especially feminists) were drastically oversensitive.

—Student, from an exam answer

In this study, I have offered the thesis that the category of feelings has a unique role in a comprehensive theory of psychological explanation: that the expression of feelings through a
diverse range of nonlinguistic and linguistic resources is the attempted communication of personal significance. To develop a model for
affective meaning, I have moved attention away from the most readily
named of feelings—the classic emotions—toward feelings that are more
personal, local, inchoate, or even idiosyncratic. I have argued that what
we feel can be individuated through expression to sympathetic interpreters and can be distorted or constricted in interpretive communities
that are unsympathetic. The necessary public nature to expression gives
others ways of controlling our affective lives.

I have developed the theory partly through a critical hermeneutics of
philosophical and feminist work on the emotions. Traditional philosophical attention to emotions as a small group of highly conceptualized feelings that might seem to find expression in easily identifiable patterns of
behavior has obscured the importance of expression in the formation of
our complex and nuanced emotional lives. Significantly, theorists, in neglecting expression, also have neglected the role of interpretation in the
formation of affective meaning and have failed to account for the many
ways in which individuals and groups are emotionally manipulated through
the unsympathetic or hostile interpretive practices of others. Feminist theorists have been particularly sensitive to the political manipulation of the

emotions and have been attracted to social constructivism as an account of affective meaning where social response plays a dominant role in constituting the personal. In Chapter 5, I expressed the concern that a theoretical commitment to the social construction of emotion, with its emphasis on conventional emotion categories, supports restrictive and ethically problematic interpretive practices. I argued that interpreting others within the narrow range of categories set by emotion types will restrict the range of affective significance that can be determined, and thus, restrict the significance to people of their own lives

The intent of this final chapter is to scrutinize further our interpretive practices by bringing a key group of critical terms associated with the expressive failure—bitterness, sentimentality, and emotionality—to greater attention. Although any of the three terms in which I have an interest can characterize a single expressive act, they are more often used as trait words that to characterize emoters on the basis of how we express ourselves, and they often characterize us in ways that imply that we need no longer be taken seriously.

In Chapter 2, I referred to bitterness, sentimentality, and emotionality as "diseases of the affections." There I made the case that expressive criticisms such as sentimentality are at the same time criticisms of the feelings expressed. They suggest that on the basis of the way someone expresses her feelings, her emotional nature is unhealthy and not, for instance, that she's simply acted or overreacted in inappropriate ways on some occasions. I am interested now in how these criticisms also are strategies of interpretive dismissal. Affective significance, for many individuals and groups, is only tentatively constituted and can easily be undermined. Perhaps sometimes an individual deserves the disregard that comes with being characterized as bitter or sentimental; my concern, however, is in isolating the strategic political use of these terms.

I choose the term "being dismissed" to capture the nuance of being told to leave the room before a conversation starts or being treated like a piece of furniture while it is going on. I shall regard being dismissed as when what we do or say, as assessed by what we would have described as our intentions in that situation, is either not taken seriously or not regarded at all in the context in which it is meant to have its effect. This definition is a counterfactual roughing-in of a kind of situation where the power of interpreters to help determine the situation may render our intentions unrecoverable and opaque. Put more simply, if no one takes my anger seriously by making any attempt to account for his or her behavior or to change it, but, instead, characterizes me as upset and oversensitive, I may be unsure, in retrospect, of how best to describe my behavior. I am interested in a particularly duplicitous kind of dismissal that does not dismiss women and others for having emotions, but characterizes our emotional lives as unhealthy, attempting to limit our ways of acting in the world, and, consequently, our effects on the world.

The analysis of bitterness, sentimentality, and emotionality that follows has evident continuity with the feminist work described in Chapter 5. However, it focuses much more strongly on the concept of expression. In the final section of this chapter, I return to the problem of concealment.

BITTERNESS AND THE POLITICS OF EXPRESSION

The accusation of bitterness implicitly acknowledges that a great many people have never been granted the social goods likely to lead to the luxury of cultivating sympathetic emotional lives. Bitterness does not always involve gender as a salient determinant of who is most likely to be accused. The angry disadvantaged of a society—visible minorities, aboriginals, the working class, the disabled, the ill, the divorced, and the old—are all targets of this critique. I wish to discuss bitterness to focus the role of uptake in affective experience and the relation of uptake to accountability for expressive failure. I use as counterpoint Audre Lorde's speeches on anger and Lynne McFall's "What's Wrong with Bitterness?," a so far lonely contribution to this particular diagnosis of emotional ill health.

McFall initially defines bitterness as "a refusal to forgive and forget. It is to maintain a vivid sense of the wrongs one has been done, to recite one's angry litany of loss long past the time others may care to listen or sympathize. 'You're so bitter' is condemnation, never praise . . . designed to silence the sufferer" (McFall, 146). In "The Uses of Anger: Women Responding to Racism" and "Eye to Eye: Black Women, Hatred, and Anger," Audre Lorde does not mention bitterness. She does, however, recite a litany of angers fueled by racist incidents neither forgotten nor forgiven. She speaks of "a symphony of anger" ("The Uses of Anger," 129), "a molten pond," and "net of rage" ("Eye to Eye," 145), the weight of her anger, her fear of it, her "sisters of Color who . . . tremble their rage under harness" ("The Uses of Anger," 127), the energy of her anger, her use of it, and the reasons for it: "Something's going on here I do not understand, but I will never forget it. Her eyes. The flared nostrils. The hate" ("Eye to Eye," 148). "I will never forget" is a commitment, a declaration of intent, and sometimes a threat—never simply a prediction.

Is Lorde angry or bitter? What makes the difference? Who has the authority to make the designation? And what might their motives be? I shall assume, for this discussion, that an expression categorized as bitterness begins its life at some point as intended anger, and I limit my analysis to expressions such as Lorde's where it is anger, and not some other feeling, that is clearly intended. I am interested in how bitterness distorts intended anger. McFall's definition of bitterness contains a strong focus on the communicative nature of the encounter. Bitterness seems to be a particular mode of expression—the recounting of incidents of injury—only in a certain context of interpretation—one in which people no longer care to listen. Both the mode of expression and the failure of uptake combine to form bitterness. We do not typically call people holding bombs bitter. They are expressing their anger so forcefully that we cannot afford not to give them our attention. Furthermore, people whose anger receives uptake are not, on that occasion at least, bitter. They are, instead, angry or even righteous.

The collaboration of a certain mode of expression (recounting of injury) with a certain mode of response (failure to listen) forms bitterness. Although if we encounter this mode of response often enough, we may call ourselves bitter, even privately and silently bitter, it is, at least, not easy to define bitterness apart from the public conditions of its formation: the performance of actions received in a particular way. However, "You're just bitter" is not a designation that characterizes mutual failure in a communicative situation. It is rather a condemnation of one of the people in that situation, the person who expresses what they had, at some point, intended as anger through a recounting of incidents to those who no longer care to listen.

In assessing the potential political force of an accusation of bitterness, then, we must keep in mind the collaboration of interpreters at some point in the formation of bitterness. Bitterness is publicly formed rather than privately formed and then revealed to others. One way to characterize this collaboration is that the refusal to forgive and forget often is related to the failure of others to listen and act. The failure of others to listen may actually determine that the form of the expression counts as a refusal. For example, my intended reluctance to do something may be read as a form of stubbornness in any situation where people are unwilling to understand the reasons for my nonparticipation. And having noted the collaboration of interpreters in the public formation of bitterness, we also must understand the strategy of calling someone bitter, and how, in particular, this criticism works against those most likely to be accused.

By placing responsibility for the failure of a communicative encounter on the expresser, the challenge of bitterness both ignores the collaboration of the interpreter and, significantly, lessens her responsibility for continuing the encounter. The not caring or no longer caring to listen, which helps determine what is a case of bitterness, becomes a reason or excuse for not listening through a critique of the mode of expression: "I speak out of direct and particular anger at an academic conference, and a white woman says, 'Tell me how you feel but don't say it too harshly or I cannot hear you.' But is it my manner that keeps her from hearing, or the threat of a message that her life may change?" (Lorde, "The Uses of Anger," 125) The interpreter may, as Lorde's critic does, defend her withdrawal by suggesting that the same feelings could be formed in quite a different manner, that Lorde could express anger while doing nothing harsh, and that this is a reasonable condition of the interpreter's continued participation. But certain modes of expression may, of course, be necessary for something to count as anger.

The further obvious strategic force to "You're so bitter" is to block the strategy of anger by shifting both attention away from blameworthy behavior to the mode of expressing blame and the responsibility from the people who could do something about the blameworthy behavior to the expresser herself, who is now meant to account for *her* behavior. The expresser cannot account for or defend her intended anger, however, because her interpreters are no longer listening. "You're so bitter" is meant to be not challenging, but silencing.

We are left with the following problem: should we ever, for ourselves or others, accept the shift in accusation or responsibility that comes with the critique of bitterness, given both the collaboration of interpreters in the formation of this response and the mechanism of silencing that is the goal of the critique? We can only generalize so far; we all know individuals in positions of exceptional privilege who are angry at their lot, and it is the rightful burden of the privileged to make a strong case that their dissatisfactions are worth the time and energy of others. I think, however, that for most people, there is good reason to resist the shift. My concern diverges here from McFall's and does so over our different assessments of the appropriateness of the language of rationality to emotional response.

Although she recognizes that accusations of bitterness are designed to silence and often ought to be politically resisted, McFall's focus is not on whether the criticism of bitterness is itself justified. Her question is rather: in what circumstances are we justified in being and staying bitter? McFall sets two questions about an emotional attitude: "What are the facts to which it is a response?" and "Is this attitude a rational response to those facts?" (McFall, 146). My concern, phrased in a general way, is that calculating rationality may put responsibility on the individual for her attitudes or actions without offering ways of assessing that individual's situation against the political options of others. If, as I believe it to be the case, assessments of rationality are connected most deeply to questions of intelligible agency, what is not within my power to affect may not provide a rational ground for my actions or responses. That others have different powers will not provide a rationale for *my* acting in a certain way in *my* situation.

What can a woman of Color in america legitimately hope for?

> Women of Color in america have grown up within a symphony of anger, at being silenced, at being unchosen, at knowing that when we survive, it is in spite of a world that takes for granted our lack of humanness, and which hates our very existence outside of its service. (Lorde, "The Uses of Anger," 129)

McFall considers bitterness a rational response to the frustration of important and legitimate hopes where a hope is not legitimate if it is patently false, that is, extremely unlikely to be realized. Once the critique of bitterness is given legitimacy—once we say we are tired of this angry litany and you are bitter, it shifts the burden of proof onto you to defend the legitimacy of your hopes. But is it legitimate for you to hope for a sort of treatment you realize you will never get and who has the authority to decide which hopes are legitimate? If the legitimacy of a hope is connected to the likelihood of its realization, then many of the frustrated hopes that lead to the intended anger characterized as bitterness may get categorized as illegitimate hopes. For this reason, we are better off in blocking the criticism than in internalizing this description of our attitude and trying to defend our bitterness, and we should block this especially for people most susceptible to the criticism of bitterness, for this is where it does its most pernicious work.

The criticism of bitterness is most powerful against people whose resources for expressing anger are limited to recounting injury in the hope that others will listen, people who are not in a position to influence politicians, bring lawsuits, make threats, or otherwise express anger irresistibly. The criticism works to maintain this impoverishment of resources because, once a group is dismissed as bitter, others feel under little obligation to work for their empowerment. The particulars of the critique also have their greatest efficacy against the most disempowered. The refusal to forgive is the refusal to break the chain of consequences instituted by another's actions. The bitter are accused of blocking the goodwill that would be exercised toward them if they were not bitter, and thus of further disadvantaging the group to which they belong: "When women of Color speak out of the anger that laces so many of our contacts with white women, we are often told that we are 'creating a mood of hopelessness,' 'preventing white women from getting past guilt' or 'standing in the way of trusting communication and action'" (Lorde, "The Uses of Anger,"

131–32). Both judgment and motives in bringing complaint are thus called into question, and this may lead to a state of paralyzing political doubt. Finally, the accusation of bitterness not only refuses to grant authority to judgments of wrongdoing but also refuses to grant authority to what counts for others as significant memory. Those most likely to be called bitter, moreover, belong to groups that already have the least support and validation for their personal memories and group history, groups for whom actively not forgetting may be the only way to establish a sense of history. The accusation of bitterness may further undermine the struggle for group memory by failing again to provide the uptake that leaves the recounting of incidents established as public record.

Lorde's speeches are angry and not bitter, but I hope my discussion has given some indication of the political fragility of this collaborative achievement. The criticism of bitterness is a powerful political tool that can be used to persuade people that the importance of how they view their lives, as marked by what is recalled and recounted as significant, is of dismissable interest to others. Anyone who speaks from and for an oppressed group can expect to encounter the criticism at its most brutely political. Emma LaRoque, in the preface to an anthology of Native Canadian women's writings, speaks of being a Native author before the days when what Natives had to say about their own lives secured any uptake:

> The interplay between audience reception and publishing cannot be minimized. As one of those earlier Native writers, I experienced and studied what might be called the Native-voice/white-audience dynamic. The interactions were often poignant. On another level, we were again rendered voiceless no matter how articulate we were. Apparently unable to understand or accept the truth of our experiences and perceptions, many white audiences, journalists, and critics resorted to racist techniques of psychologically labelling and blaming us. We were psychologized as "bitter," which was equated with emotional incapacitation, and once thus dismissed we did not have to be taken seriously. (LaRoque, xvi–xvii)

Whether the members of subordinate groups can reclaim anger, whether, in particular, they can get angry in the right way at the right time to the right people so that what they are expressing *is* anger, does not depend solely on the actions of these individuals. Viewing the feminist fight for anger in the light of insights about the crucial role of interpretation in affective encounters suggests that in the fight for situations in which our responses are taken seriously and have efficacy, we must deal with the techniques of interpretive dismissal as much as with our own reluctance to get angry. We may try to be angry through our actions and simply not succeed. The very same actions may succeed as angry actions in a different interpretive context.

I hope to emphasize, through this analysis of bitterness, that the model of interpretation I have developed is useful in understanding some of the political complexities of situations of expressive failure. I have previously argued that as feelings are formed through expression, people can exercise restrictive control over our feelings through controlling our acts of expression and thus dismiss or diminish the possibilities for finding or creating significance in our lives. They can do so in at least two ways: (1) there may be an unequal distribution of the social resources that we use to give form to our feelings. It's important to remember that opportunities for action are such a resource. For example, if I am so moved by the plight of the Tin Man that I wish to leave for Oz immediately, and I do not have the opportunity to take this action, my compassion cannot take a particular form. It may become a kind of mere sentimental wishfulness. (2) People have considerable power as interpreters of our acts of expression and may interpret these acts restrictively.

Diagnoses of bitterness—and, as I shall argue below, sentimentality and emotionality—as a sort of persistent critical uptake to emotional expression seem to serve both of the above purposes at once. They are complex attributions that both depend on and encourage a gendered and/or otherwise unequal distribution of expressive resources. They are used to interpret our expressions narrowly and critically as always either being on the edge of excess or already excessive; they are attempts to limit the range of our expressive acts and to destroy our confidence in the possible success of those acts. Furthermore, bitterness, sentimentality, and emotionality disguise their own operation by suggesting that expressive failure lies with the individual. If the individuation of feeling, however, is a collaborative undertaking, the hypothesis that expressive failure is the responsibility of the person who is trying to express herself ought to be made to bear the burden of proof.

CO-OPTING GENDER: SENTIMENTALITY AND EMOTIONALITY

Kant described the women of his time as creatures of "many sympathetic sensations, good-heartedness and compassion," as well as "very delicate feelings in regard to the least offence" (Kant, quoted in Mahowald, 194). This assessment captures perfectly the sense that to have an emotional life as a woman, to be an ideal woman, in fact, always means to be edging the excessive sensitivity that is a ground for dismissability. But many women have never been regarded as fit for the ideal that I characterize as "the

Kantian feminine," an ideal of a woman formed by white race and upper-class privilege and applicable mainly to such women. I refer to these women as "Kantian women." As bitterness may be used to dismiss those who fall outside the Kantian feminine, diagnoses of sentimentality and emotionality may corset those who fall within it. I used bitterness to discuss the public, collaborative nature of individuating feeling and noted that bitterness has its greatest efficacy as criticism against those who have the fewest resources for expressing anger. Using the framework derived from this discussion, I will use sentimentality and emotionality to show further how strategies of interpretive dismissal can both play on and promote restrictions in the range of resources that we have for communicating and acting on what, for us, is of significance.

I begin by making some uncontentious remarks about gender, expressive resource distribution, and the link between expressive resources and diseases of the affections. My remark on gender is brief. Women are encouraged to express their gender partly through various forms of women's work: for those of us under the sign of the Kantian feminine, this work is primarily nurturance that involves finding the lives of those close to us of great significance and thus, feeling for others. Men are encouraged to express their gender through men's work, whatever form this may take. Among the many types of things we can express, we can express our gender.

I have described expression as the articulation of our psychological lives through various resources. I have phrased it in this way partly to raise questions of access. Moreover, I argued in Chapter 2 that feelings involve a wide range of resources for articulation. We can express the same kind of feeling in many ways. Arguably, the successful expression of feeling also requires a wide range of resources. For example, the successful expression of anger may require resources that can move others to effect change, and what resources are efficacious may vary with circumstances. The presence or absence of kinds of expressive resources also corresponds to gendered diseases of the affections, sentimentality and emotionality. That expressive resources are differentially distributed between women and men suggests that diseases of the affections are primarily a political category of criticism.

We can see this connection between resources and gender and expressive criticism if we limit ourselves, quite crudely, to involuntary but controllable response, action, and language, as three broad categories of potentially expressive behavior and inquire into their historical relation to gender. We can see that Kantian women have been encouraged not to suppress involuntary response, but instead, been licensed and encouraged to express themselves by blushing, crying, smiling, and through a range of refined bodily and facial gesture. Their range of public action, however, has been limited, as has their access to public institutions that offer sophisticated expressive resources in the form both of participation within the institution (e.g., the art world) and in the powerful metaphorical discourse associated with the institution (e.g., the law, the military, athletics). Men have not been encouraged toward involuntary response and many have been granted the access to actions and institutions denied to women.

The restriction of feminine resources has opened the way to criticisms of sentimentality and emotionality, both of which imply that a mode of expression is indicative of an unhealthy emotional life. *Emotionality* as an assessment of expression seems directly connected to involuntary response. Those women accused of it are thought to betray emotion through voice, gesture, or other bodily reactions, and the feminine behavior that is first encouraged is later interpreted as reactive and symptomatic rather than initiatory, deliberative, and significant. In addition, certain bodily responses, especially tears, can express a range of emotions from joy to rage. The difficulty lies in discovering which emotion is being expressed. I will discuss this in more detail later. *Sentimentality* seems directly connected to action as an expressive resource. Many feelings are expressed through action. Some feelings of great importance to the Kantian feminine—compassion and love, for example—arguably must be expressed through action to be taken as genuine. In "Sentimentality," an article I have already discussed in Chapter 2, Michael Tanner offers an analysis of sentimentality as involving action not appropriately governed by the nature of the occasion. To criticize someone, then, for sentimentality, should require that that person have the opportunity to act appropriately. I shall argue that the connection between sentimentality and the lack of occasion for appropriate action is very complex and affects precisely those emotions—compassion, for example—that require active expression to be genuine.

If the perception of bitterness dismisses what is of significance, accusations of sentimentality and emotionality control what can be of significance. I believe that sentimentality and emotionality require a slightly different framework of analysis from bitterness, which is more straightforwardly dismissive. Like bitterness, sentimentality and emotionality may be used as criticisms of particular acts of expression or of the people who are expressing themselves. In general, like terms denoting virtues and vices (generous, courageous, licentious, etc.), they range both over acts and the character of the person performing these acts. Aristotle does not take up the virtues and vices of emotional expression, and, in the end, I think a virtue analysis is not adequate for these terms, but it is helpful to regard them initially as something like virtue or vice terms. There are at least three advantages to regarding them in this way: (1) we may contemplate whether the use of these terms suggests that our ways of expression are excessive, defective, or just about right for meeting the objectives of our activities. In this case, the general description of the activity is the articulation of significance. (2) Terms for virtues and vices do not arise independently of what a community values, and so a virtue-based framework will encourage us to contemplate these terms in their critical political use. (3) The activity over which these terms range, expression, requires collaborative individuation for its success, but the terms are applied primarily to persons, and to the actions and moral characters of these persons. They are thus terms that can easily be used in the service of political manipulation. Like bitterness, they assign personal responsibility for the failures of public interaction and can be used to mystify the nature of this interaction and the social stake in its outcome. And, in fact, sentimentality and emotionality operate fairly duplicitously.

Consider:

It is generally agreed that there is something unwholesome about sentimentality: it would certainly be a mistake to think it a virtue. But just what sentimentality is and why it is objectionable is something of a mystery. (Jefferson, 519)

[I]t seems to be all but agreed that sentimentality is no virtue even if it is not, like cruelty or hypocrisy, intrinsically vicious. Something is wrong with sentimentality; the only question is, what is it that is wrong? . . . I will argue that there is nothing wrong with sentimentality. (Solomon, "In Defense of Sentimentality," 305)

These remarks call for some detective work about the nature of these critical terms. Sentimentality and emotionality are particularly interesting because of their doubled nature, their ambiguous status as critical terms. Robert Solomon refers to "sentimentality" as a quasi-ethical term. Sentimentality is never a wholly positive characterization. Mark Jefferson is right that it is clearly not a virtue. Put into an Aristotelian framework, both sentimentality and emotionality are either on the mean or they are species of excess, but it is difficult to tell which. We are unsure whether it is sufficient to criticize someone for being sentimental or whether she has to be "sentimental to a fault." Is it sufficient to criticize someone that we call her "emotional," or does she have to be overemotional?

The odd status of these terms, that they are critical terms that do not unambiguously criticize, and their tie to a distribution of expressive resources that is both encouraged and gendered suggest that these terms may be a political category of criticism of the sort that is busy condemning what it is, at the same time, somehow promoting. I have argued elsewhere that many of our virtue terms are gendered (see my "The Aristotelian Mean and the Vices of Gender"). When this is the case, certain characteristics can be promoted as virtues for one gender and condemned as vices for the other. This does not quite account for the status of sentimentality or emotionality, for neither is clearly a virtue, but I intend to pursue this kind of analysis as far as it can be taken.

Sentimentality has received more attention than emotionality. Remarks on this condition are scattered through literary theory and philosophy, and recently there have been a number of philosophical articles on the subject that maintain, as their touchstone, the article by Tanner. (See Tanner, Jefferson, Solomon ("In Defense"), and Midgley.)

The attention sentimentality has received focuses on its history as a critical term that went through a rapid transformation, from a rise in the eighteenth century as a term of praise for a refined emotional life to its fall in the mid-nineteenth century to a term of ethical and aesthetic condemnation, a time that coincides with the rise of the Kantian feminine. The period of sentimentality's decline as praise also coincides exactly with the rise of women novelists. In the introduction to *Great Short Works of the American Renaissance* (selections from Emerson, Thoreau, Hawthorne, Melville, and Whitman), the editor, Willard Thorp, describes the change in the period:

> The persistent self-sufficiency of these five should be viewed against a new phenomenon of the time in which they wrote—the arrival of the best-seller. . . . In 1855 Hawthorne took note of the situation in an angry letter to his publisher:
>
> America is now wholly given over to a damned mob of scribbling women, and I should have no chance of success while the public taste is occupied with their trash—and should be ashamed of myself if I did succeed. (Thorp, xi)

This historical coincidence has not been incorporated into a philosophical analysis of sentimentality.

Tanner raises a number of interesting questions about sentimentality: (1) Is it predicated of feelings or people and in what circumstances? (2) Is it a harmful quality? (3) Is there more than a contingent relationship between sentimentality and cynicism or brutality? (4) Is it a historical phenomenon? (128). He does not, however, operate within a sensitive enough political framework to be able to answer the questions he sets: "I have found it too perplexing and difficult a subject to be able to offer more than a series of loosely related thoughts" (Tanner, 138–39). In particular, Tanner does not take up the criticism of sentimentality as a local historical phenomenon, and this is a particular methodological choice:

> There is a clear danger that in attempting to locate the central aspects of sentimentality one will oscillate between dealing with specific feelings and with the people who have them, trying to get to grips with the concept by dealing with a given emotional state, and moving outwards from there into the pattern of life of a person whom we would call sentimental, and hoping this oscillation will give the impression that it is, indeed will be, a dialectical process towards understanding. It won't. (Tanner, 138–39)

If sentimentality is a criticism that has been primarily applied to a particular group of people who are patterning their lives in a particular way, we need to understand this fact to understand what kind of criticism it is, but this is one way in which the use of the term is duplicitous.

In the philosophical treatments of sentimentality specific men (or characters) often are mentioned: Lord Alfred Douglas (by Oscar Wilde), Rousseau (by James and Southey), Rudolf Hess (by Midgley), Othello and Mendelsson (by Tanner). These men not only are mentioned as illustrations of sentimentality, but also are lambasted, despite the fact that, as Solomon notes, sentimentality is thought to be common to women and its use as a term of criticism for men arose at exactly the same time that women were beginning to write novels ("In Defense," 307–8). James's criticism of Rousseau illustrates the invective at its harshest:

> There is no more contemptible type of human character than that of the . . . sentimentalist and dreamer, who spends his life in a weltering sea of sensibility and emotion, but who never does a manly concrete deed. Rousseau, inflaming all the mothers of the mothers of France, by his eloquence, to follow Nature and nurse their babies themselves, while he sent his own children to the foundling hospital, is the classic example of what I mean. (James, *Principles*, 1:125)

James goes on to caution against excessive novel reading and theater going ("[it] will produce true monsters in this line") and offers us the portrait of a Russian woman weeping over a play while her coachman freezes waiting for her. But this woman is an imagined type and not a real named individual. The man who is attacked for sentimentality is a real man. The woman, whether she is attacked, or more likely, as Solomon suggests, forgiven, is, in discussions of sentimentality, every white woman of gentle birth, or at least, no one in particular.

I believe we have a somewhat complex historical situation, and only through this situation will we understand sentimentality. It is not that Kantian women lacked opportunities for action that gives rise to the use of sentimentality as a critical notion, but that they were acting—among other things, they were writing, and in this writing they represented women expressing their emotions through action. *Little Women*, a famous sentimental novel by Louisa May Alcott, begins with the four March girls lamenting the fact that they are poor and that it won't be much of a Christmas without presents and with their father away at war. In chapter 2, titled "A Merry Christmas," they awake, and the servant Hannah informs them that a beggar has come to the door and their mother has gone off to see what is needed. She soon returns, and they greet her in chorus:

> "Merry Christmas, Marmee! Many of them! Thank you for our books; we read some and mean to, every day," they cried, in chorus.
>
> "Merry Christmas, little daughters! I'm glad you began at once and hope you will keep on. But I want to say one word before we sit down. Not far away from here lies a poor woman with a little newborn baby. Six children are huddled into one bed to keep from freezing, for they have no fire. There is nothing to eat over there; and the oldest boy came to tell me they were suffering hunger and cold. My girls, will you give them your breakfast as a Christmas present?"
>
> They were all unusually hungry, having waited nearly an hour, and for a minute no one spoke; only a minute, for Jo exclaimed impetuously:
>
> "I'm so glad you came before we began!" (Alcott, 15)

Alcott presents women acting morally, with compassion for those in serious social circumstances, and without the guidance of any man. I suggest that the political response to this type of presentation was the establishment of sentimentality as a limiting (or policing) virtue of feminine expression. It is a virtue because Kantian women are encouraged to cultivate the tender emotions—compassion, for example—for their work as nurturers. It is a limiting virtue because its use as a critical term is to imply that feminine ethical actions when they are outside the domestic sphere, and feminine literary productions, which are outside this sphere, either are not effective or are not appropriate actions, and do not have to be taken seriously. Sentimentality is a virtue of femininity, and so in men it can be condemned as a vice. It has not received an adequate political analysis because it is falsely presented as a general character defect of women for which they are accountable but can do nothing about. Finally, it does not receive an adequate philosophical analysis because philosophers look for a clear use of sentimentality as a critical term. Its status as a clear and correctable masculine vice will be more salient than its nature as a limiting virtue of feminine expression. These remarks indicate only some of the complexities of the historical circumstances in which the notion of sentimentality emerged as a critical notion in application to expressiveness.

Emotionality has received even less attention than sentimentality as a distinctive kind of criticism tied to expressive resources, although its connection to gender has never been questioned: "Although the emotionality of women is a familiar cultural stereotype, its grounding is quite shaky. Women appear to be more emotional than men because they, along with some groups of people of color, are permitted and even required to express emotion more openly" (Jaggar, 161). This passage is somewhat disturbing in its suggestion that men might maintain a protected private life of feeling. In addition, I think there is more to be said about emotionality, for, of course, anger, the emotion that women have fought so hard for, is very freely expressed by many men.

Like sentimentality, emotionality is a limiting expressive virtue of feminine expression, though one whose imperatives seem to operate more independently of class and race. Women who are not emotional are cold. Women who are emotional are expressing themselves in such a way as to be dismissable. The important feature of emotionality is how women become dismissable. Emotionality is popularly connected to involuntary response as an expressive resource. As remarked, certain bodily responses associated with emotionality, tears notoriously, can be used to express joy, sorrow, frustration, shame, or any range of feelings. They thus give an emotional life the appearance of contingency by suggesting that nothing is any more important than anything else, because there are no discriminations in behavior that mark the importance. Insofar as women cry a lot, they cannot be reliably held to distinguish the important from the trivial. As a student pointed out to me, the deliberate vagueness of the term, which lumps all emotions together, negates the necessity for any specific uptake that would help individuate a feeling, thus promoting what it condemns.

In actual critical use the insinuation of emotionality does not remain tied to involuntary response but can be used to suggest that a woman always lacks control over her emotional life, as evidenced by nearly any manner of expression. James Dickey's review of *To Bedlam and Part Way Back* by Anne Sexton begins: "Anne Sexton's poems so obviously come out of deep painful sections of the author's life that one's literary opinions scarcely seem to matter; one feels tempted to drop them furtively into the nearest ashcan, rather than to be caught with them in the presence of so much naked suffering" (Dickey, in McClatchy, 117). Dickey, as a reviewer, is in precisely the right position to give certain expressive acts the special critical uptake that will help form for all of us Sexton's insights into her life and madness. Instead, he does not just negate the sophistication of Sexton's expressive resources, he, in fact, pretends that she is not using any special expressive resources but is symptomatically betraying an emotional life she cannot control.

I conclude, tentatively, that both sentimentality and emotionality are limiting expressive virtues of femininity. They police expression through the development or limitation of certain expressive resources that will, at the same time, allow for the dismissal of what is significant to women about our own lives when this significance is a violation of the constraints on gender performance: when we express ourselves, we must do so within the constraints of gender. The pervasiveness of these criticisms of women's affective lives suggests strongly that women are constrained to express gender roles when they express feeling.

Emotionality and sentimentality give the fight for control of anger a special importance. Anger is an emotion that requires judgment and action and is associated with a powerful range of cultural metaphors. Its control can stand as a symbol for access to a range of expressive resources that are so finely discriminated and object-directed that they cannot lead to certain expressive criticisms. But one's intended anger can still, of course, be categorized as bitterness.

HIGH NOON: THE POSSIBILITY OF INARTICULATENESS

This study can be summarized by its denial of the possibility of an inarticulate expressive life that is compatible with a well-articulated life of feeling. Without acts of expression that are publicly interpretable, we have no feelings. Even when we do express ourselves, the difficulties in the interpretation of affect will often lead to affective lives that are dominated by frustration and confusion. This is especially the case when people cannot secure adequate uptake or do not have the power to determine how the occasions of their lives are viewed.

The necessity of expression to the individuation of feeling has been obscured by a long tradition of theory that has concentrated on the classic emotions. This tradition of theory, traced in Chapter 1, has assumed that emotions can be recognized by set patterns of behavior and thus has not investigated the conditions of the interpretability of affect or the special significance of affect as an explanatory category. The theories of expression investigated in Chapter 2 assumed that feelings were individuated prior to expression, again obscuring the conceptual relation between feeling and expression. In this study, I have argued for the dependence of all feelings, including the classic emotions, on publicly interpretable acts of expression.

The importance of expression and interpretation to a theory of affect also has been mystified by an ideology that holds out the promise of a protected private life without the need of expression. This is the myth of private emotional experience: "This is a study of emotional experience. I am not directly and in the first instance concerned with emotional behavior, emotional expression, or the symptomatology of emotion" (Koch, 60). This myth of emotional experience without emotional expression is obviously very much with us. Feminist theorists, among others, have understood how affective meanings are subject to interpretation and control by the people to whom we express ourselves. They have been, in my view, wrongly, attracted toward social constructivism on the assumption that allowing our emotions to be open social constructions is the only alternative to buying into the myth of an unproblematic first-person authority and privileged access to our feelings. When we accept these myths, we fail to understand how affective meanings are subject to control and manipulation by others. I have argued that epistemic privacy versus social constructivism is a false set of options that confuses private with the personal. Nevertheless, I fully agree that first-person authority and privileged access are well-held myths that have never been applied to women in practice. A private life of feeling, although a conceptual impossibility has, however, been a myth that men have actually been encouraged to live out, at least in the American West.

I conclude this study by taking up the interesting question of the possibility of inarticulateness, a disease of the affections that is deeply involved in Western ideologies as a positive characteristic of masculinity, but should not, on the model of feelings I have been defending, be a possible affective style. To comment on inarticulateness as a possible expressive style, I first return to the discussion of concealment and restraint which I initiated in Chapter 2. I said at that point that Charles Taylor's work on desire indicated what was necessary for an adequate account of expressive success and failure: an understanding of our form of life as communicators as this concerns the communication of feeling. I hope, by this point, to have provided some of this account. Because affective significance is easily manipulated by the interpretive practices of others, our form of life is one where we have much to conceal.

Concealment and expressive restraint are often not only viable, but also necessary, emotional strategies. First, there are penalties, sometimes severe, for not viewing the significance of occasions as those dominant over us would have them viewed. In *Incidents in the Life a Slave Girl*, the protagonist, Linda, risks death because of her inability to conceal her anger: "He sprang upon me like a tiger, and gave me a stunning blow. It was the first time he had ever struck me; and fear did not enable me to control my anger. When I had recovered a little from the effects, I exclaimed, 'You have struck me for answering you honestly. How I despise you!'" (Jacobs, 61). The slaveowner Flint replies that she is lucky he does not kill her on the spot. Making clear the personal significance of occasions renders us vulnerable, and there are frequently good reasons for keeping this significance to ourselves.[1] Second, to hold on to the personal significance of occasions, we often have to protect our feelings from becoming confused by the response of others to them. But both types of circumstances seem to suppose that feelings can be individuated without their expression.

Are situations involving concealment and/or restraint situations where emotions are individuated independent of expression? If so, they are an obvious challenge to my theory. At the end of Chapter 2, I suggested that the dependence of affect on expression could take stronger or weaker forms and that concealment, as a phenomenon, is more likely to be associated with classic emotions than free-style feelings. The well-specified occasions of classic emotions and the conventions governing expression can lead to abilities to recognize these emotions in ourselves even when our expressions are restrained. The arguments of Chapter 3, the discussion of the importance of an individual's history, gave further explanation of our ability to recognize both emotions and feelings by discussing their habitual development over a history of occasions in a person's life. Our prior involvement in situation types may easily make our recognition of a situation, along with our impulses toward expression, sufficient grounds for knowing what we feel. And at points in Chapters 4 and 5, I argued that securing adequate uptake on some occasions protects our responses from being confuted by others on other occasions and may allow us some confidence about what we feel independently of our acts of expression.

I also took the phenomenon of concealment to support my concentration on expression. Concealment is a contrastive notion to expression. To conceal a feeling is by definition to *not express* it, to prevent something from becoming manifest rather than attempting to make it manifest. Concealment is given its significance within an account of expression and interpretation. Cases where we individuate through concealment or restraint are cases where we have particular expressive opportunities and behave in certain ways related to these opportunities. I do not restrain

1. The way in which Elizabeth Spelman phrases a similar point in "On Treating Persons as Persons," is that to treat others maximally as persons is to attend to their self-conceptions and because of the ways in which such knowledge of us makes us vulnerable, we do not always want to be treated maximally as persons.

myself from yelling at you when you are not there. Much of the action that Cyrano takes in *Cyrano de Bergerac* is action taken to restrain and conceal his feeling for Roxane. I concluded that there is some behavior on which the existence and individuation of a feeling depend. If Cyrano neither acts to express nor acts to conceal his love for Roxane, he would not love Roxane.

I have two further reflections on concealment. First, I was and am cautious about how possible or lasting one's confidence can be in the nature of concealed emotion without some continuing history of expressive success. Cyrano is eloquent, articulate, and familiar with love. We can well accept that he knows that he loves Roxane even while he restrains and conceals that love. A brilliant cinematic representation of the deeper costs of concealment is *The Remains of the Day*. The butler who has devoted his life to the service of the household cannot express love to the housekeeper, although he evidently values her dearly. On each occasion where we think he might express love, he conceals his feelings and talks to her instead of their household duties. The love in this story never develops, never clearly becomes love, because it is too repressed and inchoate. We can see that it could have been love. By the end of the narrative the butler, perhaps, also knows only this much.

Second, an understanding of affective restraint is interestingly complicated, in ways I can only point at, by how pervasive concealment is in the affective lives of many or most of us. Here I return to Taylor's account of the relation of expressive to the individuation of desire. Faced with the example of unconscious desire, Taylor claims that part of what we mean by an unconscious desire it that our awareness of the desire is distorted, the desire is "self-unavowable." We do not mean, however, that the desire is unexpressed: "What was utterly unmanifested . . . couldn't be a desire. (And it is difficult to see how it could play the explanatory role of desire.)" (Taylor, 85). These are related points for Taylor. Our explanatory (and self-determining) vocabulary of desire has arisen and been able to arise because, in what Taylor refers to as the "normal or basic situation," desire produces "unreluctant and unconstrained action." My desires are identified and characterized by such action, and it is the existence of this basic kind of situation that explains why my desires are fit for explaining my actions in the first place.

In "Feeling and Expression," Stuart Hampshire argues that we would not have the category of feeling without the ability to restrain our impulses: suppression of these tendencies gives rise to a feeling vocabulary by isolating the tendencies as possible objects of attention. Hampshire's point has some force for the category of desire. We would, perhaps, not have such an articulate language of desire without the suppression of our tendencies to act: "Desire and action are not separable components in the basic situation. . . . [but] begin to come apart when I am constrained from action. Then the awareness of the desire can take the form merely of a formulation to myself, or to you, of what I want; or a sense of unease, perhaps" (Taylor, 86). But I agree with Taylor that the explanatory use we make of this category points to unconstrained expression as a basic or normal situation for desire and other cases as parasitic on this normal case.

Hampshire's point seems to have a different sort of force for feeling. I have acknowledged that in our emotional lives, the phenomenon of concealment is extremely pervasive. Hampshire presents this as an unproblematic observation universal in its application to socialized adults. We can see, given, the disruptive potential of many of the classic emotions, why this would be the case.

> He was strangling Peterson to the accompaniment of Grieg's Piano Concerto in A Minor, Opus 16, third movement and it wasn't a nightmare. The music from the adjoining show room was thumping through his head, beating at his heart, pulsating through his fingers as his hands tightened around Peterson's scrawny neck while the words came screaming out of his mouth. And the bastard wouldn't stop talking. . . .
> The violence of his reaction to Peterson, albeit inwardly expressed, appalled him. (Gill, 7)

However, concealment is especially pervasive in the lives of those for whom significance conflicts with dominant ways of viewing the world. Moreover, as well as being a necessity for devalued groups in our culture, concealment is an explicit normatively imposed constraint on dominant groups through exhortations to rationality and emotional stoicism. Its desirability as an expressive strategy is further buttressed through the presentation of emotion as always potentially uncontrollable. Finally, the role of affect as an explanatory category, the understanding of personal significance, give us considerable latitude as interpreters to find significance in the unexpressed. Thus, we cannot have any security here that unconstrained expression is the normal or basic case. I believe these insights into the importance of concealment should lead us back, a final time, to reflecting on the importance of expressive resources. How do we harmonize a need for expressive success with the reality of the many constraints on our expressive opportunities?

Hampshire remarks that: "entry into . . . [an] adult form of life . . . includes among other things, the habit of deliberately controlling the natural expression of inclination, and includes also a growing knowledge of conventions of speech and behavior. It is characteristic of the more refined concepts, which we use to distinguish between one sentiment and another, that the subject's own avowals are a necessary part of the condition of their application" ("Feeling and Expression," 19). Hampshire's point is that the inappropriateness of some expressive resources will find part of its effect in the development of other resources. I have argued that there is no special group of resources that either uniquely characterizes expression as an activity or that helps delimit the expression of affect. The notion of natural expression, theoretically dominant since Darwin in discussions of emotion, has done much to inhibit our understanding of the complexities of affective expression. I would suggest that it is partly because restraint and concealment are such a dominant part of our affective lives that our resources for expressing affect are so interestingly diverse and that we are so dependent on our interpreters. We can see the value of an interpretive approach to affect by looking at purported cases of nonexpressiveness.

The philosophical and political views that underlie the positive treatment of inarticulateness as a version of emotional stoicism are views that this study has criticized: (1) a commitment to the individuation of psychological states, independently of expressive activity; and also, interestingly, (2) a rejection of interpretability. The consequence of accepting both (1) and (2) is a total distrust of either a shared or an interpretable language as a possible expressive resource. I quote from Emerson, Thoreau, and Tocqueville to illustrate the influential rhetoric that made these views popular:

[T]he reformers summon conventions and vote and resolve in multitude. Not so, O friends! will the God deign to enter and inhabit you, but by a method precisely the reverse. It is only as a man puts off all foreign support and stands alone that I see him to be strong and to prevail. He is weaker by every recruit to his banner. (Emerson, 169)

If we would enjoy the most intimate society with that in each of us which is without or above, being spoken to, we must not only be silent, but commonly so far apart bodily that we cannot possibly hear each other's voice in any case. (Thoreau, 208)

[N]ot only does democracy make each forget his ancestors, but it hides his descendants and separates his contemporaries from him; it throws him back forever upon himself alone and threatens in the end to confine him entirely within the solitude of his own heart. (de Tocqueville, 106)

Assumptions about the private nature of our psychological lives, combined with a distrust of language, both foster and are fostered by a commitment to individualism in politics where those who would interpret you or speak for you will only misrepresent you. This may seem like the picture of a life where, without the resources to articulate significance, a life cannot have significance, and so no feelings whatsoever. But a life where neither language nor involuntary response can be used to express feeling may still be a life of action.

When we interpret art, we do so through the limitations of an expressive medium. This is rarely our strategy with affect, but it seems to me appropriate in this case to ask what the medium of articulation could be that makes it possible for white Western men to have confidence in the significance of their own lives. Certainly some of this is provided by the enormous burden women and persons of color adopt as interpreters and nurturers (see Bartky, "Feeding Egos and Tending Wounds," and Tronto); the rest, I suggest, is provided by performing their gender through work:

> As we become permanent drunkards by so many separate drinks, so we become saints in the moral, and authorities and experts in the practical and scientific spheres, by so many separate acts and hours of work. Let no youth have any anxiety about the upshot of his education, whatever the line of it may be. If he keep faithfully busy each hour of the working day, he may safely leave the final result to himself. He can with perfect certainty count on waking up some fine morning, to find himself one of the competent ones of his generation. (James, *Principles* 1:127)

In these remarks, made very near the passage on sentimentality quoted in the preceding section, the aesthetic sphere has disappeared from James's thought. Part of what makes the notion of living such a inarticulate life possible, even appealing, is that the masculine gender is expressed through men's work and that the importance of lives is acknowledged and shared through a mutual understanding of the importance of men's work. This work guarantees significance and community without the need for alternative expressive resources.

The expression of significance through work has been a dominant theme of Western American novels and films. In Jack Shaffer's classic, *Shane,* the protagonist, a gunman, expresses gratitude, loyalty, and the desire profoundly to change his own life through helping the homesteader who feeds him dinner remove an old stubborn stump from the land. The homesteader participates in the work to acknowledge Shane's gratitude, to mark the profound changes that are endangering his homestead, and to show that, though he does not need help in protecting his land, he will accept Shane's. The two men do not speak for hours of work, but, as the novel develops, it is clear that each has successfully interpreted the other. They communicate, so we are asked to imagine, complex degrees of significance through these seemingly inarticulate acts.[2]

I believe that we can understand inarticulateness as an expressive style through attention to resources. However, the limited way in which affect can be expressed within this style has the unfortunate consequence that these men's lives risk losing significance to them when they are separated from their work. This consequence, also often presented in American film and literature, displays the poverty of work as a sole expressive resource.

In the classic movie *High Noon* (1952), Will Kane, played by an aging and tired-looking Gary Cooper, is retiring as town Marshal to marry Amy (Grace Kelly), a Quaker. They plan to leave town and run a store, trading men's work for women's work, and western masculinity for Quaker pacifism and community. As they celebrate their marriage, Will receives a telegram warning that Frank Miller, a man he sent to prison, is coming back on the noon train. In American westerns, the train comes in to destroy the illusion that parallel lines never meet. Your destiny will always find you. Will and Amy leave town, but before they get far, Will turns back to face Miller.

The movie has little dialogue. The significant moments occur when Amy, or the various townspeople who are no longer in community with Will, confront Will about why he is coming back to what is no longer his job. He cannot say why it is important to him.

> Amy: "I don't understand any of this."
> Will: "Well I don't have time to tell you."
> Amy: "Then don't go back, Will."
> Will: "I've got to—that's the whole thing."

Amy claims that Miller was part of a job, that Will's job is over, and that she still doesn't understand. When Will replies that he is the same man, with or without his badge, Amy says, "That isn't so." Every time someone confronts Will about why he has come back to what isn't his job, he simply says "I've got a lot to do," or "I haven't got time," or "If you don't know, I can't explain it to you," or, finally, "I don't know."

2. We may have some skepticism about these possibilities. In the contemporary Western film, *Tender Mercies* (1983), Mac Sledge, the character played by Robert Duvall, expresses his love for Rosa Lee (Tess Harper) through the work he does around her motel. His stoic masculine character, all action, no talk, and no tears, provoked film critic Pauline Kael to remark with a cheery lack of deference that Duvall should simply wear a T-shirt in the movie, reading: "Life Makes Me Wince." (Kael, 480). Kael was pointing to the defects of hard work as a sole expressive resource.

If a large part of expressing the Kantian feminine is to express feeling, then there is a social stake in expressiveness as an activity, and our critical vocabulary will extend to this activity. If to express the masculine gender is to share work, it may appear as if there is not the same stake in social control and, therefore, that the autonomy of an affective life that is articulate, but unexpressed, is left intact. But if my view of the dependence of our affective lives on our expressive lives is correct, this life is neither unexpressed nor free of social control. An ideology of restraint and concealment, as one of the ideologies that govern affective significance in this culture, controls what can be of significance by limiting available expressive resources and by positioning some groups as the inexhaustibly sensitive interpreters to the rigidly restricted expressive practices of others.

The figures of Shane and Will Kane are meant to move us deeply. Bitterness, sentimentality, and emotionality are terms of interpretive dismissal. They contrast interestingly to inarticulateness, a categorization that suggests, quite explicitly, a poverty of expressive resources that is no fault of the individual, but, in fact, challenges the interpreter to be highly sensitive to the intended effects of behavior in conveying significance.

We would do well to keep the contrast between types of expressive failure in mind when we are subject to or witness to the charge of individual accountability that comes with criticisms of bitterness or emotionality. I hope to have done something to indicate the seriousness of this kind of criticism: there is a seriousness of critical intent elided by the very use of terms that invariably suggest overreaction on the part of the person expressing her feelings. However, because of the relation of feeling to significance, when our feelings are trivialized, ignored, systematically criticized, or extremely constrained by the poverty of our expressive resources, this situation can lead to a very serious kind of dismissal—the dismissal of the significance to a person of his or her own life, in a way that reaches down deeply into what the significance of a life can be to the person whose life it is.

APPENDIX TO CHAPTER 5

YELLOW KITCHEN GLOVES
by Michael Lynch

    i.
Dressed with an eye towards changes in the day I took
the bucks American Express disbursed for bail,
joined an affinity group on the lawn
wary of, dependent on each other, who
snapped ourselves under a rainbow
flag and the Senate portico, joined the crowd
opposite the Court.

Out of museums, in Washington again—
except as Washington's its own museum
garnering, displaying
power in its plangent colonnades, displaying
us claiming our power under these oaks
to snowfences ringing the sacred grove
of camera tripods—history in our stomachs.

    ii.
Blocks away, government and science
direct their receptionists to order morning
coffee and the day: the drugs untried, the less distasteful
viruses, and who else can they test that fights back least?
A family burnt from its home in Florida
not their department, nor is
the four-letter word no one likes pronouncing:

unspeakable once, like us, now just unspoken.
A trained arm covers my shoulder, we line up in fives,
something awful is cheering on those steps,
something awful pushes us towards it.
The shouts and shoves among our own wrenches
us apart (I want him back). A man in yellow tulle has cracked
the human wall of riot-heads.

iii.
We lift rubber-gloved fists to the sun
and the shadowy heights from which assistants
peek. We are asked to cut
to the Court's unguarded north door, get inside.
This wasn't in the plan: I wonder
if we're tricked. (I want him back.) History
now churns in my gut with Norman Mailer.

Inside the Rehnquist court, what would I do
wearing a yellow kitchen glove "for Bill"?
While we hold rank in the loud push
towards the steps, a rank of lesbians
rushes the north door, almost gets in, earns
a thousand cheers. We're cheered. I'm scared.
My glove glares back distorted from a bubble.

iv.
Face to helmet now, we're here. Another cheer
goes up. We turn to the crowd to wave
and pose and look for the three
who're holding our medicine and cash.
They're there. We turn to thrust
against the helmets lined to guard American
justice. This is it. (I want him back.)

The crush of clubs on skulls I dread
relents before it happens. The human wall
parts easily—the script was well prepared—
our little rank files through. In the protected
zone we sit encircled, quieter here
and notice a new face in our midst. Only the two
of us over forty recognize Franklin Kameny.

v.

"We're making history," the others have been saying.
They mean, "we're starting history,
nothing before today." So Hank and I
play elders, telling
Kameny's past—a tribal role he rapidly
takes over, too loudly and too long.
But cops and cameras come for us,

order us to leave, record refusals, place us
under arrest. One by one they lead us
past the looming dome, rough only with Gary
who's blind and mild, to handcuffs at the bus.
"I volunteered for overtime today," says the woman
processing me, "I thought this was a Jesse rally."
The handcuffs pinch. "Mm mm. I sho was surprise."

vi.

Among six hundred taken in that day
were thirteen Sharon Kowalskis, twenty Harvey
Milks, and one (sex unrecorded) Connie Lingus.
Justice make us outlaws, rent our bonds,
slammed doors on dying men and stubborn women,
on paralyzed women and uncowering men. Two very
dry martinis help me tell the day to Victor

but the only telling is to him named on my glove
now three weeks dead after three weeks ill.
If life moves fast in this infected world
then trials delayed—of charges or of drugs—
are trials denied. Mourning that treasures
and elegies that hold convert this day
to other arts: the pageantry of protest, televised.

vii.

Pageantry converting bedsides, or friends
beneath the windows of intensive care,
or parents who make the acquaintance of lovers
over patients toxoplasmosis wracks—
converting lament to rage (*I want him back*) and fear
to action. We want you back.

We want you all beside us on these steps,
this other dancefloor, gloved fists in the air
defying the empowered who deny
our lives and deaths, our fucking, and our hate.
We too can organize, and camp
inside whatever colonnade. We should have known
we're tough, our fist in yellow kitchen glove
transformed by the outer fingers in the air.[1]

1. Note to "Yellow Kitchen Gloves":

On October 13, 1987, a massive action of nonviolent civil disobedience took place on the steps of the United States Supreme Court. At particular issue were two recent rulings in the court system: one denying Karen Thompson access to her paralyzed lover Sharon Kowalski, and one upholding the criminalization of same-sex sodomy. Beyond the particulars, these two represented a broad complicity between the courts and other offices of American homophobia—a complicity which continues to increase the epidemic's toll.

Several weeks earlier, Washington police donned yellow rubber gloves before arresting a smaller group protesting government indifference to the epidemic. The media—which would barely cover the Supreme Court action—widely propagated the image of police in rubber gloves. In the action on October 13, protestors countered that image by wearing yellow kitchen gloves themselves. Many inscribed the gloves to friends or lovers who had died.

Franklin Kameny, founder of the Washington, D.C., Mattachine Society in 1961, led the earliest public challenges to the anti-gay policies of U.S. federal agencies.

REFERENCES

Alcott, Louisa May. *Little Women or Meg, Jo, Beth, and Amy.* Boston: Little, Brown, [1868] 1968.

Alston, William P. "Expressing." In Black, ed., 1965.

———. "Feelings." *The Philosophical Review* 78 (1969): 3–34.

Aristotle. *Nichomachean Ethics.* Trans. Sir David Ross. Oxford: Oxford University Press, 1953.

———. *The Rhetoric of Aristotle.* Trans. Lane Cooper. New York: D. Appleton, 1932.

Arnold, Magda B., ed. *The Nature of Emotion.* Harmondsworth: Penguin, 1968.

Atkinson, Brooks, ed. *The Selected Writings of Ralph Waldo Emerson.* New York: Random House, 1968.

Aune, Bruce. "On the Complexity of Avowals." In Black, ed., 1965.

Austin, John L. "Intelligent Behaviour." Review of *The Concept of Mind,* by Gilbert Ryle. *Times Literary Supplement* (1950). Rpt. in Wood and Pitcher, eds., to which citations refer, 1970.

———. "Other Minds." In Urmson and Warnock, eds., 1961.

———. "Performative Utterances." In Urmson and Warnock, eds., 1970.

Averill, James R. "The Acquisition of Emotions during Adulthood." In Harré, ed., 1986.

Bartky, Sandra. "Feeding Egos and Tending Wounds." In Bartky, 1990.

———. *Femininity and Domination: Studies in the Phenomenology of Oppression.* New York: Routledge, 1990.

———. "On Psychological Oppression." In Bartky, 1990.

———. "Shame and Gender." In Bartky, 1990.

Bass, Rick. *An Oilman's Notebook: Oil Notes.* Excerpted in Halpern, ed., to which citations refer, 1988.

Bergmann, Frithjof. "A Monologue on the Emotions." In Thomas Attig and Fred D. Miller, eds., *Understanding Human Emotions.* Bowling Green, Ohio: Bowling Green Studies in Applied Philosophy, vol. 1, 1979.

Bersani, Leo. *Homos.* Cambridge: Harvard University Press, 1995.

References

Bilgrami, Akeel. "An Externalist Account of Psychological Content." *Philosophical Topics* 15 (1987): 191–226.

Black, Max, ed. *Philosophy in America.* Ithaca: Cornell University Press, 1965.

Block, Ned, ed. *Readings in the Philosophy of Psychology.* 2 vols. Cambridge: Harvard University Press, 1980.

Browning, Frank. *The Culture of Desire: Paradox and Perversity in Gay Lives Today.* New York: Vintage Books, 1994.

Butler, Judith. "Performative Acts and Gender Constitution: An Essay in Phenomenology and Feminist Theory." In Sue-Ellen Case, ed., *Performing Feminisms: Feminist Critical Theory and Theatre.* Baltimore: Johns Hopkins University Press, 1990.

Calhoun, Cheshire. "Subjectivity and Emotion." *The Philosophical Forum* 20, no. 3 (1989): 195–210.

Calhoun, Cheshire, and Robert C. Solomon, eds. *What Is an Emotion? Classic Readings in Philosophical Psychology.* Oxford: Oxford University Press, 1984.

Campbell, Sue. "The Aristotelian Mean and the Vices of Gender." *Eidos* 6, no. 2 (1987): 177–200.

——. "Being Dismissed: The Politics of Emotional Expression." *Hypathia* 9, no. 3 (1994): 24–65.

——. "Love and Intentionality: Roxane's Choice." In Roger Lamb, ed., *Love Analyzed.* Boulder, Colo.: Westview Press, 1996.

Cannon, William B. "James-Lange Theory of Emotion: A Critical Examination and an Alternative Theory." *American Journal of Psychology* 39 (1927): 106–24.

Clarke, Stanley G. "The Emotions: Rationality without Cognitivism." *Dialogue* 25 (1986): 663–74.

Collingwood, R. G. *The Principles of Art.* Oxford: Oxford University Press, [1938] 1969.

Cornwell, Patricia. *Post-Mortem: A Kay Scarpetta, M.E., Mystery.* New York: Avon Books, 1990.

Darwin, Charles. *The Expression of the Emotions in Man and Animals.* Chicago: University of Chicago Press, [1872] 1965.

Davidson, Donald. "Actions, Reasons, and Causes." *The Journal of Philosophy* 60 (1963): 685–700. Rpt. in Davidson 1980, to which citations refer.

——. "Communication and Convention." *Synthese* 59 (1984): 3–15.

——. "The Conditions of Thought." In Johannes Brandl and Wolfgang Gombocz, eds., *The Mind of Donald Davidson.* Grazer Philosophischen Studien, Bard 36. Amsterdam: Rodopi, 1989.

——. "Epistemology Externalized." *Dialectica* 45 (1991): 191–202.

——. *Essays on Actions and Events.* Oxford: Clarendon Press, 1980.

——. "Problems in the Explanation of Action." In Philip Pettit, Richard Sylvan, and Jean Norman, eds., *Metaphysics to Morality: Essays In Honor of J. J. C. Smart.* London: Basil Blackwell, 1987.

——. "Rational Animals." *Dialectica* 36 (1982): 318–427.

——. "Three Varieties of Knowledge." In A. Philips Griffiths, ed., *A. J. Ayer: Memorial Essays.* Cambridge: Cambridge University Press, 1991.

Davies, Steven. "The Expression Theory Again." *Theoria* 52 (1986): 146–67.

Dennett, Daniel C. *Consciousness Explained.* Boston: Little, Brown, 1991.

——. *Content and Consciousness.* London: Routledge & Kegan Paul, 1969.

——. *The Intentional Stance.* Cambridge: MIT Press, 1989.

——. "Three Kinds of Intentional Psychology." In R. Healy, ed., *Reduction, Time and Reality.* Cambridge: Cambridge University Press, 1981. Rpt. in Dennett 1989, to which citations refer.

Dewey, John. *Art as Experience.* New York: Capricorn Books, [1934] 1958.

——. "A Theory of Emotion." *Psychological Review* 1 (1894): 553–69; 2 (1894): 13–52. Rpt. in *John Dewey: The Early Work, 1882–1898*, vol. 2. Carbondale: Southern Illinois University Press, 1967, to which citations refer.

Dinnerstein, Dorothy. *The Mermaid and the Minotaur.* New York: Harper & Row, 1976.

Dretske, Fred. *Explaining Behavior: Reasons in a World of Causes.* Cambridge: MIT Press, 1988.

Ducasse, Curt. *The Philosophy of Art.* New York: Dover, [1929] 1966.

Emerson, Ralph Waldo. "Nature." In Atkinson, ed., 1968, to which citations refer.

——. "Self-Reliance." In Atkinson, ed., 1968, to which citations refer.

Ferguson, Ann. "Is There a Lesbian Culture?" In Jeffner Allen, ed., *Lesbian Philosophies and Cultures.* Albany: State University of New York Press, 1990.

Fodor, Jerry. "Methodological Solipsism Considered as a Research Strategy in Cognitive Psychology." In *Representations: Philosophical Essays on the Foundations of Cognitive Science.* Cambridge: MIT Press, 1981.

Freud, Sigmund. *Civilization and Its Discontents.* Trans. and Ed. James Strachey. New York: Norton and Norton, 1961.

Fridlund, Alan. "Darwin's Anti-Darwinism in *Expression of the Emotions in Man and Animals.*" In K. T. Strongman, eds., *International Review of Studies in Emotion.* vol. 2. John Wiley, 1992.

Frye, Marilyn. "A Note on Anger." In *The Politics of Reality: Essays in Feminist Theory.* Freedom, Calif.: Crossing Press, 1983.

Garden, Nancy. *Annie on My Mind.* New York: Farrar, Straus & Giroux, 1982.

Gill, B. M. *Dying to Meet You.* London: Hodder & Stoughton, 1988.

Gombrich, Ernst H. "Expression and Communication." In *Meditations on a Hobby Horse.* London: Phaidon Press, 1965.

Gordon, Robert M. *The Structure of Emotion: An Investigation in Cognitive Psychology.* Cambridge: Cambridge University Press, 1987.

Greenspan, Patricia S. *Emotions and Reasons: An Inquiry into Emotional Justification.* New York: Routledge, 1988.

Halpern, Daniel, ed. *Our Private Lives.* New York: Anataeus, 1988.

Hampshire, Stuart. "The Analogy of Feeling." *Mind* 61 (1952): 1–12. Rpt. in Hampshire 1971, to which citations refer.

——. "Feeling and Expression." Inaugural Lecture. University College London, 1961.

——. *Freedom of Mind and Other Essays.* Princeton: Princeton University Press, 1971.

——. "Sincerity and Singlemindedness." In Hampshire 1971, to which citations refer.

——. *Thought and Action.* New York: Viking, 1960.

——, ed. *The Philosophy of Mind.* New York: Harper & Row, 1966.

Harré, Rom, ed. *The Social Construction of Emotions.* London: Basil Blackwell, 1986.

Hill, Aaron. "Dramatic Passions." In Toby Cole and Helen Krich Chinoy, eds., *Actors on Acting.* New York: Crown, 1970.

Hobbes, Thomas. *Leviathan*. Ed. C. B. Macpherson. Harmondsworth: Pelican Books, [1651] 1971.

Hunter, J. Paul., ed. *The Norton Introduction to Poetry*. New York: Norton & Norton, 1973.

Irons, D. "Professor James's Theory of Emotion." *Mind* 3 New Series (1894): 77–97.

Jacobs, Harriet. *Incidents in the Life of a Slave Girl*. The Schomburg Library of Nineteenth-Century Black Women Writers. Oxford: Oxford University Press, 1988.

Jaggar, Alison. "Love and Knowledge: Emotion in Feminist Epistemology." *Inquiry* 32 (1989): 151–76.

James, William. "The Physical Basis of Emotion." *Psychological Review* 1 (1894): 516–29.

——. *The Principles of Psychology*. 2 vols. New York: Dover, 1950.

——. "What Is an Emotion?" *Mind* (1884). Rpt. in Arnold, ed., 1968, to which citations refer.

Jefferson, Mark. "What Is Wrong with Sentimentality?" *Mind* 92 (1983): 519–29. In Kruschwitz and Robert, ed., 1987, to which citations refer.

Kael, Pauline. *Taking It All In*. New York: Holt, Reinhart, & Winston, 1984.

Kaufmann, Linda. *Ways of Desire*. Ithaca: Cornell University Press, 1986.

Keefer, Janice Kulyk. *Rest Harrow*. Toronto: Harper Collins, 1992.

Kesterbaum, Victor. *The Phenomenological Sense of John Dewey: Habit and Meaning*. Atlantic Heights, N.J.: Humanities Press, 1977.

Koch, Philip. "Bodily Feeling in Emotion." *Dialogue* 26 (1987): 59–75.

Kraut, Robert. "Feelings in Context." *Journal of Philosophy* 83 (1986): 642–52.

——. "Love De Re." *Midwest Studies in Philosophy* 10 (1986): 413–30.

Kruschwitz, Robert B., and Robert C. Roberts, eds., *The Virtues: Contemporary Essays on Moral Character*. Belmont, Calif.: Wadsworth, 1987.

LaRoque, Emma. "Preface." In Jeanne Perreault and Sylvie Vance, eds., *Writing the Circle*. Edmonton: NeWest Publishers, 1990.

Leibniz, G. W. *Discourse on Metaphysics*. 1790. Trans. George Montgomery. In *The Rationalists*. New York: Doubleday, 1960.

Lipking, Lawrence. *Abandoned Women and Poetic Tradition*. Chicago: University of Chicago Press, 1988.

Lorde, Audre. "Eye to Eye: Black Women, Hatred and Anger." In Lorde, 1984.

——. *Sister Outsider*. Trumansburg: Crossing Press, 1984.

——. "The Uses of Anger: Women Responding to Racism." In Lorde, 1984.

Lynch, Michael. "Yellow Kitchen Gloves." In *These Waves of Dying Friends*. New York: Contact II Publications, 1989.

Mahowald, Mary Briody, ed. *Philosophy and Women*. Indianapolis, Ind.: Hackett, 1983.

McClatchy, J. D., ed. *Anne Sexton: The Poet and Her Critics*. Bloomington: Indiana University Press, 1978.

McFall, Lynn. "What's Wrong with Bitterness?" In Claudia Card, ed., *Feminist Ethics*. Lawrence: University of Kansas Press, 1991.

McGinn, Colin. *Mental Content*. London: Basil Blackwell, 1989.

Merleau-Ponty, Maurice. *The Prose of the World*. Ed. Claude Lefort and trans. John O'Neill. Evanston, Ill.: Northwestern University Press, 1973.

Midgley, Mary. "Brutality and Sentimentality." *Philosophy* 54 (1979): 385–89.

Montgomery, William. "Charles Darwin's Thought on Expressive Mechanisms in Evolution." In Gail Zivin, ed., *The Development of Expressive Behavior: Biology-Environment Interactions.* Orlando, Fla: Academic Press, 1985.

Monture-Angus, Patricia. *Thunder in My Soul: A Mohawk Woman Speaks.* Halifax: Fernwood Press, 1994.

Morton, Adam. "Character and the Emotions." In Rorty, ed., 1980.

Nissenbaum, Helen F. *Emotion and Focus.* Stanford, Calif.: Centre for the Study of Language and Information, 1985.

Ostriker, Alicia. "The Americanization of Sylvia." *Writing Like a Woman.* Ann Arbor: University of Michigan Press, 1983.

Pineau, Lois. "Date Rape: A Feminist Analysis." *Law and Philosophy* 8 (1989): 217–43.

Pitcher, George. "Emotion." *Mind* 74 (1965): 326–46.

Plath, Sylvia. "Cut." *Ariel.* London: Faber & Faber, 1965.

Putnam, Hilary. "The Meaning of Meaning." In *Mind, Language and Reality: Philosophical Papers.* vol. 2. Cambridge: Cambridge University Press, 1980.

Quine, Wilfrid Van Orman. *Word and Object.* Cambridge: MIT Press, 1960.

Rich, Adrienne. "Interview." *The Ohio Review* 13, no. 1 (1971): 28–46. In Hunter, ed., 1973, to which citations refer.

Richards, Robert. *Darwin and the Emergence of Evolutionary Theories of Mind and Behavior.* Chicago: University of Chicago Press, 1987.

Rorty, Amélie O. "Explaining Emotions." In Rorty, ed., 1980.

——. *Explaining Emotions.* Berkeley: University of California Press, 1980.

——. "The Historicity of Psychological Attitudes: Love Is Not Love Which Alters Not When It Alteration Finds." *Midwest Studies in Philosophy* 10 (1986): 399–412.

Rosenthal, David, ed. *The Nature of Mind.* Oxford: Oxford University Press, 1991.

Rostand, Edmond. *Cyrano de Bergerac.* Trans. Brian Hooker. New York: Bantam Books, 1959.

Ryle, Gilbert. *The Concept of Mind.* Chicago: University of Chicago Press, 1949.

Sarbin, Theodore R. "Emotion and Act: Roles and Rhetoric." In Harré, ed., 1986.

Scheman, Naomi. "Anger and the Politics of Naming." In Sally McConnell Ginet, Ruth Borker, and Nelly Forman, eds., *Women and Language in Literature and Society.* New York: Praeger, 1980.

——. "On Sympathy." *Monist* 62 (1979): 320–30.

Sellars, Wilfrid. "Philosophy and the Scientific Image of Man." *Science, Perception and Reality.* London: Routledge & Kegan Paul, 1963.

Shaffer, Jack. *Shane.* New York: Bantam Books, 1983.

Shakespeare, William. *Othello.* Oxford: Clarendon Press, [1622] 1975.

Solomon, Robert C. "In Defense of Sentimentality." *Philosophy and Literature* 14 (1990): 304–23.

——. *The Passions: The Myth and Nature of Human Emotions.* Garden City, N.Y.: Anchor Books, 1976.

Sousa, Ronald B. de. *The Rationality of Emotion.* Cambridge: MIT Press, 1987.

Spelman, Elizabeth. "Anger and Insubordination." In Ann Garry and Marilyn Pearsall, eds., *Women, Knowledge, and Reality.* Boston: Unwin Hyman, 1989.

——. "On Treating Persons as Persons." *Ethics* 88 (1978): 150–61.

Stevenson, C. L. *Ethics and Language.* New Haven: Yale University Press, 1958.

Tanner, Michael. "Sentimentality." *Proceedings of the Aristotelian Society* 77 (1976): 125–47.

Taylor, Charles. "Action as Expression." In Cora Diamond and Jenny Teichman, eds., *Intention and Intentionality: Essays in Honour of G. E. M. Anscombe.* Brighton: Harvester Books, 1979.

Tennyson, Lord Alfred. "In Memoriam A. H. H." In *The Complete Works of Alfred Lord Tennyson.* London: Macmillan, 1906.

Thomas, Laurence. "Moral Deference." *Philosophical Forum* 24, nos. 1–3 (1992–93): 233–50.

Thoreau, Henry David. *Walden and Other Writings.* Toronto: Bantam Books, [1854] 1962.

Thorp, Willard, ed. *Great Short Works of the American Renaissance.* New York: Harper & Row, 1968.

Tlali, Miriam. *Between Two Worlds.* Longman African Writers Series. New York: Longman, 1987.

Tocqueville, Alexis de. *Democracy in America,* vol. 2. New York: Random House, [1840] 1945.

Tormey, Alan. *The Concept of Expression: A Study in Philosophical Psychology and Aesthetics.* Princeton: Princeton University Press, 1971.

Tronto, Joan C. *Moral Boundaries: A Political Argument for an Ethic of Care.* New York: Routledge, 1993.

Urmson, J. O., and G. J. Warnock, eds. *Philosophical Papers.* Oxford: Clarendon Press, 1961.

——. *Philosophical Papers,* 2d ed. Oxford: Oxford University Press, 1970.

Veron, Eugene. *Aesthetics.* Trans. W. H. Armstrong. London: Chapman & Hall, 1879.

Walzer, Michael. *Spheres of Justice.* New York: Basic Books, 1983.

Wohlgemut, Sharon Alice. "The Shame of It All." M.Ed. thesis. Queen's University, 1995.

Wollheim, Richard. *Art and Its Objects: An Introduction to Aesthetics.* New York: Harper & Row, 1971.

——. "Expression." *The Human Agent.* Royal Institute of Philosophy Lectures, vol. 1, 1966–67. London: Macmillan, 1968.

Wood, Oscar P., and George Pitcher, eds. *Ryle: A Collection of Critical Essays.* Garden City, N.Y.: Anchor Books, 1970.

Worcester, W. L. "Observations on Some Points in James's Psychology. II. Emotion." *The Monist* 3 (1893): 285–98.

INDEX

Abandonment, 144–45, 153, 154
Affect:
  defined, 10
  fragmentation of, 14, 31
Affective explanation, 104, 120, 126,
    142, 144, 150, 165
  in Alston, 42
  in James, 26–28, 29
  narrative, 32, 38, 39, 126–27. *See
    also* Autobiography
  problem of redundancy, 16, 20, 21,
    24, 29, 30, 37–39, 89
  in Ryle, 33
  simplicity and comprehensiveness,
    14, 15, 127
  See also Explanation of behavior
Affective meaning:
  authority over. *See* Authority, first
    person
  indeterminacy of, 109, 117–19, 130,
    137, 152
  linguistic analogy, 112–20, 138, 141
  new, 162–64
  occasion, 143–48, 151, 152, 156,
    159, 162, 181
  oppositional, 156–64
  rules. *See* Social constructivism
  shared, 141, 144, 147, 162
  as significance, 3, 71, 111, 116–17,

    119, 126, 128, 131, 133, 136–37,
    144
  social meaning, contrast to, 136–43,
    146, 150, 161, 181
Affective response:
  ambivalence, 8
  appropriateness, 143
  associational, 95–97. *See also* Emo-
    tion: properties
  confusion, 81, 83, 84, 86–87, 95,
    109, 110, 117, 130
  determining of emotion, 91, 95, 99
  importance of history, 143, 150
  in learning emotion, 90–91
  See also Concealment
Alston, William:
  expression, 49, 53, 55–57, 62
  feelings, account of 40–44
  relation to Ryle, 40, 41
Anger, 35, 42, 53, 66, 136, 179, 182
  feminist accounts of, 147–151, 158
  object formation, 90–95
  and racism, 167, 169–70, 171. *See
    also* Bitterness; "Thunder in my
    soul"
Annie on My Mind (Garden), 129
Aristotle, 90, 174
Articulation, 58, 105, 107–9, 164, 173
Austin, J. L., 40, 82, 86

Authority, first person, 80, 108–10, 112, 118–20, 128, 147–49, 155, 181

Autobiography, 11, 32, 33, 38, 39, 126–28

Averill, James, 138, 142–43

Avowals, 33–35, 80–87, 94, 148, 149, 150, 156, 185

Bartky, Sandra, 1, 90, 151–52, 186

Bass, Rick, 4–7, 10, 11, 35, 36, 44, 64, 66, 67, 125, 128, 153, 158

Belief:
in belief/desire explanation, 127–28
content of, 111, 115, 131–32
hope, contrast with, 110
individuation, 29–30, 32, 59, 93

Bergmann, Frithjof, 103, 104

Bersani, Leo, 163–64

Between Two Worlds (Tlali), 7–10, 11, 14, 32, 35, 36, 64, 66, 67, 119, 127

Bilgrami, Akeel, 141

Bitterness, 166, 167–72
and communication, 168–69
justified, 169–70

Block, Ned, 1

Browning, Frank, 163–64

Calhoun, Cheshire, 1, 127

Causes, mental, 31, 32, 36, 38

Character, moral, 174–76, 178–79

Clarke, Stanley, 42

Cognitive/perceptual theory, 75, 82, 84, 85, 88–95, 97, 140

Collingwood, R. G., 59, 67, 68, 69, 72–73

Concealment, 8, 9
and individuation of feeling, 66, 103, 183
and restraint, 181–84
socialization, 184–85

Consciousness, 14, 15, 33, 39–42

Consciousness-raising. *See* Anger: feminist accounts of

Contempt, 109–10

"Cut" (Plath). *See* "Weird sinking hilarity"

Cyrano de Bergerac, 75–88, 97, 118, 183

Darwin, Charles, expression of emotions, 2, 11, 15, 16–23, 27, 28, 37, 42, 63, 89, 106, 120

Date-rape, 130–31, 152

Davidson, Donald:
explanation of action, 36, 37, 38, 120, 123–24
externalism, 104, 132–33
meaning, 112–16, 139, 141, 151, 152–53, 156, 164

Dennett, Daniel, 1, 25

Desire, 1, 2,
expression of, 56–62, 65, 183
sexual, 129, 163

Dewey, John:
emotional attitudes, 95, 99–102, 108
as evolutionist, 20, 22, 99
expressionism, 67, 69, 72–73

Dinnerstein, Dorothy, 144

Dispositions. *See* Ryle, Gilbert

Dretske, Fred, 1

Ducasse, Curt, 67, 69, 71–73

Emerson, Ralph Waldo, 185

Emotion:
ambivalence, 8
appropriateness, 161
causal history, 76, 79, 80, 85, 86, 88, 95, 101–2
cause/object ambiguity, 94, 101–2
complexity, 3, 104
concepts, 10, 71, 72, 114, 136, 148, 154
correctness, 98, 153–54, 159
cross-cultural, 3, 138, 144
as epiphenomenal, 26–27
in evolutionary theory. *See* Darwin
feminist, 161–62
formed by expression, 76, 80–83, 87
history of theories, 1–2
importance in James, 23
judgment. *See* Emotion: object
object, 75, 76–95, 99, 100

Emotion (*continued*)
  outlaw, 160–62
  properties, 6, 78, 79, 88, 97–99,
    119, 136
  as a psychological kind, 2, 7
  rationality, 169–70
  relation to feeling, 10, 12, 24
  variety of, 3, 104, 138
  vocabulary for, 3, 6, 90, 91, 119,
    149, 153–54
  See also Cognitive/perceptual theory;
    Social constructivism
Emotion categories, 1–3, 6, 8–9, 12,
    71, 82, 104, 119, 138, 180
  in Alston, 44
  control of, 147–51
  and conventions, 83, 88, 90, 145,
    157
  in Darwin, 22–23
  in expressionist theory, 69–70
  and interpretation, 135–36, 150
  in James, 24
  paradigm scenarios, 90–91, 95–98,
    102
Emotionality, 51, 54, 166, 174–75
Evolutionary theory, 15, 41, 89, 90,
    100
  and creationism, 17–19
  instinct, 19, 20, 24, 30
  See also Darwin, Charles
Explanation of behaviour, 13
  and emotions, 1–2
  in evolutionary theory, 16–17
  intentional, 11, 21, 123–25, 127–
    28, 136
  levels of, 14, 125, 127
  objectives, 37–38, 123–24
Expression:
  as activity, 50, 56–59, 64–64, 66
  animal, 17, 19, 20
  as communication, 47, 56, 58, 60,
    61, 63, 66, 69, 70, 104, 115, 130–
    31, 181
  control by others, 12, 82, 135
  criticism of, 49–50. *See also* Bitter-
    ness; Emotionality; Sentimentality
  defined, 10, 48, 67–70

facial, 11, 16, 22, 56, 60, 63, 64, 65
  and inference, 52, 54, 55, 59–60
  involuntary, 11, 56, 179
  medium of, 60, 69, 70, 73, 105,
    106, 137
  politics of, 2, 67, 68
  range of states, 47, 48, 59, 64, 67
  and reporting, 56–58
  as revealing, 52, 55, 62, 81
  See also Affective meaning; Articula-
    tion; Desire: expression of; Ex-
    pressive behavior; Interpretation
Expressionist theory, 50, 67–73, 106,
    115, 155
  critique of, 68, 70
  motivation for, 68–69
Expressive behavior:
  as action 76, 78–79, 81, 82, 84–88,
    92–93, 130, 174
  in cognitive/perceptual theory, 89–
    90
  and externalism, 104, 112
  description of, 122–26
  gendered, 7, 55, 172, 178, 180
  patterned, 13, 16, 17, 20, 29–31,
    36, 136, 148, 149
  recognition of, 16, 61, 82, 103, 104,
    120, 132, 165
  serviceable, 18–21, 23, 30
  targets of, 91–95
  variety, 16, 21–22, 149–50
  See also Interpretation; Interpreters;
    Pictionary
Expressive resources, 12, 48, 55, 59,
    60, 64–65, 67
  action. *See* Expressive behavior: as
    action
  gendered, 172–73, 175, 179
  limited, 158, 168, 170, 173, 179,
    180, 186–87
  linguistic, 57, 65, 82, 94, 136
  naturalness, 62–64, 65
  variety, 48, 105, 133, 185, 186–
    87
Expressive success and failure, 6–7,
    12, 51, 60, 66, 106, 111, 119,
    129–31, 172

Externalism, 104, 112, 120–23, 131, 133, 137, 141, 145, 147–48

Fear, 27–28, 30, 76, 98, 100
Feelings:
  bodily, 28, 41
  cause, 80–81, 84, 110, 117, 124–25
  defined, 10
  epistemology of, 42–43, 110, 161
  examples of. *See* Bass, Rick; *Between Two Worlds*; "Sunday melancholy"; "Thunder in my soul"; "Weird sinking hilarity"
  free-style, 67, 71, 104, 138, 160, 182
  neglect of, 4–5, 11, 13–14
  oppositional, 144–45. *See also* Emotion: outlaw
  reduced to sensations, 4, 10, 15, 23, 27, 28–29, 31, 33, 35, 41, 140, 150
  shared, 10, 68, 69, 71, 73, 119, 147
  and social practice, 5
  uniqueness of, 71–73, 112
  variety of, 23, 44, 67, 71, 153–54
  vocabulary, 32, 153
  See also Individuation of feelings
Fodor, Jerry, 121
Fridlund, Alan, 17, 19
Frustration, 6, 8
Frye, Marilyn, 158

Gay sexuality, 129, 163–64
Gombrich, Ernst, 55, 70, 115
Gordon, Robert, 1, 77
Greenspan, Patricia, 1
Grief, 28, 100, 142, 145, 189–92

Habit:
  in Darwin, 18–21
  in Dewey, 99–103
Hampshire, Stuart, 1, 40, 47, 59, 110, 112, 183–85
Harré, Rom, 1, 3, 137–38, 142
Hawthone, Nathaniel, 176
High Noon (film), 187
Hill, Aaron, 2
Hobbes, Thomas, 1, 2

Inarticulateness, 181–88
  and masculinity, 7, 181, 186
  and political individualism, 184–85
Incidents in the Life of a Slave Girl (Jacobs), 181–82
Individuation, 103–11. *See also* Articulation
Individuation of feelings, 66–67, 103–5, 120, 131
  assumed for expression, 48–49, 51–52, 55, 65, 180
  by categorization, 135–36, 159
  in cognitive/perceptual theory, 75–76
  collaborative, 104, 108, 111, 134, 137, 151, 168, 172
  in Darwin, 21–22
  defined, 49
  in expressionist theory, 72–73
  failure in *Cyrano*, 76, 78, 81, 84, 86
  in James, 28
  problems with, 6, 10, 14
  See also Expression: as activity
In Memoriam (Tennyson), 100
Intention, 47, 51, 166, 168
  in action explanation, 124, 125
  in Darwin, 13, 16, 19, 21
  unnecessary for expression, 58, 60–61, 63
Intentionality, 75–76, 81, 88, 89, 92–94, 123
Interpretation:
  and communication, 61, 63
  conditions of, 115–20, 129, 137, 157
  and constraints, 152
  contestable, 164
  correct, 152–53, 159
  and deference, 155–60
  dismissive, 164–66, 172, 180. *See also* Bitterness; Emotionality; Sentimentality
  ethics of, 8–9, 135, 146–64
  labelling, 156
  and meaning. *See* Affective meaning
  restrictive, 135, 145, 146, 150, 153, 172

Interpretation (*continued*)
  and uptake, 106, 108, 128, 149,
    160, 180, 182
Interpreters:
  communities, 161–64
  power, 135–37, 145, 147, 150–52,
    166
  responsibilities, 130, 143, 149–51,
    155, 157, 159, 186, 188

Jaggar, Alison, 1, 15, 75, 137, 138,
    140, 161–64, 179
James, Williams, 5, 13, 15, 21, 23–31,
    89, 120
  critics of, 27, 30
  reductionism, 24–27, 29
  relation to Darwin, 24, 27, 28
  on sentimentality, 177, 186
Jealousy, 121–26, 144
Jefferson, Mark, 175, 176

Kael, Pauline, 187
Kant, Immanuel, 172–73
Kaufmann, Linda, 144
Koch, Phillip, 181
Kraut, Robert, 79

LaRoque, Emma, 171
Lipking, Lawrence, 144–45
Little Women (Alcott), 178
Lorde, Audre, 167–71
Love, 30, 75–88, 97, 129, 143, 183

Matisse, Henri, 50–51
McFall, Lynn, 167, 169–70
McGinn, Colin, 121, 132
Memory, 155, 171
Merleau-Ponty, Maurice, 45, 50–51, 66
Midgley, Mary, 176
Montgomery, William, 17, 18
Monture-Angus, Patricia. *See* "Thunder
    in my soul"
Motives, 1, 31, 33, 34, 36, 39, 89

Nissenbaum, Helen Fay, 1, 91, 114, 126

Objectivity, 98, 111, 116, 153, 154

Ostriker, Alicia, 44
Othello, 53–54, 60, 88, 177

Passions. *See* Emotion categories
Pictionary (game), 107–11
Pineau, Lois, 130
Privacy, mental, 40, 62, 112, 128, 135,
    140, 146, 147
Psychology, 13, 23, 40
Putnam, Hilary, 121, 132–33

Quine, Wilfrid Van Orman, 112, 118

Racism. *See* Anger: and racism; *Between
    Two Worlds*
Remains of the Day (film), 183
Response of others. *See* Interpretation;
    Interpreters; *Pictionary*
Rich, Adrienne, 47
Richards, Robert, 17, 18
Rorty, Amélie, 76, 77, 89, 94, 100, 140
Rosenthal, David, 1
Ryle, Gilbert, 2, 5, 14, 15, 31–39, 80,
    105, 120, 128
  analysis of vanity, 33, 34, 36
  behaviorism, 32, 34, 61
  relation to James, 31, 33, 37
  See also Avowals
Sarbin, Theodore, 2, 142
Scheman, Naomi, 1, 126, 137, 144,
    147–51, 160
Sensations, 4, 10, 28, 35
Sentimentality, 49, 51, 172–79
  and femininity, 172–73, 178
  Tanner's account 53, 54, 174, 176–77
Shame, 90, 160
Social categories:
  downwardly constituted, 155
  oppositional communities, 161–62
Social constructivism, 132–145, 159
  and feminism, 17, 146, 160, 161–
    67, 181
  and rules, 142, 143, 144
  politics of, 146
  and social roles, 142
  See also Affective meaning: social
    meaning, contrast to

Sellars, Wilfrid, 26, 153
Sexton, Anne, 179–80
Shane (Shaffer), 186
Solomon, Robert, 1, 175, 176, 177
de Sousa, Ronald, 1, 75, 76, 77, 89–91, 94, 95, 97, 102
Spelman, Elizabeth, 1, 15, 158, 182
"Sunday melancholy," 140–42, 153, 160

Tanner, Michael. *See* Sentimentality: Tanner's account
Taylor, Charles, 49, 50, 59–66, 105, 181, 183–84
Thomas, Laurence, 155, 159–60
Thoreau, Henry David, 185
"Thunder in my soul," 156–62
Tocqueville, Alexis de, 185

Tormey, Alan, 37, 49, 52, 55, 56, 57, 58, 59, 62, 68, 91
Tronto, Joan, 186

Veron, Eugene, 67, 68–69

Walzer, Michael, 152–53
"Weird sinking hilarity," 43–44, 64, 67, 119, 153, 160
"White-master's-well-fed-dog." *See Between Two Worlds*
Wilde, Oscar, 49, 177
Wittgenstein, private language argument, 112
Wollheim, Richard, 49, 52, 55, 56, 57, 58, 62, 70

Yellow Kitchen Gloves (Lynch), 145, 189–92